Art and Cultural Heritage Law

Art and Cultural Heritage Law
A Practical Guide

Martin Bradley

Published by
Clarus Press Ltd,
Griffith Campus,
South Circular Road,
Dublin 8.
www.claruspress.ie

Typeset by
Gough Typesetting Services,
Dublin

Printed by
SprintPrint
Dublin

ISBN
978-1-911611-99-8

A catalogue record for this book is available from the British Library

All rights reserved. No part of this publication may be reproduced, or transmitted in any form or by any means, including recording and photocopying, without the written permission of the copyright holder, application for which should be addressed to the publisher. Written permission should also be obtained before any part of the publication is stored in a retrieval system of any nature.

Disclaimer

Whilst every effort has been made to ensure that the contents of this book are accurate, neither the publisher nor the author can accept responsibility for any errors or omissions or loss occasioned to any person acting or refraining from acting as result of any material in this publication.

Copyright © Martin Bradley 2024

For Síne

Foreword

In 1903 the Viennese banker Ferdinand Bloch commissioned a painting of his wife by the artist Gustav Klimt. An oil on canvas with gold leaf, *Portrait of Adele Bloch-Bauer I* hung in the Bloch family home until Ferdinand, who was Jewish, fled Austria in 1938 following the Anschluss. The Nazis seized the painting, changed the name to *Lady in Gold* (at Hitler's instigation), and installed it in the Galerie Belvedere in Vienna. Hugely popular, *Lady in Gold* quickly became known as 'Austria's Mona Lisa'. But Ferdinand – who had died penniless and in exile in 1945 – had willed his entire estate, including the painting, to his nephew and two nieces, one of whom was Maria Altmann. In 2000 Altmann, now living in America, began a lengthy legal battle in the Austrian and US courts to have the painting returned to her. The Austrian gallery stoutly resisted but Altmann eventually prevailed. The painting, which had probably cost Ferdinand 5,000 kronen (about €42,000), was sold by Altmann for $135m in 2006, making it at the time the world's most expensive painting: it now hangs in the Neue Galerie in New York.

The story of *Portrait of Adele Bloch-Bauer I* has everything: the intersection of law (national and international) and moral obligation, the avarice of occupying forces, and a magnificent – and extremely valuable–work of art. In such a labyrinth of litigation, a reliable guide is vital, which is why Martin Bradley's book is so important. As well as his fascinating examination of the legal implications of art crimes, and the restitution and repatriation of stolen art works, Bradley's clear exposition of the intricacies of topics such as copyright, provenance, data protection, contracts, tax, and import and export restrictions, is welcome. The author also considers the comprehensive codifying legislation that is the Historic and Archaeological Heritage and Miscellaneous Provisions Act 2023 (a number of sections of which came into effect earlier this year) as well as the National Monuments legislation. In a helpful innovation, Bradley provides a 'case study' at the end of each chapter, which vividly illustrates the practical effect of the complex legal and other principles at play in respect of various artefacts, including the Derrynaflan Hoard, Rory Gallagher's Stratocaster guitar, and the letter of surrender written in 1916 by Padraig Pearse.

Written in fluent and engaging prose, the book is also studded with gems, as befits its subject-matter. Bradley is as comfortable recounting the sack of Constantinople (whose 'Horses of the Hippodrome' ended up in St Mark's Square in Venice) as he is outlining the staggering amounts earned by Disney ($3-6 billion per year) from Winnie-the-Pooh. The accessibility of the language means non-lawyers as well as lawyers will learn much from these pages; the reach of the myriad of applicable laws is so extensive, and so well explained here, that every cultural institution, auction house, and legal practice in Ireland would do well to acquire a copy of this book.

Bradley's research is rigorous, but he wears his learning lightly, and is judiciously alert to popular culture. Inevitably, the saga of the Bloch-Bauer painting became a film, *Woman in Gold*, with Helen Mirren playing Maria Altmann. Mirren later testified to the US Senate Committee, and Bradley provides a link to her testimony. "The right thing to do," she said, "is to return the art to its rightful owner." He also quotes counsel's observation in *Donaldson v Becket*, an early (1774) case on copyright, that "booksellers had not, till lately, ever concerned themselves about authors," which will sound ruefully familiar to anyone who has written a book.

"*They've taken the skeleton/Of the Great Irish Elk/Out of the peat, set it up/An astounding crate full of air.*"[1] As suggested with characteristic imaginative deftness by Seamus Heaney in his poem 'Bogland,' the process of investigating our culture is endless. Our museums and institutions play a vital role in protecting what we find, but we cannot absolve ourselves of our personal responsibility in this regard. We may scorn how section 3(4) of the British Museum Act, which prevents the disposal of objects vested in the Trustee as part of the Museum's collection, provides a fig-leaf for the Museum's refusal to repatriate the Parthenon (Elgin) Marbles; but, as Bradley points out, Irish institutions may also have held—or hold— objects originally acquired by donors in questionable circumstances. And there are other conundrums: for example, we refer to some writers and artists as 'national treasures,' yet we still have no clear formal process as to how we identify and designate what constitutes a 'national monument.' I believe Martin Bradley's timely and necessary book— unique of its kind in this jurisdiction—will provide answers to the many legal issues surrounding art and cultural heritage, and I am happy to commend it to legal practitioners, and to all involved in the administration and protection of the arts and heritage in Ireland.

John O'Donnell
22 September 2024

---

[1] Extract from 'Bogland', from *Door into the Dark* © Estate of Seamus Heaney. Published by Faber and Faber. Used by kind permission of the Estate of Seamus Heaney.

Preface

> "This book makes no pretensions to be a guide to the perplexed. I am myself perplexed. But I have tried, as best I can, to convey the nature of my perplexity."
>
> RD Laing[1]

What is art and cultural heritage law? As you will see when you read this book it is a mixture of a wide range of disciplines, national and international laws, ethics, practicalities, codes of conduct, treaties and conventions. It addresses such diverse issues as copyright and moral rights of authors; data protection and freedom of information; title and provenance; crime and money laundering; ethics of acquisition; restitution, repatriation and deaccessions; Nazi-era spoliation and colonial looting; contracts and agreements; archaeology, monuments and metal-detecting; protected structures; shipwrecks; UNESCO and UNIDROIT conventions; tax and inheritance; donations and loans; import and export conditions and restrictions and, in the case of paintings by John Bratby, Derrick Greaves, Edward Middleditch and Jack Smith, *The Kitchen Sink*. As a result of trying to cover such a massive and diverse area of law there will inevitably be some errors, which are the author's alone. This book is correct to the author's best knowledge at the time of publication in October 2024. Any lacunae will be addressed in future editions.

Art and cultural heritage law has been in the news with great frequency in the months leading up to the publication of this book. Rory Gallagher's guitar has been put up for sale with resulting calls for it to be secured as an iconic symbol of Irish culture; Bronze Age axe heads have been posted to the National Museum anonymously with a resulting plea for the finder to supply more information, which was subsequently forthcoming thus allowing the museum's staff to locate a possibly important new Bronze Age site, and to remind the public of its legal responsibilities in relation

---

[1] Quotation from 'The Facts of Life', by R D Laing (c) The RD Laing Estate. Used by kind permission of The RD Laing Estate.

to antiquities via plentiful press coverage; residents of Kenilworth Square in Dublin 6 are mounting a challenge to redevelopment of the Victorian square into an all-weather rugby pitch with lights and seating, partially based on the protected status of the buildings that surround the park; the Parthenon Marbles dispute shows signs of moving towards a resolution whereby the statues might be loaned to the Acropolis Museum in Athens; Benin Bronzes have been repatriated to Nigeria from Germany and the US; artworks that were purchased under duress or stolen during the Nazi-era have been returned to the heirs of their rightful owners. Readers may be familiar with the cases of the Derrynaflan Hoard, or the protests over the development of the Wood Quay site in Dublin. Some of these issues are considered in the 'Case Study' section at the end of each chapter, which tries to put the concepts that have been discussed into a meaningful context.

This book is for two audiences: gallery, library, archive and museum ('GLAM') professionals and legal practitioners. Lawyers can skip over parts of the book that explain basic legal concepts (you'll know which parts as you read them) but there will hopefully be enough to engage — there will most likely be aspects of national and international law, treaties and conventions that you may not have come into contact with during your legal training or professional practice, especially as this is a rapidly evolving area in Irish law.

Similarly, some of the content of this book will be familiar to GLAM professionals, but I am confident that there will plenty to learn in terms of the legal frameworks that underpin much of your professional work, as well as some case law and interpretation that may be new to you. GLAM professionals should not be afraid to ask a lawyer for advice. For any matters that are non-contentious; that is work that involves deals, transactions, contracts or advisory work, you can speak directly with a barrister or a solicitor. For anything contentious — involving a dispute between two or more parties — you must first consult a solicitor who will instruct a barrister if and as appropriate.

Ireland is a common law jurisdiction, which means that much of our law is based on decisions of the courts and is contained in precedent. This is why you will see court cases referred to throughout the body of this text. Common law originated in the King's Courts in England in the period following the Norman Conquest in 1066. UK cases are also referred to in this text as these are viewed as being persuasive by the Irish courts, if not binding on their decisions, especially if issued after 1922. In contrast

Preface

countries such as France and Italy (and c.120 others worldwide) operate a civil law system, based on the *Code Napoléon*, which stresses a heavily codified clearly written law.

As part of the European Union, Ireland is bound by the doctrine of supremacy of EU law. What this means is that EU law takes precedence over national law

> "based on the idea that where a conflict arises between an aspect of EU law and an aspect of law in an EU Member State (national law), EU law will prevail. If this were not the case, Member States could simply allow their national laws to take precedence over primary or secondary EU legislation, and the pursuit of EU policies would become unworkable. The principle of the primacy of EU law has developed over time by means of the case law (jurisprudence) of the Court of Justice of the European Union. It is not enshrined in the EU treaties, although there is a brief declaration annexed to the Treaty of Lisbon in regard to it."[2]

Art and cultural heritage law is also bound up in a series of international conventions, recommendations and declarations, such as the UNESCO Convention on the Means of Prohibiting and Preventing the Illicit Import, Export and Transfer of Cultural Property 1970; the Hague Convention for the Protection of Cultural Property in the Event of Armed Conflict 1954; the UNIDROIT Convention on Stolen or Illegally Exported Cultural Objects 1995; the UNESCO 2001 Convention for the Protection of Underwater Heritage; the UNESCO 2003 Convention for the Safeguarding of Intangible Cultural Heritage; the Convention on International Trade in Endangered Species of Wild Fauna and Flora 1973; and the UN Declaration on the Rights of Indigenous Peoples 2007. The purpose of each of these conventions and their impact on Irish law are discussed at the appropriate junctures in the text.

One of the biggest developments for art and cultural heritage law in Ireland was the passage of the Historic and Archaeological Heritage and Miscellaneous Provisions Act 2023, a 230-page statute with a broad remit. There are 13 parts to the 2023 Act, which address the law as it applies to, among others, monuments, archaeological objects, underwater wrecks and heritage, offences, licencing schemes and amendments to existing legislation. Most chapters of the 2023 Act have yet to be commenced at the time of writing, aside from those that came into operation under SI No 252 of 2024.

---

[2] EUROPA, 'Primacy of EU law (precedence, supremacy)' < https://eur-lex.europa.eu/EN/legal-content/glossary/primacy-of-eu-law-precedence-supremacy.html> accessed 21 August 2024.

These changes have been addressed in detail in an appendix, while the ramifications of the changes are addressed in the relevant chapters throughout the book; as well as the potential future impact of different sections of the act, particularly in relation to the UNESCO 1970 and UNIDROIT 1995 conventions, where these would not be unduly confusing in relation to the law as it stands at the time of writing.

An annotated version of the Historic and Archaeological Heritage and Miscellaneous Provisions Act 2023 may be required once it is commenced in full, but that is an undertaking beyond the remit of this book.

Contents

Foreword vii
Preface ix
Acknowledgments xvii
Table of Cases xix
Table of Legislation xxi

Chapter 1
Copyright and Moral Rights 1
    Copyright: A Brief History 1
    Copyright in Ireland 3
    Copyright Exhaustion 6
    Copyright Duration 7
    Copyright Exceptions 8
        Orphan Works 8
        Fair Dealing 9
        Exemptions for Librarians and Archivists 11
        DSM 12
        Lending of Works 14
        PLR and e-Books 15
        Moral Rights 17
        Artist's Resale Right 18
        Digitisation and Copyright 19
    Case Study: *Winnie-the-Pooh* 21

Chapter 2
Data Protection, Freedom of Information and Open Data 23
    Data Sharing: A Brief History 23
    GDPR 26
    Records Less than 100 Years Old 29
    Who is the Data Controller? 30
    Data Protection Officers 32
    Freedom of Information 34
    Refusal of Access Requests 36
    Publication Scheme 38
    Appeals 39
    The Open Data Directive 40
    Case Study: FOI Section 35 Exemptions 42

Chapter 3
Title and Provenance 45
    What is Title? 45
    Provenance 46
    Gifts and Loans 48
        Bailment 48
        Gifts 50
        Loans 52
    Civil Recovery of Objects 53
    Where Can Claims be Brought? 55
    International Cultural Object Protection Laws 56
    Compulsory Acquisition 58
    Limitation Periods 60
    The UNESCO 1954 Convention 63
    Case Study: The Derrynaflan Hoard 64

Chapter 4
Art Crime and Acquisitions 69
    Introduction 69
    Elements of a Crime 71
    Fraud and Theft Offences 73
    Handling Stolen Property 74
    Possession of Stolen Property 75
    Money Laundering 75
    Proceeds of Crime 76
    Ethics of Acquisition — International Conventions 77
    Ethics of Acquisition — Codes of Ethics 81
    Case Study: *Qatar Investment & Projects Development Holdings Co v Eskenazi* 83

Chapter 5
Restitution, Repatriation and Deaccession 87
    Ethical and Legal Considerations of Deaccession 88
    Sale and Disposal 90
    Human Remains and Ethnological Items 91
    The UNESCO 1970 Convention 94
    The UNIDROIT 1995 Convention 95
    Nazi-Era Spoliation 100
    The Washington Principles 101
    Holocaust Expropriated Art Recovery Act (2016) 103
    Foreign Sovereign Immunities Act 105
    Case Study: Rue Saint-Honoré in the Afternoon—Effect of Rain 106

Chapter 6
Contracts 109
    Introduction to Contract Law 109
    Essential Terms 110
    Other Terms 111

Contents

Loan Agreements..113
Digitisation and Cataloguing Contracts..115
Public Procurement..116
Auctions..117
Case Study: Dating Damien Hirst..119

Chapter 7
Archaeology and Monuments..123
National Monuments..123
Protected Structures and their Contents..129
Fixtures and Chattels..131
An Taisce...132
Battlefield Sites...133
Wrecks and Underwater Sites...134
Case Study: The *SS Gairsoppa and SS Mantola*...136

Chapter 8
Tax...141
Tax on Cultural Objects...141
Tax and Inheritance..141
Gifts and Inheritances of Heritage Property..142
Donation of Heritage Items..143
Loan of Art Objects...145
Expenditure on Approved Buildings, Gardens and Objects.......................146
Imports, Exports and Tax..148
VAT and Artists..149
Basic Income for the Arts...150
The Margin Scheme...151
Imports and Exports..151
Free Ports..152
NFTs..153
Case Study: The Rory Gallagher Stratocaster..155

Chapter 9
Imports, Exports and Loans..159
Imports into the EU...162
Exports from the EU..164
Exports within the EU...165
Imports within the EU...168
International Loans...170
Immunity from Seizure..173
International Examples..175
    United States..175
    United Kingdom..176
    European Union..176
    Australia..177
Case Study: The Padraig Pearse Surrender Letter..177

Appendix
SI No 252 of 2024 the Historic and Archaeological Heritage and
    Miscellaneous Provisions Act 2023 (Commencement) Order 2024....................181

Index 195

Acknowledgements

Thanks to my family Síne, Daniel, Benjamin and Poppy for support and sets of sympathetic ears through long years of legal studies and even longer months of book writing; my publisher David McCartney at Clarus Press; The Beynacers; my graduating class from King's Inns; Group 3; Garret Cooney BL; Ruaidhrí Giblin BL; Andrew Lindsay BL; John Michell BL; Mark Tottenham BL; Ronan Bergin; Rory Bresnihan; Chris Heaney; Mick Heaney; Ciarán Walsh; Kate Nolan; Ruairí Quinn; Scott Burnett; Dr Kirsty March; Eimear Ashe and everyone else who encouraged, assisted with or tolerated the writing of this book. You know who you are.

Table of Cases

Andy Warhol Foundation for the Visual Arts Inc v Goldsmith et al, (2023) No 21-869 111
Antiquesportfolio.com plc v Rodney Fitch & Co Ltd [2001] FSR 34 20

Barton & Booth v R [2020] EWCA Crim 57 85
Begley & Clarke v An Bord Pleanála,[2003] IEHC 137 .... 130, 134

Cassirer v Thyssen-Bornemisza Collection No 19-55616 (9th Cir. 2024) 105–108
Commission v Italy, Case 7/68 [1968] ECR 42 .... 169n

Deckmyn and Vrijheidsfonds v Vandersteen & Ors, Case C-201/13 [2014] ECLI:EU:C:2014:2132 .... 10n
Deely v The Information Commissioner (2001) IEHC 91 4 35
Donaldson v Becket (1774) Hansard, 1st ser, 17 (1774): 953-1003 2
DPP v Bartley (HC, 13 June 1997) (Carney J) 71n
DPP v Murray [1977] IR 360 72

Federal Republic of Germany v Philipp, No. 19-351, 592 US (2021) 105

Hollins v Fowler (1875) LR 7 HL 757, 76 55

John Burns, The Sunday Times and the Arts Council [2022] OIC-119922-V5G3G 42

Kuwait Airways Corporation v Iraqi Airways Company (Nos 4&5) [2002] AC 88 55

Ladbroke (Football) Ltd v William Hill (Football) Ltd [1964] 1 WLR 27 5
Ladbroke (Football) Ltd v William Hill (Football) Ltd [1980] RPC 544 5

New Zealand v Ortiz [1984] AC 56

Odyssey Marine Expl Inc v Shipwrecked & Abandoned SS Mantola, 333 F Supp 3d 292 (SDNY 2018) 139

Philipp v Federal Republic of Germany, 894 F.3d 406, 410-11 (DC Cir 2018) 105
Poole v Burns [1944] Ir Jur Rep 2 54

Qatar Investment & Projects Development Holdings Co & His Highness Sheikh Hamad Bin Abdullah Al Thani v John Eskenazi Limited & Mr John Eskenazi [2022] EWH 83, 84, 85

R (Simonis) v Arts Council England [2018] EWHC 1822 (Admin) 164
R v Gibbins and Proctor [1918] 13 Cr App Rep 13 71
R v Miller [1983] 1 All ER 97 .... 71n
R v Moloney [1985] 1 All ER 102 72
Reif, Fraenkel and Vavra v Nagy and Richard Nagy Ltd [2018] 175 AD 3d 10 103
Republic of Iran v Barakat Galleries [2007] EWCA Civ 1374 57
RGRE Grafton Ltd v Bewley's Café [2023] IEHC 2 132
RGRE Grafton Ltd v Bewley's Café Grafton Street Ltd & Bewley's Ltd
   [2024] IECA 19 132

Skatteverket v David Hedqvist, Case C-264/14 (ECJ, 22 October 2015 154

The London Borough of Tower Hamlets v The London Borough of Bromley
   [2015] EWHC 1954 C 61
THJ Systems Limited & Anor v Daniel Sheridan & Anor [2023] EWCA Civ 135 19
Thompson, Case 7/78 [1978] ECR 224 .... 169n
Tidy v Trustees of the Natural History Museum [1996] 39 IPR 50 18

United States v Frederick Schultz, 178 F.Supp. 2d 445 (SDNY 2002), aff 'd,
   333 F.3d 393 (2d Cir 2003) (New York, United States) 56

Vereniging Openbare Bibliotheken v Stichting Leenrecht
   [2016] ECLI:EU:C:2016:85 15

Webb v Ireland [1988] IR 35 .... 54, 127
Webb v Ireland and the Attorney General [1987] IESC 2 .... 50, 65
Winkworth v Christie Manson and Woods Ltd [1980] 1 Ch 496 55

Zuckerman v Metropolitan Museum of Art 928 F.3d 186 (2d Cir 2019 104

Table of Legislation

CONSTITUTION OF IRELAND

Constitution of Ireland 1922 and 1937	67
art 10.1	67
art 11	67
art 34.3.1°	70

PRE-STATE STATUTES

Copyright Act 1842	2
Copyright Act 1911	3
Engraving Copyright Act 1734	3
Fine Arts Copyright Act 1862	3
Licensing of the Press Act 1662	1
Petty Sessions (Ireland) Act 1851 s 10(4)	192
Sale of Goods Act 1893	110
s 4	110
s 21	48
s 22(1)	48
s 23	48
Statute of Anne 1710	1
Statute of Frauds (Ireland) 1695	110
s 2	110

ACTS OF THE OIREACHTAS

Architectural Heritage (National Inventory) and Historic Monuments (Miscellaneous Provisions) Act 1999	130, 182
s 5	182
s 5(2)	182
s 5(3)	182
s 5(4)	182
Arts Act 2003	
s 2(1)	150
Capital Acquisitions Tax Act 2003	141, 142
s 76(2)	157
s 77	142, 154
s 78	142, 154
Civil Service Regulation Act 1956	30

Civil Service Regulation Act 1956—*contd.*
    s 2(1)(a) 30
    s 2(1)(b) 30
    s 2(1)(c) 30
    s 2(1)(d) 30
Continental Shelf Act, 1968 .... 135, 138
    s 2(1) 138
    s 2(1)(a) 135
    s 2(1)(b) 135
Copyright Act 1963 3
Copyright and Related Rights Act 2000 3
    Ch 7 17
    s 17 4
    s 17(1) 4
    s 17(3) 4
    s 21 3
    s 21 6
    s 21(a) 5
    s 21(b) 5
    s 21(c) 5
    s 21(d) 5
    s 21(e) 5
    s 21(f) 5
    s 21(g) 5
    s 21(h) 5
    s 23(1) 115
    s 330(A)(6) 13
    s 37 6
    s 37 3
    s 37(1) 6
    s 37(1)(a) 6
    s 37(1)(b) 6
    s 39 6
    s 40 6
    s 40(1)(a) 6
    s 40(1)(b) 6
    s 40(1)(c) 6
    s 40(1)(d) 6
    s 40(1)(e) 6
    s 40(1)(f) 6
    s 40(1)(g) 6
    s 42A(5) 15
    s 50(1)(f) 9
    s 50(4)(g) 9
    s 58(3) 13
    s 58A(1) 13
    s 58A(1)(a) 13
    s 58A(1)(b) 13
    s 58A(1)(c) 13
    s 65 11
    s 68 11

Table of Legislation

Copyright and Related Rights Act 2000—*contd.*
    s 68(3) 11
    s 69(A) 11, 12
    s 70 12
    s 94(1)(a) 9
    s 94(1)(b) 9
    s 95 11
Criminal Assets Bureau Act 1996 77
    s 4(a) 77
    s 4(b) 77
    s 4(c) 77
    s 4(d) 77
Criminal Justice (Amendment) Act 2009 70
Criminal Justice (Money Laundering and Terrorist Financing) (Amendment)
    Act 2021 .... 75, 118
    s 25 118
Criminal Justice (Money Laundering and Terrorist Financing) Act 2010 75
    Pt 2 75
    s 7 75
    s 7(5) 76
    s 8(1)(a) 76
    s 8(1)(b) 76
    s 8(1)(c) 76
    s 8(1)(d) 76
    s 33 118
Criminal Justice (Money Laundering and Terrorist Financing) Act 2013 75
Criminal Justice (Theft and Fraud Offences) Act 2001 46
    s 2(1) 73
    s 4(1) 73
    s 4(5) 73
    s 16(2) 46, 73
    s 17 .... 46, 47, 74
    s 18 .... 47, 75
    s 18(2) 75
    s 45 68
    s 56 47
Criminal Justice (United Nations Convention against Torture) Act 2000. 70
Criminal Justice Act 1964 s 4(2) 72
Criminal Justice Act 1994 75
Criminal Law Act 1997 191
Data Protection Act 1988 26
Data Protection Act 2003 26
Data Protection Act 2018 .... 26, 28
    s 3(1) 30
    s 14(4) 31
    s 42 30
    s 61 29
    s 71(6)(a) 29
    s 84(1) 31
    s 88 32
    s 88(4) 32

Data Protection Act 2018—*contd.*
    s 88(5) 33
    s 88(5)(a) 33
    s 88(5)(b) 33
    s 88(5)(c) 33
    s 88(5)(d) 33
    s 88(5)(e) 34
    s 90(2) 30
    s 90(4)(b) 30
Freedom of Information Act 1997 35
Freedom of Information Act 2014 35
    s 8(2) 39
    s 8(2)(a) 39
    s 8(2)(b) 39
    s 8(2)(c) 39
    s 8(2)(d) 39
    s 15(1) 36
    s 15(2) 36
    s 15(3)(2) 37
    s 24 39
    s 32 37
    s 33 37
    s 34 37
    s 35 .... 37, 42
    s 35 (1)(a) 42
    s 35 (1)(b) 42, 43
    s 36 .... 37, 42
    s 37 .... 37, 42
    s 41 37
Geneva Conventions Act 1962 70
Genocide Act 1973 70
Health Identifiers Act in 2014 28
Historic and Archaeological Heritage and Miscellaneous Provisions Act 2023 181
    s 1(7) 98, 181
    s 2(1) 123, 134, 181
    s 2(1)(a) 124, 181
    s 2(1)(b) 124, 181
    s 2(1)(c) 124, 181
    s 2(1)(d) 124, 181
    s 2(1)(e) 124, 181
    s 2(1)(f) 124, 181
    s 2(1)(g) 124, 181
    s 2(1)(h) 124, 181
    s 3 181
    s 4 181
    s 5 181
    s 6 181
    Part 2 .... 124, 133
    Part 3 183
    Part 4 134
    Part 5 ch 1 .... 124, 133

Historic and Archaeological Heritage and Miscellaneous Provisions Act 2023—*contd.*

Part 5 ch 2	134, 139
Part 8	184
Part 8 ch 2	185
Part 8 ch 3	185
Part 9	185, 186
Part 10 ch 7	190
Part 10 ch 11	193
s 43	170
s 96	45, 128
s 96(1)	58
s 96(2)	58
s 96(3)	58
s 96(4)(a)	58
s 96(4)	58, 68
s 96(5)	74
s 97(1)	62
s 98(3)	60
s 98(4)	60
ss 117–124	98
ss 125–130	98
s 131(1)	45, 48
s 131(2)	48
s 131(3)(a)	48
s 131(3)(a)	48
s 132	134
s 133	134
s 154	190
s 158(3)	184n
s 159	187
s 159(2)	188
s 159(4)	187
s 172	187, 188
s 174	187, 188
s 175	187
s 175(3)(a)	187
s 175(3)(b)	187
s 175(4)	190
s 175(7)	188
s 175(8)	188
s 178(2)	188
s 179	188
s 179(1)	188
s 179(2)	188
s 182	189
s 188	189
s 189	189
s 190	189
s 194	190
s 195	190
s 195(6)	190

Historic and Archaeological Heritage and Miscellaneous Provisions Act 2023—*contd.*
    s 196 190
    s 196(1) 190
    s 197 190
    s 204 191
    s 207 192
    s 209 192
    s 210 192
    s 210(3) 192
    s 217 193
    s 218 193
    s 220 193
    s 220 s 3(2) 193
    s 221 ....193, 194
    Schedule 3 ....193, 194
Land and Conveyancing Law Reform Act 2009 s 3 117
Local Government (Sanitary Services) Act 1964 182
    s 3(1) 182
    s 3(2) 182
    s 32 13
Local Government Act 2001 s 77(1) 15
Merchant Shipping (Salvage and Wreck Act) 1993 136
National Archives Act 1986 38
    s 2(2)(ii) 36
    s 8(2) 38
    s 8(4)(a) 38
    s 8(4)(b) 38
    s 8(4)(c) 38
National Cultural Institutions Act 1997 ....50, 90
    s 2 166
    s 11(2) 53
    s 18(2) 90
    s 28(1) 50
    s 28(2) 50
    s 28(3) 50
    s 42 ....50, 52
    s 43(1) 50, 53
    s 47 90
    s 48 ....165, 166, 178
    s 49 ....165, 169
    s 49(1)(a) 165
    s 49(1)(b)(i) 166
    s 49(1)(b)(ii) 166
    s 49(1)(c) 166
    s 49(1)(d) 166, 178
    s 49(1)(e) 166
    s 49(1)(f) 166
    s 49(1)(g) 166
    s 49(2) 166
    s 49(3) 166
    s 50 ....166, 167, 170

Table of Legislation

National Cultural Institutions Act 1997—*contd.*
    s 50(2) 167, 178
    s 50(2)(a) 167
    s 50(2)(b) 167
    s 50(2)(c) 167
    s 50(3) 167
    s 50(6) to (8) 167
    s 51(1) 168
    s 52 58
    s 53(1) 59
    s 53(2) 59
    s 57 59
    s 58 59
    s 59(1) 59
    s 59(3) 59
    s 59(7) 59
    s 68 90
National Monuments (Amendment) Act 1987 .... 124, 133, 134, 182
    s 1 138
    s 1(1) 135, 137
    s 2 124
    s 2(1)(b) 124
    s 2(1)(c) 124
    s 3(1) 135, 137, 138
    s 3(1)(a) 137
    s 3(1)(b) 137
    s 3(4) 135, 138
    s 3(5) 136
    s 3(6)(b) 136
    s 4(2) 125
    s 5(1) 125
    s 7 124
    s 8(1) 124
    s 8(2) 124
    s 8(2) 124
    s 9 124
National Monuments (Amendment) Act 1994 .... 135, 136
    s 4(1) 68, 127
    s 5 128
    s 5(2) 128
    s 7(1)b 138
    s 11 126
    s 11(a) 124
    s 11(b) 124
    s 11(c)(i) 124
    s 11(c)(ii) 125
    s 11(d) 125
    s 12(1) 125
    s 12(3) 126
    s 13 128
National Monuments (Amendment) Act 2004 124

National Monuments (Amendment) Act 2004—*contd.*
    s 5 124
National Monuments Act 1930 .... 64, 124, 137
    s 8 64
    s 14 .... 66, 126
    s 14(3)(d) 126
    s 23 128
National Monuments Acts 1930 to 2014 90
Offences against the State Act 1939 70
Offences against the State Act 1998 70
Planning and Development Act 2000 129
    s 2(1) 129
    s 10(2)c 186
    s 28 186
    s 51(1) 129
    s 52 186
    s 52(a) 186
    s 52(b) 186
    s 53(1) 130
    s 57(1) 131
Proceeds of Crime (Amendment) Act of 2005 s 10 77
Proceeds of Crime Act 1996 76
Statute of Limitations 1957 60
    s 12(1)(a) 61
    s 12(1)(b) 61
    s 12(2)(a) 61
    s 12(2)(b) 61
    s 12(2)(c) 61, 77
Succession Act 1965 s 78 .... 51, 52
Taxes Consolidation Act 1997 .... 142n, 143
    s 118 145
    s 195 .... 150n
    s 195(12) 149
    s 236 .... 145, 154, 157, 158
    s 436 145
    s 482 .... 146, 147
    s 606 .... 145, 157
    s 1003 45
    s 1003 .... 45, 143, 144, 154, 158
    s 1003(2)(a) 143
Wildlife Act 1976 s 53(A) 162
Wireless Telegraphy Act 1926 38
Wireless Telegraphy Act 1988 38

STATUTORY INSTRUMENTS (IRELAND)

Copyright and Related Rights (Public Lending Remunerations Scheme)
    Regulations 2008 SI No 597/2008 .... 14, 15
European Union (Award of Public Authority Contracts) Regulations 2016
    SI No 284/2016 116

European Union (Certain Permitted Uses of Orphan Works) Regulations 2014 SI No 490/2014 8
    r 5(1) 8
    r 5(3) 8
    r 8(1)(a) 8
    r 8(3) 9
    r 8(4) 9
    r 8(5) 9
    r 8(1)(b) 9
European Union (Copyright and Related Rights in the Digital Single Market) Regulations 2021 SI No 567/2021 12
    r 8 14
    r 8(1) 12, 13
    r 8(9) 13
    r 9(1) 13
European Union (Open Data and Re-use of Public Sector Information) Regulations 2021, SI No 376/2021 40
    r 3(2)(j) 40
    r 5 41
    r 6(5)(c) 41
    r 8(3)(b)(i) 41
    r 8(3)(b)(ii) 41
    r 8(3)(b)(iii) 41
    r 14(3)(b) ....
Historic and Archaeological Heritage and Miscellaneous Provisions Act 2023 (Commencement) Order 2024 SI No 252/2024 181
Irish Copyright and Related Rights (Public Lending Remunerations Scheme) Regulations 2008 SI No 597/2008 16
National Archives Act 1986 (Prescription of Classes of Records) Order 1997 SI No 281/1997 38

ENGLAND & WALES STATUTES

British Museum Act 1963 s 3(4) 89
Digital Economy Act 2017 16
Holocaust (Return of Cultural Objects) Act 2009 .... 89, 101
Human Tissue Act 2004 s 47(2) 92
Limitation Act 1980 s 3(2) 62
National Heritage Act 1993 s 6(3) 89
State Immunity Act 1978 173
Tribunals, Courts and Enforcement Act 2007 177
UK Museums and Galleries Act 1992 90

USA STATUTES

5 United States Code (USC) 34
Foreign Sovereign Immunities Act 1976 .... 105, 173
    ss 1602 to 1611 105
    ss 1605 to 1607 105

Foreign Sovereign Immunities Act 1976—*contd.*
    s 1605(a)(3) 105
Freedom of Information Act 1966 34
    s 552 34
Holocaust Expropriated Art Recovery Act 2016 .... 95, 103
    s 5(c) 104, 105
    s 5(d) 104
    s 5(e) 104
    s 5(e)(1) 104
    s 5(e)(2) 104
Immunity from Judicial Seizure Statute 1965 175
National Stolen Property Act 1934 56
Sonny Bono Copyright Term Extension Act 1998 (USA) 7

SWEDEN STATUTES

His Majesty's Gracious Ordinance Relating to Freedom of Writing and the
    Press 1766 34

TURKEY STATUTES

Turkish Law no 2863 1983 art 5 57

IRAN STATUTES

Iranian Legal Bill Regarding Prevention of Unauthorised Excavations and
    Digging 1979 art 1 57

AUSTRALIA STATUTES

Protection of Cultural Objects on Loan Act 2013 177

EGYPT STATUTES

Egyptian Law No 117 1983 art 9 56

EUROPEAN UNION DIRECTIVES

2014/52/EU 185
93/7/EEC 1993 169
Copyright Term Directive 2006/116/EC 7
Copyright Term Directive 2006/116/EC, art 1 7
Council Directive 2006/112/EC of 28 November 2006 on the common system of
    value added tax [2006] OJ L 347/1 .... 151, 152n
        art 2(1) 151

Table of Legislation

Council Directive 2006/112/EC of 28 November 2006 on the common system of value added tax [2006] OJ L 347/1—*contd.*
    art 135(e) 154
Data Protection Directive of 1995... 26
Directive (EU) 2019/1024 Open Data Directive 40
Directive (EU) 2019/790 Copyright and related rights in the Digital Single Market (DSM) 12
    art 14 20
    art 8 12
    art 8(5) 12
Directive 2001/84/EC Resale right for the benefit of the author of an original work of art... 18
    art 2 19
Directive 2006/115–Rental right and lending right and on certain rights related to copyright in the field of intellectual property 14, 15, 16
    art 2(1)(b) 14
    art 3 14
    art 3(1) 14, 15
    art 3(3) 14, 16
    art 6 14
Directive 2014/60/EU on the Return of Cultural Objects Unlawfully Removed from the Territory of a Member State 169, 176
    art 2(2)(b) 176
    art 9 169
EIA Directive 2011/92/EU.. 185
EU Third Money Laundering Directive (Directive 2005/60)............................... 75
InfoSoc Directive 2001/29/EC 49 3

EUROPEAN UNION REGULATIONS

Council Regulation (EC) No 116/2009... 164
    art 2(1) 164
    art 2(2) 164
    annex 1(A) 165
EU Regulation 2019/880... 162
    art 3(1) 162
    art 3(2) 162
    art 3(4)(c) 162
    art 4(1) 163
    art 4(4) 163
    art 5 163
    art 5(2) 163
    art 8 164
    art 8(2) 162
    part A Annex 162
    part B Annex 162, 164
    part C Annex 162, 164
EU Wildlife Trade Regulation (Regulation 338/97) 162
General Data Protection Regulation (GDPR)... 25, 26
    art 5 29

General Data Protection Regulation (GDPR)—*contd.*
    art 15 27
    art 27 28
    art 30(1) 31
    art 30(2) 31
    art 32 28,
    art 49(1) 31
    art 89(1) 29
Regulation (EU) No 1081/2012 165
Regulation (EU) No 386/2012 8

IRELAND CONVENTIONS AND AGREEMENTS

National Museum of Ireland Collections Disposal Policy 91
    s 3(1) 91
    s 3(2) 91
    s 5(5) 91

EUROPEAN UNION CONVENTIONS AND AGREEMENTS

Charter of Fundamental Rights of the European Union 2000 .... 16, 26
    art 8 26
    art 11 16
    art 14 16
Convention for the Protection of the Architectural Heritage of Europe (Grenada
    Convention) 1985 129
    art 3 129
    art 4(2)(c) 129
EC Treaty (Treaty of Maastricht) 1992 168
European Convention on State Immunity 173
    art 5 174
Lisbon Treaty (TEU) 2007 168
TFEU (Treaty on the Functioning of the European Union) 168
    art 2(2) 170n
    art 34 169
    art 35 169
    art 36 .... 169, 170
Treaty of Rome 1957 (EEC) 168

INTERNATIONAL CONVENTIONS AND AGREEMENTS

Berne Convention for the Protection of Literary and Artistic Works 1886 4
Berne Convention for the Protection of Literary and Artistic Works 1979 .... 4, 17
Berne Convention 1979 s 10(1) 10
Convention on International Trade in Endangered Species of Wild
    Fauna and Flora 1973 .... 77, 78, 80, 160, 161
    art 10(6) 77, 80, 81, 161

Table of Legislation

Draft Convention on Immunity from Suit and Seizure for Cultural Objects Temporarily Abroad for Cultural, Educational or Scientific Purposes by the International Law Association 175
Hague Convention for the Protection of Cultural Property in the Event of Armed Conflict 1954 .... 63, 77, 78, 87, 159, 160
    part 1 160
International Council of Museums Guidelines on Deaccessioning of the International Council of Museums 89, 90, 91
International Council of Museums, 'Code of Ethics' 1986 .... 81, 112
    art 2.1 82
    art 2.2 82
    art 2.3 82
International Council of Museums, 'ICOM Guidelines for Loan Agreements' 172
International Foundation for Art Research, 'Professional Guidelines established by International Association of Dealers in Ancient Art annex 1(2) 83
UN Declaration on the Rights of Indigenous Peoples 2007 77
UNESCO 'International Code of Ethics for Dealers in Cultural Property 1999 82
    art 1 82
    art 4 82
UNESCO 2001 Convention for the Protection of Underwater Heritage 77, 78, 79, 134, 139
UNESCO 2003 Convention for the Safeguarding of Intangible Cultural Heritage; 77, 79
UNESCO Convention concerning the Protection of the World Cultural and Natural Heritage 1972 .... 183, 194
    art 11 .... 183, 184
UNESCO Convention on the Means of Prohibiting and Preventing the Illicit Import, Export and Transfer of Cultural Property 1970 .... 77, 78, 94, 95, 97, 98, 99.159
    art 7(b)(i) 159
    art 7(b)(ii) 159
    art 9 159
UNIDROIT Convention on Stolen or Illegally Exported Cultural Objects 1995 ...... 77, 78, 88, 91, 94, 95, 96, 97, 98, 99, 159
    art 3 96
    art 3(1) 78, 95, 96
    art 3(2) 96
    art 3(4) 97
    art 3(5) 97
    art 3(6) 97
    art 3(8) 97
    art 4 .... 96, 99
    art 4(4) 99
    art 5 .... 96, 160
    art 10(1) 96
    art 10(1)(a) 96
    art 10(1)(b) 96
    art 10(2) 96
    art 10(3) 96, 160
UNIDROIT Model Provisions on State Ownership of Undiscovered Cultural Objects (2011) 58

United Nations Convention on Jurisdictional Immunities of States and
    Their Property 173
United Nations Convention on the Law of the Sea 137
    Part V1 (s 3(3)!! unclear on page 135) 135
    art 56 137
United Nations Declaration on the Rights of Indigenous Peoples
    (UNDRIP) 2007 91
    art 12 .... 81, 92

Chapter 1

Copyright and Moral Rights

Copyright: A Brief History

Ireland's first recorded instance of copyright enforcement dates back to the 6th century, when King Diarmaid ruled in a dispute between St Columba (also known as St Colmcille) and St Finian. Columba had borrowed a psalter from Finian and secretly copied it in order to have a copy to study at his leisure. Diarmaid famously stated, ruling in Finian's favour, that "to every cow belongs its calf, to every book its copy." In other words, each copy of a book belonged to the owner of the original. This resulted in the battle of Cúl Dreimhne, also known as the Battle of the Book, and Columba's banishment.

Some nine hundred years later, in or around 1450, Johannes Gutenberg perfected the oil-based movable type printing press, having previously failed in such enterprises as the manufacture and sale of polished metal mirrors which were claimed to capture and retain 'holy light' from religious relics. In 1455, Gutenberg completed printing some 180 copies of his 42-line Bible, known to history as the *Gutenberg Bible*.

As printing technology spread throughout Europe, different regulations emerged relating to the control of printing presses. In England, control was vested in the Stationers' Company, a livery company formed in London in 1403 and receiving a Royal Charter in 1557. The Stationers' Company held a Crown monopoly over publishing under the Licensing of the Press Act 1662, which required them to act as censors in return for the exclusive power to print. It was this power of censorship that led to increasing protests by authors, who sought to prevent the renewal of the Act that was required on a two-yearly basis. In 1694, Parliament refused to renew the Licensing of the Press Act.

After a period of deadlock lasting from 1694, the Stationers hit on the strategy of emphasising the benefits of licensing to the authors of works, rather than to the publishers. This resulted in the passage of the Statute of Anne in 1710. The Statute of Anne prescribed a copyright term of 14 years, while allowing an extension of a further term of 14 years — during which term only the printers to whom the author had licensed their work would be allowed to print it. Once this 28-year term expired works entered the public domain and could be reproduced freely.

London publishers who found their income eroded by Scottish printers publishing public domain works sought to persuade the English Courts that the Statute of Anne merely supplemented perpetual protection at common law that, they believed, the first publisher should enjoy. This interlude, known as 'The Battle of the Booksellers' culminated in the case of *Donaldson v Becket*[1] in 1774, where many of the issues we currently understand as being governed by considerations of copyright were first aired in detail.

> "Mr. Attorney General Thurlow opened as counsel for the appellants. He first entered into a minute investigation of the idea inculcated by what is called a publication; he then dwelt much upon the sense of the word 'property,' defining it philosophically, and in the separate lights of being corporeal and spiritual; the term Literary Property, he in a manner laughed at, as signifying nothing but what was of too abstruse and chimerical a nature to be defined. The booksellers, he observed, (exemplifying his observations by several cases) had not, till lately, ever concerned themselves about authors, but had generally confined the substance of their prayers to the legislature, to the security of their own property; nor would they probably have, of late years, introduced the authors as parties in their claims to the common law right of exclusively multiplying copies, had not they found it necessary to give a colourable face to their monopoly. He was very diffusive upon grants, charters, licences, and patents from the crown, both to corporate bodies and individuals, tracing them far back, and asserting, that they all specifically proved, that if there had been any inherent right of exclusively multiplying copies, such instances of exerting the royal prerogative would have been unnecessary. He particularly adverted to the statute of the 8th of queen Anne, maintaining that it was not merely an accumulative act declaratory of the common law, and giving additional penalties, but that it was a new law to give learned men a property which they had not before."[2]

The right to reproduce works after the 28-year period of protection had elapsed was conclusively held by the courts.

This status quo remained until the passage of the Copyright Act of 1842, which set copyright protection at the author's lifetime plus seven years, or, if their death occurred less than 42 years after publication, for 42 years from the date of publication. Changes to the categories of work protected

---

[1] *Donaldson v Becket* (1774) *Hansard*, 1st ser, 17 (1774): 953-1003.
[2] 'Cobbett's Parliamentary History of England' (1806-1820) vol XVII quoted in Karl-Erik Tallmo 'The History of Copyright: A Critical Overview With Source Texts in Five Languages' (unpublished) at https://www.copyrighthistory.com/donaldson.html accessed 21 August 2024.

by copyright resulted from case law in the matter of musical compositions; and through legislation such as the Engraving Copyright Act of 1734 and Fine Arts Copyright Act of 1862 which extended copyright to engravings, paintings, photographs and drawings.

The Copyright Act of 1911 was the last copyright act of the UK Parliament to have direct effect in Ireland. The 1911 Act implemented changes arising from the 1908 Berne Convention for the Protection of Literary and Artistic Works — namely abolishing common law copyright in unpublished works and adding sound recordings to the categories of works to which copyright applied. The 1911 Act also extended the duration of copyright to 50 years after the author's death, among other amendments — specifically in relation to copyright exemptions — while implementing copyright law throughout the UK and British Empire.

The Industrial and Commercial Property (Protection) Act 1927 was the first copyright legislation passed by the Oireachtas of the Irish Free State, which retained a 50-year post-death copyright period. The Copyright Act 1963 *inter alia* added new media to the works protected by copyright, including television broadcasts; and the Copyright Act 1987 introduced a new offence of public performance of copyright material where it was known to be copyright.

Copyright in Ireland

In Ireland, copyright is now governed by the Copyright and Related Rights Act 2000 as amended ('CRRA'), although in many respects copyright law has largely been harmonised across the European Union through a number of directives. One such directive is 2001/29/EC 49 of the European Parliament and of the Council of 22 May 2001 on the harmonisation of certain aspects of copyright and related rights in the information society, known colloquially, and more manageably, as the InfoSoc Directive.

The InfoSoc Directive states:

> "(10) If authors or performers are to continue their creative and artistic work, they have to receive an appropriate reward for the use of their work, as must producers in order to be able to finance this work…
>
> (11) A rigorous, effective system for the protection of copyright and related rights is one of the main ways of ensuring that European cultural creativity and production receive the necessary resources and of safeguarding the independence and dignity of artistic creators and performers."

Copyright protection is also governed by international law under the Berne Convention for the Protection of Literary and Artistic Works, completed at Paris in 1886 and most recently amended on 28 September 1979.

The basic principles of the Berne Convention are that works originating in one contracting state must be afforded the same protection in other contracting states as in the state of origin; protection must not be conditional upon compliance with any formality — in other words it must be automatic; and protection is independent of protection in the country of origin, subject to potential expiry of protection in a contracting state if the country of origin defines shorter protection periods. What this means is if a contracting state defines a longer period of protection than the country from which the work originates, then the work in question must be protected for the longer period.

As of October 2022, the 178 states comprising the United Nations, together with the Cook Islands, The Holy See and Niue, a self-governing island country in free association with New Zealand, are parties to the convention.

In Irish law, the CRRA defines copyright protection in the following terms at s 17:

> "1) Copyright is a property right whereby, subject to this Act, the owner of the copyright in any work may undertake or authorise other persons in relation to that work to undertake certain acts in the State, being acts which are designated by this Act as acts restricted by copyright in a work of that description."

Section 17 goes on to state that copyright subsists, in accordance with the Act, in "original literary, dramatic, musical or artistic works"; "sound recordings, films, broadcasts or cable programmes"; "the typographical arrangement of published editions"; and "original databases".

At s 17(3) the CRRA notes that copyright protection "shall not extend to the ideas and principles which underlie any element of a work, procedures, methods of operation or mathematical concepts and, in respect of original databases, shall not extend to their contents and is without prejudice to any rights subsisting in those contents."

A 'literary work' means any written or printed composition. The requirement for originality relates to the expression of something in writing or print rather than the originality of the ideas expressed *per se*. To meet the threshold of originality it is merely required that the author has made use of their "skill, judgement and labour"[3] in its creation.

This threshold was set by the judgment at appeal of the case brought between bookmakers William Hill and Ladbroke for infringement of copyright in compiled lists of fixed odds football betting coupons. Despite the opinion of Lord Denning that the coupons had "no more appeal to the aesthetic sense than a set of logarithm tables or an income tax return, which are more apt to produce a feeling of revulsion than a sense of beauty,"[4] the work of compiling the lists required skill, judgment and labour and was therefore copyright. While, as a UK ruling, this judgment is not binding in Ireland, it is persuasive.

In this sense the majority of 'works,' for instance records, books, audio recordings, video recordings or films, documents and databases, held by any gallery, library, archive or museum, are literary works.

In the case of records created by a state body or institution, any records created before 1922 and before the foundation of the Irish state are Crown copyright. State records created after 1922 and after the foundation of the Irish state are government copyright. Any 'works' which are not state records are the copyright of the author.

Defined at s 21 of the CRRA 'author' means the person who creates a work and includes:

"(a) in the case of a sound recording, the producer;
(b) in the case of a film (including the soundtrack accompanying the film), the producer and the principal director;
(c) in the case of a broadcast, the person making the broadcast or in the case of a broadcast which relays another broadcast by reception and immediate retransmission, without alteration, the person making that other broadcast;
(d) in the case of a cable programme, the person providing the cable programme service in which the programme is included;
(e) in the case of a typographical arrangement of a published edition, the publisher;
(f) in the case of a work which is computer-generated, the person by whom the arrangements necessary for the creation of the work are undertaken;
(g) in the case of an original database, the individual or group of individuals who made the database; and
(h) in the case of a photograph, the photographer."

In relation to litigation brought for copyright infringement, the CRRA

---

[3] *Ladbroke (Football) Ltd v William Hill (Football) Ltd* [1964] 1 WLR 273.
[4] *Ladbroke (Football) Ltd v William Hill (Football) Ltd* [1980] RPC 544.

presumes that copyright exists in a work until otherwise proven, and that the plaintiff is the holder of the copyright unless the contrary is proven.

Section 37 of the CRRA provides for the nature of the rights possessed by the copyright holder, and that anyone who performs one of these acts without the permission of the copyright holder is guilty of an infringement. The rights under s 37(1) are to copy the work; to make available to the public the work and to make an adaptation of the work.

Section 39 of the CRRA details copying a work, as described in s 37(1)(a), under the heading of 'reproduction right', and states that copying will be construed as meaning "storing the work in any medium". For instance, digitising a book or recording and storing it on a server.

Section 40 of the CRRA expands on what constitutes making a work available under s 37(1)(b):

"(a) making available to the public of copies of a work, by wire or wireless means, in such a way that members of the public may access the work from a place and at a time chosen by them (including the making available of copies of works through the internet)
(b) performing, showing or playing a copy of the work in public
(c) broadcasting a copy of the work
(d) including a copy of the work in a cable programme service
(e) issuing copies of the work to the public
(f) renting copies of the work
(g) lending copies of the work"

Copyright Exhaustion

The principle of exhaustion is an international legal doctrine which acts to limit the control an original copyright holder can have over goods after their first sale by the copyright owner, or their first sale on consent — for instance by a publisher to whom they have assigned rights to sell their work. What this means in broad effect is that the copyright owner cannot prevent the resale or loan of the work as the copyright is 'exhausted' by the sale. It is this principle that supports the lending of books by *inter alia* public libraries, despite libraries themselves predating the concept of copyright law by almost two thousand years — the oldest known library being that of Ashurbanipal in Nineveh in modern Iraq, founded in the 7th century BC.

Copyright Duration

The Copyright Term Directive 2006/116/EC is a European Union Directive which harmonises the term of copyright protection across the EU and was transposed into Irish law by the CRRA. Article 1 of the Directive states that copyright "shall run for the life of the author and for 70 years after his death, irrespective of the date when the work is lawfully made available to the public." The rights of 'performers' last 50 years under the Directive, which is significant as a sound recording accordingly only attracts 50 years' protection from the date upon which it is made, or from the date of its first lawful broadcast, whichever is later. A musical 'work' is protected for 70 years from the death of the author.

Films are protected for 70 years after the death of the last author or director of the film; broadcasts are protected for 50 years after the broadcast was legally transmitted.

On the expiry of the term of copyright protection works are deemed to have entered the 'public domain' and can be freely copied, distributed and republished, including in translation.

There are, of course, variations in copyright term internationally. In the US, for instance, following the Sonny Bono Copyright Term Extension Act of 1998, for works published between 1923 and the end of 1977, Copyright lasts until 95 years after the year of first publication (provided that for editions published in the US, the work was published with a copyright notice and copyright in works published between 1923 and the end of 1963 was renewed). In Spain Copyright lasts for 70 years after death for authors that died on or after 7 December 1987, and for 80 years for authors that died before 7 December 1987.

To give a practical example, the works of James Joyce, who died in Zurich in 1941, are now public domain throughout Europe as 70 years (or 80 years in Spain's case) have expired. In the US *Pomes Pennyeach*, published in 1927 is in the public domain. *Ulysses*, published in the US in 1934 by Random House will not enter public domain until 2030.

In 2004 when Joyce's works were still in copyright in Ireland, Stephen Joyce, his grandson, threatened to sue the National Library of Ireland for breach of copyright by displaying manuscripts and draft notebooks in a 'James Joyce and Ulysses' exhibition, as well as threatening to sue if any public readings of Joyce's work featured in any celebrations — for instance annual Bloom's Day events on 16 June.

The first film to feature the character Mickey Mouse, *Steamboat Willie*, entered the public domain on 1 January 2024 having first been released in 1928. Under US copyright law, 'characters' can receive protection for 95 years. However, more modern iterations of Mickey Mouse remain under copyright and the name *Steamboat Willie* is itself a trademark of Disney. The film has been available on YouTube for many years courtesy of Disney, so very little is liable to change with it entering public domain.

Copyright Exceptions

Orphan Works

An 'orphan work' is a work whose author(s) either cannot be identified, or if identifiable cannot be located. It is governed under Irish law by the European Union (Certain Permitted Uses of Orphan Works) Regulations 2014. The regulations require that a 'diligent search' be carried out, to include, as specified at r 5(1),

> "the database established and managed by the Office for Harmonization in the Internal Market in accordance with Regulation (EU) No 386/2012; the appropriate sources relevant to the category of relevant work as specified in the Schedule; and if there is evidence to suggest that relevant information on rightholders is to be found in other countries, sources of information available in those other countries."

The 'relevant body' seeking to use the work must maintain a record of each such diligent search and provide the following information to the Controller of Intellectual Property, based at the Intellectual Property Office of Ireland, as specified in the regulations at r 5(3),

> "the results of the diligent searches which the relevant body has carried out and which have led to the conclusion that the relevant work is considered to be an orphan work; the use that the relevant body makes of the orphan work concerned; any change, pursuant to Regulation 7, of the orphan work status of any relevant work used by the relevant body; and the relevant contact information of the relevant body."

The Controller will then forward that information to the Office for Harmonization in the Internal Market in order for the recording of that information on the online database established and managed by that office in accordance with Regulation (EU) No 386/2012. Once recorded on this database, certain uses of orphan works are permitted as described at r 8 of the regulations, namely

(a) making the orphan work available to the public

(b) an act of reproduction of the orphan work, for the purposes of digitisation, making available, indexing, cataloguing, preservation or restoration.

Regulation 8(3) states that the orphan work exemptions listed in the above paragraph only relate to instances where a relevant body shall use the orphan work only

> "in order to achieve aims related to its public interest mission, and in particular in relation to the preservation of, the restoration of and the provision of, cultural and educational access to, relevant works contained in its collection."

Regulation 8(4) allows for the generation of revenue, only so far as is necessary to cover the costs of digitisation and making available to the public and r 8(5) states that identified authors and rightsholders in the orphan work must be credited.

As a result, relevant bodies are free, having carried out 'diligent searches,' to digitise and make orphan works available to the public, while covering their costs as long as the authors or rightsholders are credited where they can be identified and the motivation for the digitisation is that body's public interest mission.

Fair Dealing

Chapter 6 of the CRRA details *'Acts Permitted in Relation to Works Protected by Copyright.'* The first of these acts is detailed at s 50(1), which explains that:

> "fair dealing with a literary, dramatic, musical or artistic work, sound recording, film, broadcast, cable programme, or non-electronic original database, for the purposes of research or private study, shall not infringe any copyright in the work."

And, at s 50(4), that:

> "'fair dealing' means the making use of a literary, dramatic, musical or artistic work, film, sound recording, broadcast, cable programme, non-electronic original database or typographical arrangement of a published edition which has already been lawfully made available to the public, for a purpose and to an extent which will not unreasonably prejudice the interests of the owner of the copyright."

Fair dealing is allowable for the purposes of criticism or review, making copies of part of a work (other than photograph) on current economic, political or religious matters made by a media business, making copies in the course of education or of preparation for education, unless carried out by a reprographic process (in which case an Irish Copyright Licensing Agency (ICLA) licence is required — see below), and that sufficient acknowledgement is included.

The ICLA provides licences to educational establishments, general business/administration, law firms and pharmaceutical companies, which allow for copying and making available copyright material under strict restrictions — typically no more than 10%, or one chapter of a book (temporarily increased to 20% during the COVID-19 pandemic).

Fair dealing is also addressed within the Berne Convention at article 10(1) which provides that quotations from a work which has already been lawfully made available to the public are permissible and that their extent does not exceed that justified by the purpose, as long as mention is made of the work and the author is credited where known.

Caricature, parody and pastiche are also regarded as fair dealing and will not infringe the copyright in that work. The UK Intellectual Property Office guidance from 2014 states that caricature "portrays its subject in a simplified or exaggerated way," the CJEU defined parody as evoking "an existing work while being noticeably different from it," and constituting "an expression of humour or mockery."[5]

While there appear to have been no significant judgments addressing the exact meanings of 'pastiche' it has been suggested that following an Oxford English Dictionary definition as "[a]n artistic work consisting of a medley of pieces imitating various sources" might be applicable, which would have obvious implications for, for example, AI generated artworks.[6]

For artworks, a number of exceptions are defined within the CRRA. Under s 94(1):

> "It is not an infringement of the copyright in an artistic work to copy it, or to make available to the public copies of it, for the purpose of advertising the sale or public exhibition of the work if the copying is done, and the copies are used—
> (a) only to an extent reasonably justified for achieving that purpose, and
> (b) for no other commercial purpose."

---

[5] Case C-201/13 *Deckmyn and Vrijheidsfonds v Vandersteen & Ors* [2014] ECLI:EU:C:2014:2132.

[6] Gillian Davies, Nicholas Caddick & Gwilym Harbottle, *Coppinger and Skone James on Copyright* (18th edn, Thomson Reuters Sweet & Maxwell 2021), 9-82.

Under s 95:

> "Where the author of an artistic work is not the copyright owner, it is not an infringement of the copyright in the work to copy the work in making another artistic work, where the author does not repeat or imitate the main design of the earlier work."

Exemptions for Librarians and Archivists

The CRRA allows for a number of important exemptions for librarians and archivists to allow them to carry out their core functions of preserving works and making them available to researchers. Under s 64 of the CRRA, librarians or archivists are allowed to make and supply to another prescribed library or prescribed archive a copy of a periodical or articles or the contents page contained therein and the whole or part of a work, which has been lawfully made available to the public. It is important to note these exemptions only apply where the librarian or archivist could not reasonably have obtained the consent of the author or rightsholder.

An exemption allowing for copying for preservation purposes is detailed at s 65, to allow the preservation or replacement of a work in addition to or in place of the original, or replacement of a work from the permanent collection of another prescribed library or archive which has been lost, destroyed or damaged. These exemptions do not apply where it is reasonably practical to purchase a copy of the work concerned, but the CRRA does not provide guidance on what it deems to be 'reasonably practical' steps to take to make a purchase.

Section 68 of the CRRA allows for the making of a copy of a work in the permanent collection of a prescribed library or archive in a different form, in other words digitisation, if lawful means are used to make the copy and the copy is made solely for preservation or archival purposes that are not directly or indirectly commercial. It is, of course, arguable that the best way to preserve any book or document is to digitise it and then only make the digital copy available to researchers to reduce wear and tear on the original. Section 68(3) states that "any contractual provisions contrary to this section shall be unenforceable", which means that a rightsholder cannot impose conditions on a library or archive to prevent preservation digitisation.

Under s 69A of the CRRA, the librarian or archivist of a prescribed library or prescribed archive may make available to members of the public "copies of works in the permanent collection of the library or archive, by dedicated terminals on the premises of the library or archive" where undertaken "for the sole purpose of education, teaching, research or private study, and accompanied by a sufficient acknowledgement."

It is important to note that s 70 states that where a copy is made under one of the exceptions listed above it cannot be sold, rented or lent or it will be treated as an infringing copy.

In summary, making of copies, for instance by digitisation, is allowable by librarians and archivists for preservation purposes, to supply a copy of a work to another library that has lost that work and cannot replace it, for non-commercial preservation or archival purposes or to make copies available at dedicated terminals on the premises of the library or archive.

DSM

The EU Directive on Copyright in the Digital Single Market (DSM) was transposed into Irish law by European Union (Copyright and Related Rights in the Digital Single Market) Regulations 2021 (SI No 567 of 2021). Article 8 of the DSM addresses the use of out-of-commerce works and other subject matter by cultural heritage institutions.

DSM defines out-of-commerce at article 8(5) as follows:

> "A work or other subject matter shall be deemed to be out of commerce when it can be presumed in good faith that the whole work or other subject matter is not available to the public through customary channels of commerce, after a reasonable effort has been made to determine whether it is available to the public."

While DSM does not define a 'cultural heritage institution' (and neither does SI No 567 of 2021), it does state in the recitals that

> "Cultural heritage institutions should be understood as covering publicly accessible libraries and museums regardless of the type of works or other subject matter that they hold in their permanent collections, as well as archives, film or audio heritage institutions. They should also be understood to include, inter alia, national libraries and national archives, and, as far as their archives and publicly accessible libraries are concerned, educational establishments, research organisations and public sector broadcasting organisations."

Regulation 8(1) of SI No 567 addresses the use of 'out of commerce' works by cultural heritage institutions.

> "A collective management organisation may, in accordance with its mandates

from rightholders, conclude a non-exclusive licence for non-commercial purposes with a cultural heritage institution for the reproduction, distribution, communication to the public or making available to the public of out-of-commerce works or other subject matter that are permanently in the collection of the said cultural heritage institution, irrespective of whether all rightholders covered by the licence have so mandated the collective management organisation."

In the case of Ireland this collective rights organisation is, presumably, the Irish Copyright Licensing Agency (ICLA). Provision is also made for rightsholders to exclude their works from this licensing mechanism.

Regulation 8(9) requires that

"At least 6 months before the work or other subject matter licensed under paragraph (1) is distributed, communicated to the public or made available to the public, cultural heritage institutions, collective management organisations and library authorities within the meaning of section 32 of the Local Government Act 1994 (Act No 8 of 1994) shall provide the following information on the Out-of-Commerce Works Portal established by the European Union Intellectual Property Office under the Directive: the title, where possible, the author, and a brief summary of the contents of an out-of-commerce work that is proposed to be the subject of a license under paragraph (1)".

This portal[7] is maintained by the European Union Intellectual Property Office (EUIPO) and at the time of writing there are no entries from Ireland.

Use of out-of-commerce works and other subject matter by cultural heritage institutions where no collective management organisation exists is addressed at regulation 9(1) which amends the CRRA by the insertion of the following s 58A after s 58:

"Cultural Heritage Institutions. (1) It is not an infringement of the rights conferred by this Part for a cultural heritage institution to make available, for non-commercial purposes, out-of-commerce works or other subject matter that are permanently in its collections, where – (a) no collective management organisation exists ... in relation to that database right, (b) it is accompanied by sufficient acknowledgment, and (c) such work is only made available on non-commercial websites".

Provision is also made for rightsholders to exclude their works from this licensing mechanism and there is a similar requirement for publication on the EUIPO portal.

---

[7] EUIPO, 'Out of Commerce Works Portal' <https://euipo.europa.eu/out-of-commerce/#/> accessed 21 August 2024.

Regulation 8 does not apply to sets of out-of-commerce works or other subject matter if they predominantly consist of works, other than cinematographic or audiovisual works, first published or, in the absence of publication, first broadcast in a third country; cinematographic or audiovisual works, of which the producers have their headquarters or habitual residence in a third country, or works of third country nationals, where after a reasonable effort no Member State or third country could be determined.

Lending of Works

Directive 2006/115/EC of the European Parliament and the Council of 12 December 2006 on rental right and lending right and on certain rights relating to copyright in the field of intellectual property states, at (3):

> "The adequate protection of copyright works and subject matter of related rights protection by rental and lending rights as well as the protection of the subject matter of related rights protection by the fixation right, distribution right, right to broadcast and communication to the public can accordingly be considered as being of fundamental importance for the economic and cultural development of the Community."

Article 2(1)(b) of Directive 2006/115/EC states that "'lending' means making available for use, for a limited period of time and not for direct or indirect economic or commercial advantage, when it is made through establishments which are accessible to the public." Article 3(1) states that the exclusive right to authorise or prohibit rental and lending shall belong to "the author in respect of the original and copies of his work." Article 3(3) states that "the rights referred to in paragraph 1 may be transferred, assigned or subject to the granting of contractual licences."

The effect of these rights is that an author, or the rightsholder if they have transferred their rights, may object to the lending of their work. However, a derogation exists at article 6 of the Directive, under which "Member States may derogate from the exclusive right provided for in Article 1 in respect of public lending, provided that at least authors obtain a remuneration for such lending". This remuneration is known as Public Lending Remuneration (PLR). Member States are allowed to exempt certain categories of establishments from paying PLR. In Ireland, educational bodies are exempt from paying PLR, but public libraries are required to pay PLR.

The Copyright and Related Rights (Public Lending Remunerations Scheme)

Regulations 2008 established a scheme to be known as the 'Public Lending Remuneration Scheme,' the purpose of which, as outlined at article 3(1), is to remunerate authors

> "out of moneys voted by the Oireachtas for the purpose, for the lending by public libraries of qualifying works, the qualifying works being eligible books and posthumously eligible books within the meaning of Article 7 and Article 8 of the Scheme respectively."

Section 42A(5) of the CRRA defines a public library as "a library to which members of the public have access that is operated by or under the direction of a library authority within the meaning of section 77(1) of the Local Government Act 2001." Section 77(1) of the Local Government Act 2001 states that a county council, a city council and a city and county council are all 'library authorities.'

In Ireland, PLR is managed by the Local Government Management Agency (LGMA) and paid to authors by the Irish Copyright Licensing Agency (ICLA).

PLR and e-Books

The position in EU law on whether Directive 2006/115/EC of the European Parliament and the Council of 12 December 2006 on rental right and lending right applied to e-books was in doubt since the introduction of e-books as a reading format until a landmark ECJ ruling in 2016.

In *Vereniging Openbare Bibliotheken v Stichting Leenrecht Vereniging Openbare Bibliotheken*,[8] a library association to which every public library in the Netherlands belongs (VOB) brought an action against Stichting Leenrecht, a foundation entrusted with collecting PLR, by which it sought a declaratory judgment to the effect that the regime for traditional books should also apply to digital lending.

VOB's action concerned lending under the 'one copy, one user' model, namely the lending of an electronic book carried out by placing that copy on the server of a public library and allowing the user concerned to reproduce that copy by downloading it onto their own computer, bearing in mind that only one copy may be downloaded during the lending period

---

[8] Case C-174/15, *Vereniging Openbare Bibliotheken v Stichting Leenrecht* [2016] ECLI:EU:C:2016:856.

and that, after that period has expired, the downloaded copy can no longer be used by that user.

This ruling clarifies that lending of electronic materials falls within the scope of Directive 2006/115/EC of the European Parliament and the Council of 12 December 2006 on rental right and lending right. This means that libraries can derogate from the rights of authors and rightsholders to prevent lending, providing PLR is paid, subject to certain bodies being exempt from PLR, and that provision is made for e-books in national PLR regulations.

Article 7(2)(a) of the Irish Copyright and Related Rights (Public Lending Remunerations Scheme) Regulations 2008 defines a 'book' as "a printed and bound publication (including a paperback edition)." There is no reference to e-books or audio books within the regulations.

In the UK, PLR was extended to e-books and audio books by the Digital Economy Act 2017, which crucially included the caveat that it "applies to an e-book or an e-audio-book only if... lending is in compliance with any purchase or licensing terms to which the book is subject." This allows publishers and third party intermediaries to continue to set terms in relation to price, availability, Technical Protection Measures (TPM), Digital Rights Management (DRM), bundling of titles with other titles and remote removal of access to titles; in contrast with the regime that exists for physical books.

In Irish law, as there is no provision for PLR for e-books or audio books within the Copyright and Related Rights (Public Lending Remunerations Scheme) Regulations 2008, the practice of e-book and audio book lending in Ireland is carried out under licence on an ad-hoc basis by libraries and educational establishments contracting directly with publishers or third party intermediaries, relying *inter alia* on article 3(3) of Directive 2006/115/EC. This allows publishers to set terms as detailed in the above paragraph.

The problems in relation to e-book lending were characterised by Ligue des Bibliothèques Européennes de Recherche (LIBER), a professional association of national and university research libraries throughout Europe, thus:

> "Article 11 and Article 14 of the European Charter of Fundamental Rights of the EU give European citizens the right to receive information regardless of frontiers, and the right to education and continued training. Lending and eLending by public libraries support both these rights. With eBooks, however,

the right of libraries to buy any book and lend it is currently being severely challenged.

Public libraries are not able to support education and learning in the way they used to because they are no longer free to buy and lend any book available in the marketplace. Libraries across Europe are reporting problems buying, licensing and lending eBooks to members of the public. Even where books are not available electronically, libraries don't have the right to digitise and then lend books, while applying payment to authors in line with the public lending right.

The problems are not technological. In fact, technology can be used to ensure that 'frictions' or differentiators exist, so as not to undermine viable eBook markets. In some cases, libraries are unable to purchase the material because publishers refuse to sell to them. Some publishers offer artificially higher pricing to libraries, making it difficult for libraries to purchase the range of titles their patrons want. Impractical licensing models are not uncommon, and not all books are available in electronic form."[9]

Moral Rights

A moral right is "a proprietary right which protects the personality of authors as expressed in their creations alongside their economic interests in exploitation."[10]

Under the Berne Convention the recognition of two 'moral rights' of authors are required — the 'attribution right,' or the right to be identified as the author, and the 'integrity right,' which is the right to object to any distortion, mutilation of or modification of, or other derogatory action in relation to the work which would prejudice his or her reputation. The 'integrity right' shall also apply in relation to an adaptation of the work.

In Irish law, moral rights are addressed at Chapter 7 of the CRRA. In addition to the 'attribution right,' a 'paternity right' exists, in that the author's right to be identified as the author of a work also applies to the right to be identified as the author of any adaptation of the work. Subject to exceptions similar in scope to those outlined under 'fair dealing' above, the author's 'integrity right' is also detailed in language mimicking the Berne Convention.

---

[9] LIBER, 'Limitations and Exceptions in EU Copyright Law for Libraries, Educational and Research Establishments: A Basic Guide' <https://libereurope.eu/wp-content/uploads/2020/09/A-Basic-Guide-to-Limitations-and-Exceptions-in-EU-Copyright-Law-for-Libraries-Educational-and-Research-FINAL-ONLINE-1.pdf> accessed 21 August 2024.

[10] William Cornish, David Llewellyn and Tanya Aplin, *Intellectual Property: Patents, Copyright, Trade Marks and Allied Rights*, (7th edn, Sweet and Maxwell 2010), p 513.

In August 2023, the British Museum settled a case in relation to the moral rights of Yilin Wang after using her translations of Chinese poet Qiu Jin "without permission, credit or payment" in the *China's Hidden Century* exhibition. The museum stated that it is

> "reviewing the permissions process it has in place for temporary exhibitions, particularly with regard to translations, to ensure that there is a timely and robust methodology underpinning our clearance work and our crediting of contributors going forward."[11]

The 1996 case of *Tidy v Trustees of the Natural History Museum*[12] was brought by cartoonist Bill Tidy on the basis that reproductions of his cartoons of dinosaurs in reduced size and against yellow and pink backgrounds (as opposed to the original white backgrounds) was a breach of copyright and moral rights. It was held that reproducing the cartoons without permission was a breach of Tidy's copyright, but the assertion that reducing their size and printing them on different backgrounds was derogatory treatment was dismissed.

Artist's Resale Right

The concept of Artist's Resale Right (ARR) originated in France as 'droit de suite,' to ensure that artists who sell a work in the early stages of their career for a small sum benefit from subsequent sales of the work by galleries and collectors, as their prominence and collectability increase.

Under the terms of Directive 2001/84/EC an ARR has been in existence in Ireland since June 2006. In order to qualify for ARR the work must be in copyright (claims can be made by heirs of the artist within 70 years of their death), it must be a second or subsequent sale of the work, the work must sell for €3,000 or more and the work must be sold through a gallery, auction house or art dealer. ARR is payable on a sliding scale based on the sale price of the work, subject to a ceiling of €12,500.

Liability for payment rests with the seller and the art market professionals responsible for the sale. ARR in Ireland is collected by the Irish Visual Artists Rights Organisation, to whom the seller or their agent must provide

---

[11] Anny Shaw, "British Museum settles case with translator after using work 'without permission, credit or payment', *The Art Newspaper* <https://www.theartnewspaper.com/2023/08/08/british-museum-settles-case-with-translator-after-using-work-without-permission-credit-or-payment> accessed 21 August 2024.

[12] *Tidy v Trustees of the Natural History Museum* [1996] 39 IPR 501.

such information as may be necessary to secure payment of the royalty within 90 days of the sale.

Article 2 of Directive 2001/84/EC defines which artworks are included in ARR:

> "1. For the purposes of this Directive, "original work of art" means works of graphic or plastic art such as pictures, collages, paintings, drawings, engravings, prints, lithographs, sculptures, tapestries, ceramics, glassware and photographs, provided they are made by the artist himself or are copies considered to be original works of art.
>
> 2. Copies of works of art covered by this Directive, which have been made in limited numbers by the artist himself or under his authority, shall be considered to be original works of art for the purposes of this Directive. Such copies will normally have been numbered, signed or otherwise duly authorised by the artist."

Outside of the EU, ARR is enforced in the UK and Australia, but is not enforced in the US, China, Switzerland or Japan. Consequently, sales to those countries from an EU country will not result in a payment to the artist.

Digitisation and Copyright

We have addressed the issue of the digitising and lending of copyright works within a library framework above.

Museums and libraries often assume that a digitised image of an item which is in the public domain is subject to copyright, as they believe that the act of generating the image is sufficient to meet the CRRA requirement that copyright subsists in "original literary, dramatic, musical or artistic works." The key question is, 'what is original'?

In November 2023, this issue was addressed by a judgment of the UK Court of Appeal in *THJ v Sheridan*,[13] which stated "[w]hat is required is that the author was able to express their creative abilities in the production of the work by making free and creative choices so as to stamp the work created with their personal touch," and that "this criterion is not satisfied where the content of the work is dictated by technical considerations, rules or other constraints which leave no room for creative freedom."

Typically, galleries, libraries, archives and museums have claimed full

---

[13] *THJ Systems Limited & Anor v Daniel Sheridan & Anor* [2023] EWCA Civ 1354.

copyright over digitised materials or have used 'creative commons licences,' while demanding fees for reproduction for commercial purposes. What this judgment indicates is that no new copyright arises in the production of faithfully digitised images of public domain materials, where the original work being digitised is two-dimensional.

While, as a UK ruling, this judgment is persuasive but not binding, it would seem to be supported by article 14 of Directive (EU) 2019/790 of the European Parliament and of the Council of 17 April 2019 on copyright and related rights in the Digital Single Market (DSM) which states:

> "Member States shall provide that, when the term of protection of a work of visual art has expired, any material resulting from an act of reproduction of that work is not subject to copyright or related rights, unless the material resulting from that act of reproduction is original in the sense that it is the author's own intellectual creation."

The situation in relation to images of objects, or three-dimensional works, would appear to be different. In the UK case of *Antiquesportfolio.com v Rodney Fitch and Co Ltd*,[14] it was held that copyright protection did extend to images of antiques, as the capture of the images required skill and effort in positioning the items, lighting the items, choice of details to highlight and the angle of the photograph. This protection could safely be assumed to extend to plastic arts.

Photographing a painting arguably also requires skill and effort to ensure the image is appropriately lit. Oil paintings are certainly three-dimensional. What might be harder to defend is the use of a flatbed scanner, book scanner or other orbital camera when used to capture a series of documents or photographs using pre-determined resolution, colour and size settings.

It is worth noting however that the J Paul Getty Museum in Los Angeles released 88,000 images of artworks in its collections under a CC0 licence – which licence in effect is a mechanism to announce to potential users that the creator of the digitised works asserts no copyright over them. Indeed the museum has actively promoted the free re-use of the works through its social media channels and in a press release has stated "users can download, edit, and repurpose high resolution images of their favourite Getty artworks without any legal restrictions [resulting in] ... an uptick in image downloads on our site, averaging about 30,000 per month."[15]

---

[14] *Antiquesportfolio.com plc v Rodney Fitch & Co Ltd* [2001] FSR 345.
[15] Brigitte Vézina, 'Getty Museum releases 88K+ images of artworks with CC0' <https://creativecommons.org/2024/03/13/getty-museum-releases-88k-images-of-artworks-with-cc0/> accessed 21 August 2024.

Case Study: *Winnie-the-Pooh*

Winnie-the-Pooh and his associated copyright wrangles are a useful illustration of how copyright durations in different jurisdictions can interoperate. It also demonstrates the potential difficulties rights-holders can be confronted with in the event that copyright duration is later altered by legislation in a country in which the rights have been acquired. This can lead to a requirement to renegotiate previously settled contracts.

The creator of Winnie-the-Pooh, AA Milne, died on 31 January 1956 in Hartfield, Sussex. From 1 January 2027, seventy years after the year of Milne's death, the Winnie-the-Pooh books will be out of copyright in the EU and the UK.

Milne wrote *Winnie-the-Pooh* in 1926, *Now We are Six* in 1927 and *The House at Pooh Corner* in 1928. While Milne held the copyright in his works until his death, in 1930 he sold the North American merchandising and recording rights to Stephen Slesinger for $1,000 plus a royalty on sales. In 1953, Slesinger died and in 1961, his widow sold the rights he had acquired under the 1930 agreement to Walt Disney.

On his death in 1956, Milne's widow inherited a portion of his rights, which were also divided among Milne's alma mater, Westminster School; his club, The Garrick Club; and The Royal Literary Fund. Disney concluded separate deals with each of these rights-holders in relation to payment of royalties when it bought out the rights entailed in the 1930 Slesinger agreement in 1961.

At the time of Milne signing the agreement with Slesinger in 1930, his works were subject to the copyright duration set out in the US Copyright Act 1909. Under the terms of this Act, copyright in his works would expire 56 years after their publication, in the early 1980s. The US 1976 Copyright Act extended this period of protection to 50 years after the death of the author, into the early 2000s.

Significantly the US 1976 Act included a termination right for authors, in recognition that authors are frequently in a disadvantaged bargaining position compared to large corporations, particularly early in their careers. For any agreements reached before 1978, the Act provided that authors could terminate licensing agreements during a five-year period starting at the end of 56 years from the date of the beginning of copyright. In the case of the Slesinger deal, this meant that the estate of Milne could terminate the agreement reached in 1930 between 1982 and 1987, thus rendering

Disney's rights acquired under this agreement void. Disney would, though, have retained rights in 'derivative works' — in this case the series of Winnie-the-Pooh animated films.

In 1983, new negotiations took place between Slesinger's widow, and Christopher Robin Milne, who had inherited the rights after his mother's death. This resulted in the 1930 and 1961 agreements being rescinded and a new agreement being reached which granted rights to Slesinger's widow, who in turn granted the rights to Disney — for undisclosed sums. In 2001, Disney bought out all the rights owned by the four other rights-holders for a reported $350 million. Disney currently makes an estimated $3-$6 billion a year from Winnie-the-Pooh, so the undisclosed sums paid by Disney in 1961, 1983 and again in 2001, were certainly excellent investments.

Chapter 2

Data Protection, Freedom of Information and Open Data

Data Sharing: A Brief History

Large scale data sharing for scientific, research and other less noble purposes is not a new phenomenon — indeed it has been with us for almost 150 years.

The earliest known data sharing protocol dates to 1873, when the Vienna International Meteorological Congress tasked a permanent meteorological committee to draft a set of rules and statutes for the creation of an international meteorological organisation to allow for cross border sharing of weather information. This task was completed by 1878, and in 1879, the resulting International Meteorological Organisation was founded. Countries across the world have made meteorological data available on a daily basis at an ever-increasing rate since then — for instance "1,632 Indian stations provided daily data in 1901 and 2,536 stations in 1970."[1]

Throughout the 1880s a variety of technological innovations changed the way in which data was stored and disseminated. The computing scale was patented in 1885 and the dial recorder in 1888. In 1889 a clock to record workers' arrival and departure times on ticker tape was invented. The electric tabulating machine, also known as the 'Hollerith Machine' for its inventor Edmund Hollerith — designed to assist in summarising information stored on punch cards — was developed to assist in processing of data for the 1890 US census. The Hollerith Machine was the first instance of data being recorded on a machine readable medium and signalled the start of mass data processing as we now know it.

In 1911, IBM was founded as the Computing-Tabulating-Recording Company, renamed as International Business Machines in 1924. By the 1930s in Germany the negative possibilities of data collection, processing

---

[1] Joan Sieber, 'Data Sharing in Historical Perspective', Journal of Empirical Research on Human Research Ethics (2015) Vol 10 (3) 215–216.

and sharing were being felt as the Nazis implemented Hollerith Machine technologies via a wholly owned IBM subsidiary Deutsche Hollerith-Maschinen to carry out repeated censuses of Germany and occupied territories to facilitate the identification, roundup, internment and liquidation of Jews and other targeted groups.

By the 1950s, IBM had taught a computer to play checkers and learn from its mistakes, thus demonstrating the possibility of developing Artificial Intelligence, as well as pioneering breakthroughs such as the storing of computer programs on vacuum tubes, then hard discs, as well as developing some of the first programming languages.

The internet dates back to the 1960s as a mechanism by which researchers working on government projects could share information stored on computers. At this point 'mainframe' computers were often the size of a room, and sharing information meant either physically visiting the site of a computer or transferring information onto a reel-to-reel tape and transporting or posting that tape to the location with which you wished to share your data.

The Cold War accelerated the development of the internet as the US Defence Department began to think of ways that information might continue to be shared in the event of a nuclear attack from the Soviet Union, which would render postal systems inoperative and make travel perilous if not impossible. The Advanced Research Projects Agency Network (ARPANET) was the result. ARPANET was a limited network of research institutions and universities, all of whom carried out defence contracts. In 1975, the US Defence Communication Agency took over the operation of ARPANET and created a new program known as the Defence Data Network (DDN).

The internet as we know it is generally considered to have been 'born' on 1 January 1983, which is the date from which Transfer Control Protocol / Internetwork Protocol (TCP/IP), a new protocol that allowed different types of computers on different networks to communicate with each other, was adopted as the primary communications protocol for ARPANET and the DDN.

The World Wide Web was launched in 1991 allowing users from any connected computer to access resources and web pages from any connected computer using Uniform Resource Locators (URLs) which act as an address to allow a computer to find a resource on the internet. Users can then download content from these resources using Hypertext Transfer Protocol (HTTP) or create their own resources using Hypertext Markup Language (HTML).

In 1993, the internet accounted for 1% of information passing through two-way communications networks, 51% by 2000 and more than 97% by 2007.[2] Use of the internet continues to grow, with social networks, entertainment streaming and e-commerce all driving the extent to which it has become part of the everyday fabric of life in the 21st century. Consequently, never has so much personal information on so many people been made available to the corporations that provide these services.

In many cases, the harvesting of data on users' demographics and their likes and dislikes and then either packaging and reselling it, in order to allow third parties to more effectively market to those users, or using it to create targeted advertising services to third parties, have been the primary revenue model of internet businesses.

Large-scale storage of personal data sets is also exposed to the possibility of attack and ransom by bad actors. In 2023, the British Library was subject to a cyber-attack by a hacker gang known as 'Rhysida,' which broke in via the library's Virtual Private Network (VPN), designed to allow employees to work remotely. Rhysida stole personal details on employees from their contracts and scans of identification — such as passports — and offered it back to the British Library for a £600,000 ransom. When the library refused to pay the ransom some 500,000 files were made available for free download on the dark web. Aside from the possible negative consequences for the individuals whose data had been made available — ranging from impersonation to hacking of personal bank accounts — the British Library's core systems were rendered inoperative, making access to its 170 million items impossible.

The EU's response to threats posed to its' citizens data by a rapidly changing technological environment was the General Data Protection Regulation (GDPR).

---

[2] Martin Hilbert and Priscila López, 'The World's Technological Capacity to Store, Communicate, and Compute Information' (April 2011) Science 332 (6025): 60–65.

GDPR

Under article 8 of the EU Charter of Fundamental Rights 2000, which came into force in December 2009,

> "[e]veryone has the right to the protection of personal data concerning him or her… [s]uch data must be processed fairly for specified purposes and on the basis of the consent of the person concerned or some other legitimate basis laid down by law. Everyone has the right of access to data which has been collected concerning him or her, and the right to have it rectified."

GDPR was adopted into EU Law in 2016, replacing the earlier Data Protection Directive of 1995. GDPR was designed to address the impact of the internet on all EU citizens' lives and the myriad uses to which their personal data might be put with or without their permission, none of which could have been foreseen in 1995 during the early days of the internet.

Following the principle of 'direct effect' GDPR is directly applicable in Ireland, while allowing for issues to be given further effect in national law. In Ireland, the Data Protection Act 2018 (2018 Act) was enacted for the purpose of giving effect to GDPR. The 2018 Act gives effect to the limited exclusions and restrictions permitted under GDPR (about which more below) and provides for a number of amendments to the 1988 and 2003 Data Protection Acts as a result. GDPR has prospective effect, which means that it only has application in relation to a data protection complaint from 25 May 2018 onwards, any complaints that predate that period will be dealt with under the Data Protection Act 1988.

Under GDPR, 'personal data' is data that relates to or can identify a living person either on its own or together with other available information. Personal data might, for instance, comprise a person's name, phone number, address, date of birth, banking details, medical history, location history from a mobile phone or internet browsing history. The data subject (person to whom the personal data relates) has certain rights under GDPR, including a right of access as well as the right of rectification or correction of inaccurate personal data.

Bodies that hold personal data are divided into two categories: data controllers and data processors. Processors must only process personal data on the instruction of a controller, whereas controllers define the purpose and means of the processing of data. Processors must carry out any processing under the terms of a legally binding contract, and must undertake to implement appropriate technical and organisational measures to ensure compliance with GDPR and data subjects' rights.

The definition of what counts as 'processing' under GDPR is a broad one, encompassing

> "a wide range of operations performed on personal data, including by manual or automated means. It includes the collection, recording, organisation, structuring, storage, adaptation or alteration, retrieval, consultation, use, disclosure by transmission, dissemination or otherwise making available, alignment or combination, restriction, erasure or destruction of personal data."[3]

It is clear on this basis that activities carried out by galleries, libraries, archives and museums comprise processing.

The rights of a data subject under GDPR include the right of access, the right to rectification (correction of incorrect information about the data subject), the right to erasure, the right to restrict processing, the right to data portability (being allowed to move, copy or transfer personal data from one IT environment to another), the right to object to data being used for certain purposes (such as direct marketing), where the right to object is absolute, but also tasks where data is processed in the public interest and the right not to be subject to a decision which was reached solely through the automated processing of their data.

Article 15 of the GDPR gives individuals the right to obtain from a data controller confirmation as to whether or not personal data concerning them are being processed and if such personal data exists, a copy of that data. Requests made under the provisions of article 15 are often referred to as data subject access requests (DSARs) or access requests.

Article 15 also provides for a right to access to the following information:

> "the purposes of the processing; the categories of personal data concerned; the recipients or categories of recipient to whom the personal data have been or will be disclosed, in particular recipients in third countries or international organisations; where possible, the envisaged period for which the personal data will be stored, or, if not possible, the criteria used to determine that period; the existence of the right to request from the controller rectification or erasure of personal data or restriction of processing of personal data concerning the data subject or to object to such processing; the right to lodge a complaint with a supervisory authority; where the personal data are not collected from the data subject, any available information as to their source; the existence of automated decision-making, including profiling."

---

[3] 'What constitutes data processing?' European Commission Official Website, https://commission.europa.eu/law/law-topic/data-protection/reform/what-constitutes-data-processing_en# accessed 21 August 2024.

Where such profiling has taken place, the data subject may request "meaningful information about the logic involved, as well as the significance and the envisaged consequences of such processing for the data subject."

The provision for DSARs under GDPR has led to widespread concern among holders of historical archives that contain personal data, for instance personnel records, records of legal complaints or corporate records, that they will be expected to search through, rectify, export or anonymise millions of records.

However, in the words of MB Donnelly, Deputy Commissioner and Head of Governance, Finance and Risk at the Data Protection Commission,

> "[t]here was a culture of monetised fear… because there was such anticipation and anxiety about what GDPR would mean for organisations. People working in this space are moving out of that state of fear, which is something we never wanted and never advocated."[4]

This culture of monetised fear will be familiar to readers who remember the Y2K bug and to those following current pronouncements on the future of AI.

The first and most important thing to remember in relation to personal data contained in galleries, archives, libraries and museums is that, under recital 27 of GDPR "[t]his Regulation does not apply to the personal data of deceased persons." As a rule of thumb it is usually accepted that records over 100 years old will not contain any data on living persons. This has long been the rationale for setting the date of release of census records.

The one exception to this in Irish law relates to 'Individual Health Identifiers'. On the enactment of the Health Identifiers Act in 2014, residents and former residents in Ireland with a Personal Public Services Number (PPSN) were given an Individual Health Identifier (IHI) number. The 2014 Act, as amended by the 2018 Act states that article 32 of GDPR applies to data relating to Individual Health Identifiers, whether living or deceased and as a result:

> "the controller and processor shall take steps to ensure that any natural person acting under the authority of the controller or the processor who has access to

---

[4] PWC Ireland, 'GDPR five years on: successes, shortcomings and the road ahead' <https://www.pwc.ie/services/consulting/insights/gdpr-five-years-on.html> accessed 21 August 2024.

personal data does not process them except on instructions from the controller, unless he or she is required to do so by Union or Member State law"

Records Less than 100 Years Old

Article 5 of GDPR sets out that personal data must be processed lawfully, fairly and transparently, that it must be collected for specified, explicit and legitimate purposes and not further processed in a manner that is incompatible with those purposes. Article 5 allows an exemption that personal data processed for "archiving purposes in the public interest, scientific or historical research purposes or statistical purposes" is not considered to be stored for a purpose incompatible with the purpose for which it was originally collected.

Section 61 of the 2018 Act gives effect to that exemption by restricting the rights of data subjects where processing of data is for "archiving purposes in the public interest, scientific or historical research purposes or statistical purposes." The rights restricted under this section are the rights to access, rectification, restriction of processing, data portability and the right to object. Where the processing of data is carried out for archiving purposes in the public interest the rights restricted are done so to the extent that "the exercise of any of those rights would be likely to render impossible, or seriously impair, the achievement of those purposes, and such restriction is necessary for the fulfilment of those purposes."

Black's Law Dictionary[5] defines public interest as

> "1. The general welfare of a populace considered as warranting recognition and protection.
> 2. Something in which the public as a whole has a stake; esp., an interest that justifies governmental regulation."

It is therefore reasonable to assume that any gallery, library, archive or museum that holds archival materials does so in the public interest, or for scientific or historical research purposes – certainly any such institution which operates on a not-for-profit basis or is funded centrally by the state or a state or semi-state body.

Article 89 (1) of GDPR provides that

> "[p]rocessing for archiving purposes in the public interest, scientific or historical

---

[5] *Black's Law Dictionary* (12th edn, Thompson West 2024).

research purposes or statistical purposes, shall be subject to appropriate safeguards, in accordance with this Regulation, for the rights and freedoms of the data subject."

The safeguards are required to ensure that technical and organisational measures are in place in order to ensure respect for the principle of data minimisation and may include pseudonymisation provided that those purposes can be fulfilled in that manner. Where processing can be done in a manner which does not identify data subjects it should be done in such a manner. This exemption is given effect in Irish law under s 42 of the 2018 Act.

Section 71(6)(a) of the 2018 Act allows for the processing of data that was initially collected by that controller or another controller for "archiving purposes in the public interest" for the prevention, investigation, detection or prosecution of criminal offences, including the safeguarding against, and the prevention of, threats to public security, or the execution of criminal penalties, and by means that are wholly or partly automated, or by non-automated means where the personal data form part of a filing system.

Section 90(4)(b) limits the right to access categories of information detailed at s 90(2), such as the purpose for which personal data is intended to be processed, the period for which data is to be retained and the legal basis for the processing of the data where "in the case of archiving purposes in the public interest… the provision of the information proves impossible or would involve a disproportionate effort."

Who is the Data Controller?

The Civil Service Regulation Act 1956 s 2(1) defines an 'appropriate authority' as follows:

"(a) in relation to a civil servant holding a position to which he was appointed by the Government, the Government,
(b) in relation to a civil servant who is a member of the staff of the Houses of the Oireachtas or an officer of the Attorney General, the Taoiseach,
(c) in relation to a civil servant who is a member of the staff of the office of the Revenue Commissioners, the Minister, or
(d) in relation to any other civil servant, the Minister of State by whom the power of appointing a successor to him would for the time being be exercisable."

Under s 3 (1) of the 2018 Act an appropriate authority may, as respects all or part of the personal data kept by that authority, designate a civil servant to be a data controller and while the designation is in force the civil servant so designated shall, other than for disciplinary or regulatory purposes, which remain the responsibility of the authority, be deemed, for the purposes of this Act and the Data Protection Regulation, to be the controller in respect of the data concerned. In brief, individual civil servants can be appointed as data controllers, but they are not personally subject to administrative fines for infringements or failures, which offers some reassurance as these fines can be as high as €1,000,000 under s 141(4) of the 2018 Act.

For private institutions with a legal personality of their own, for instance organisations running as a limited company, a charity or under the terms of a trust then that legal entity is itself the data controller.

Article 30(1) of GDPR states that each data controller must maintain a record, in writing, of processing activities under its responsibility, and article 30(2) states that the same categories of information must be retained for data processing carried out on behalf of the data controller. We have seen above that 'processing' means collection, recording, organisation, structuring, storage, alteration, retrieval, consultation, use, transmission, making available, combination, restriction, erasure or destruction of personal data.

The categories of information that are required to be kept are (a) the name and contact details of the controller and, where applicable, the joint controller, the controller's representative and the data protection officer; (b) the purposes of the processing; (c) a description of the categories of data subjects and of the categories of personal data; (d) the categories of recipients to whom the personal data have been or will be disclosed including recipients in third countries or international organisations; (e) where applicable, transfers of personal data to a third country or an international organisation, including the identification of that third country or international organisation and, in the case of transfers referred to in the second subparagraph of article 49(1), the documentation of suitable safeguards; (f) where possible, the envisaged time limits for erasure of the different categories of data; (g) where possible, a general description of technical and organisational security measures. The resulting record is known as a Record of Processing Activities (RoPA).[6]

Under s84(1) of the 2018 Act, a data controller must conduct a data protection impact assessment. Where having regard to its nature, scope,

---

[6] Detailed guidance on preparing a RoPA is available from the Data Protection Commission at <https://www.dataprotection.ie/en/dpc-guidance/records-of-processing-article-30-guidance> accessed 21 August 2024.

context and purposes, a type of processing, and in particular a type of processing using new technology, is likely to result in a high risk to the rights and freedoms of individuals, the controller that is proposing to carry out the processing shall conduct an assessment of the likely impact of the proposed processing operations on the protection of personal data (in this Part, referred to as a 'data protection impact assessment') prior to carrying out the processing. It is unclear what is meant by 'new technology' in this instance, but it is probably reasonable to assume it does not refer only to technologies invented after 2018, but rather to existing technologies such as digitisation, publishing online and data analysis of the content. New technology can certainly be construed to apply to AI systems.

The data protection impact assessment must include:

"(a) a general description of the proposed processing operations to which it relates;
(b) an assessment of the potential risks to the rights and freedoms of data subjects as a result of the proposed processing; and
(c) a description of any safeguards, security measures or mechanisms proposed to be implemented by the controller to mitigate any risk referred to in paragraph (b) and to ensure the protection of the personal data in compliance with this Part."

Examples of potential risks might include inadvertent publication of personal data of living persons, infringement of moral rights or publication of material which is subject to copyright (see Chapter 1).

Where the controller has conducted a data protection impact assessment and it appears that the processing concerned would, despite the implementation of safeguards, security measures or mechanisms referred result in a high risk to the rights and freedoms of individuals the controller must consult the Data Protection Commission in writing before commencing that processing.

Data Protection Officers

Section 88 of the 2018 Act sets out the requirement for the appointment of a Data Protection Officer (DPO). A data controller other than a court or independent judicial authority must appoint a person to carry out the functions of a DPO. Two or more controllers may, by reference to the structure and size of their organisation, appoint a single DPO. When appointing a DPO, a controller must do so on the basis of the person's expert knowledge of the law and the practice relating to the protection of personal data, and his or her ability to carry out the functions specified in subsection (5). In practice, for many galleries, libraries, archives and museums, this means outsourcing their DPO function to an individual or consultancy that specialises in this area.

Section 88(4) of the 2018 Act states that when a DPO is appointed the data controller shall

(a) publish or cause to be published the contact details of the data protection officer,
(b) inform the Commission of the appointment of the data protection officer and provide the Commission with his or her contact details, and
(c) ensure that the data protection officer reports directly to the highest level of management of the controller. The DPO must not receive any instructions regarding the exercise of the functions set out under s 88(5) and must be involved in an appropriate and timely manner in all matters relating to the protection of personal data and support the data protection officer in performing his or her functions under subsection (5).

The support that the controller must provide the DPO comprises providing them with the resources that they require to perform those functions, ensuring that they have access to processing operations carried out by the controller, and assisting them to maintain their expert knowledge in the law and practice relating to the protection of personal data. This requirement has led to the development of a significant industry of private companies and third level institutions offering qualifications in data protection law aimed at DPOs.

Section 88(5) of the 2018 Act sets out the functions of a DPO and states that they shall include:

(a) informing and advising the controller, and the employees of the controller who carry out processing, of their obligations under the 2018 Act and under any other law of the European Union or law of the state that relates to the protection of personal data;
(b) monitoring the compliance of the controller with the 2018 Act, any other law of the European Union or law of the state that relates to the protection of personal data, and the policies of the controller in relation to the protection of personal data, including the assignment of responsibilities in the controller in relation to the protection of personal data, the raising of awareness and the training of staff involved in processing operations in that regard, and any audit activity related to the protection of personal data;
(c) providing advice, where requested to do so, in relation to the carrying out of a data protection impact assessment in accordance with section 84 (see above) and monitoring any steps taken on foot of that assessment;
(d) acting as the contact point for data subjects with regard to all issues related

to the processing of their personal data and to the exercise of their rights under this Part;

(e) cooperating with the Data Protection Commission and acting as a contact point for the Data Protection Commission for issues related to processing carried out by the controller, including consultation by the controller with the Data Protection Commission under section 84.

Freedom of Information

Freedom of Information (FOI) is a right of access to official information that is qualified by exceptions and subject to independent adjudication by a third party. It has long been associated with the idea of press freedom, recognising the importance of an independent fourth estate, but has developed into a universal right in jurisdictions that have adopted FOI legislation.

The earliest known such legislation dates to 1766 when 'His Majesty's Gracious Ordinance Relating to Freedom of Writing and the Press' came into force in Sweden. This Ordinance stated that "free access should be allowed to all archives, for the purpose of copying such documents in loco or obtaining certified copies of them."[7]

The 1946 UN General Assembly Resolution 59(1) on Freedom of Information states that

> "Freedom of Information is a fundamental right and is the touchstone of all the freedoms to which the United Nations is consecrated. Freedom of Information implies the right to gather, transmit and publish news anywhere and everywhere without fetters. As such it is an essential factor in any serious effort to promote the peace and progress of the word."

Though it is doubtful whether this resolution was intended to imply freedom of access to documents, but rather freedom of the press to source and publish without fear of censure.

In 1966, the US Freedom of Information Act (FOIA) was enacted establishing the public's right to obtain information from federal government agencies. Under 5 USC s 552 any person can file an FOIA request, to include US citizens, foreign nationals, organisations, associations and third level institutions. Following the revelations of the Watergate scandal of

---

[7] Anders Chydenius, *'The World's First Freedom of Information Act: Anders Chydenius'*, (Anders Chydenius Foundation 2006) <https://www.access-info.org/wp-content/uploads/worlds_first_foia.pdf> accessed 21 August 2024.

1972-1974, the FOIA was amended to change existing exemptions in relation to national defence and foreign policy records and investigatory law enforcement records. A 1996 amendment to FOIA allowed for greater access to information stored in electronic formats.

The Council of Europe Recommendation No R (81) 19 of 1981 was a non-binding recommendation encouraging member states to ensure that

> "[e]veryone within the jurisdiction of a member state shall have the right to obtain, on request, information held by the public authorities other than legislative and judicial bodies."

In Ireland, the Freedom of Information Act 1997 (FOI Act), commenced in 1998, gave statutory weight to Recommendation No R (81) following a long period of debate within government and the civil service as to the desirability and practicality of such legislation. In his judgment in *Deely v The Information Commissioner*, Mr Justice McKechnie described the FOI Act as "on any view, a piece of legislation independent in existence, forceful in its aim and liberal in outlook and philosophy."[8]

The FOI Act was amended in 2003, introducing fees to access non-personal information and a mandatory class exemption for records which concern security, defence or international relations of the state or matters relating to Northern Ireland and exemption for communications between ministers relating to a matter before government.

The Freedom of Information Act 2014 (the 2014 Act) repealed the 1997 and 2003 Acts and widened the remit of bodies to which FOI applies unless specifically exempt. The 2014 Act provides a legal right of access to government records, predominantly those created after 1998, the right to amend personal information held in those records where that information is incomplete, incorrect or misleading and the right to be given reasons for decisions taken by FOI bodies that impact on the person making the request. There are, however, exceptions to these rights.

The 1998 cut-off date is of particular relevance to galleries, libraries, museums and archives as it means that FOI requests only relate to records of the last 26 years (at time of writing).

The definition of a 'record' in the 2014 Act is broad and includes

---

[8] *Deely v The Information Commissioner* (2001) IEHC 91 4.

"(a) a book or other written or printed material in any form (including in any electronic device or in machine readable form),
(b) a map, plan or drawing,
(c) a disc, tape or other mechanical or electronic device in which data other than visual images are embodied so as to be capable, with or without the aid of some other mechanical or electronic equipment, of being reproduced from the disc, tape or other device,
(d) a film, disc, tape or other mechanical or electronic device in which visual images are embodied so as to be capable, with or without the aid of some other mechanical or electronic equipment, of being reproduced from the film, disc, tape or other device."

Unlike the National Archives Act 1986, which talks about 'departmental records' in terms of being the records to be transferred to the National Archives and specifically states at s 2(2)(ii) that these do not include "any part of the permanent collection of a library, museum or gallery," the 2014 Act doesn't make this distinction, so it is possible that a member of the public could make an FOI request relating to the content of an archive or library, subject to the grounds for refusal below – specifically in relation to containing sufficient particulars.

Refusal of Access Requests

Under s 15(1) of the 2014 Act, a head to whom an FOI request is made may refuse to grant the request under the following circumstances: the record concerned does not exist or cannot be found; the FOI request does not contain sufficient particulars in relation to the information concerned to enable the record to be found; in the opinion of the head, granting the request would require the retrieval and examination of such number of records or kind of records as to cause a substantial and unreasonable interference with or disruption of work of the FOI body concerned; the information is already in the public domain; publication of the record is required by law and is intended to be effected not later than 12 weeks after the receipt of the request by the head; the FOI body intends to publish the record and such publication is intended to be effected not later than six weeks after the receipt of the request by the head; the request is, in the opinion of the head, frivolous or vexatious or forms part of a pattern of manifestly unreasonable requests from the same requester or from different requesters who, in the opinion of the head, appear to have made the requests acting in concert; a fee or deposit payable under section 27 has not been paid, or the request relates to records already released, either to the same or a previous requester.

Section 15(2) states that a head may also refuse to grant access to a record that is available for inspection by members of the public whether upon payment or free of charge, or a record a copy of which is available for purchase or removal free of charge by members of the public.

Section 15(3) is rather unhelpfully worded as "a record shall not be within subsection (2) by reason only of the fact that it contains information constituting… personal data." The wording doesn't suggest that the personal data in question is restricted to that of the person making the request, so it would appear that a head cannot refuse to grant access to a record on the grounds of it being available to the public if it contains personal data.

Section 32 of the 2014 Act states that a head may refuse to grant an FOI request if access to the record concerned could reasonably be expected to prejudice or impair the prevention, detection or investigation of offences. Section 33 provides for a number of security, defence and international relations exemptions. Section 34 states that a minister of the government or the head of an FOI body other than a Department of State may declare by certificate that a record is an exempt record by virtue of ss 32 and 33.

An exemption for information obtained in confidence is detailed at s 35 of the 2014 Act, where the record concerned contains information given to an FOI body in confidence and on the understanding that it would be treated by it as confidential and, in the opinion of the head, its disclosure would be likely to prejudice the giving to the body of further similar information from the same person or other persons and it is of importance to the body that such further similar information should continue to be given to the body, or where disclosure of the information concerned would constitute a breach of a duty of confidence provided for by a provision of an agreement or enactment.

Section 36 of the 2014 Act allows for the refusal to grant access to commercially sensitive information.

Section 37 of the 2014 Act allows for refusal to grant access to a record if access to the record would involve the disclosure of personal information, including information relating to a deceased individual, with the exception that the information relates to the requester themselves, the individual to whom the information relates consents to its release, the information is already publicly available, the individual who gave the information to the body was informed that the information might be made publicly available, or disclosure is required to prevent a serious and imminent danger to the life or health of an individual.

Section 41 of the 2014 Act provides for the refusal of access requests made in respect of records to which non-disclosure provisions of laws of the EU or other enactments apply. For instance, under the terms of the National Archives Act 1986, s 8(4), an officer of a Department of State may, with the consent of an officer of the Department of the Taoiseach so authorised (except in relation to records of the Department of the Taoiseach), certify, in relation to particular departmental records, or a particular class or classes of departmental records which are more than 30 years old and are specified in the certificate, that to make them available for inspection by the public (a) would be contrary to the public interest, or (b) would or might constitute a breach of statutory duty, or a breach of good faith on the ground that they contain information supplied in confidence, or (c) would or might cause distress or danger to living persons on the ground that they contain information about individuals, or would or might be likely to lead to an action for damages for defamation.

Records in respect of which certificates have been issued under s 8(4) of the National Archives Act are therefore exempt from disclosure under FOI. The existence of the certificate stating the file titles and or reference numbers is not exempt from disclosure.

The National Archives Act 1986 (Prescription of Classes of Records) Order 1997 prescribes certain classes of record for the purposes of s 8(2) or s 8(4) of the National Archives Act, regardless of which department, scheduled body or court they emanate from, particularly relating to details relating to personnel, pensions, wages, and salaries paid. Other classes of records are prescribed relating to particular departments, scheduled bodies or courts, with a high degree of specificity — for instance records relating to examinations for certificates in Marine Radar Maintenance at various technical colleges, under the Wireless Telegraphy Acts 1926 to 1988, are exempt from inspection.

Publication Scheme

As we have seen above, one of the bases for refusal of an FOI request is if the request does not contain sufficient particulars in relation to the information concerned to enable the record to be identified by the taking of reasonable steps.

However s 8(2) of the 2014 Act sets out that bodies subject to the Act must prepare and publish a scheme (publication scheme) to include

> "(a) the classes of information that the FOI body has published or intends to publish,
> (b) the terms under which it will make such information available and, where the material is not available without charge, the charge,
> (c) a general description of its structure and organisation, functions, powers and duties, any services it provides for the public and the procedures by which any such services may be availed of by the public,
> (d) a general description of the classes of records held by the body concerned, giving such particulars as are reasonably necessary to facilitate the exercise of the right of access."

When this requirement was first made known there was great excitement among archivists and records managers who assumed that the "general description of the classes of records... giving such particulars as are reasonably necessary to facilitate the right of access" would result in widespread cataloguing and organisation of departmental records — and thus more work for them. What transpired in practice was that this bar was set quite low, and instead publication schemes have tended to give very broad overviews of records by category, rather than getting into very much detail as to their content.

Appeals

A person making an FOI application who is not satisfied with the result of that application may request the body of whom the request has been made to conduct an internal review of the relevant decision. If the result of the internal review is not deemed acceptable by the person making the application, they can refer the decision to the Information Commissioner for review via an online application form.[9]

Section 24 of the 2014 Act allows that a party to a review by the Information Commissioner may appeal to the High Court on a point of law from the decision or where the party or person concerned contends that the release of a record concerned would contravene a requirement imposed by EU law, on a finding of fact set out or inherent in the decision. Any person

---

[9] Office of the Information Commissioner, 'Apply for a review' <https://www.oic.ie/apply-for-a-review/start-application/> accessed 21 August 2024.

affected by the issue of a certificate under s 34 of the 2014 Act (see 'Refusal of access requests' above) may also appeal to the High Court on a point of law against such issue or from such decision.

The Open Data Directive

Directive (EU) 2019/1024 of the European Parliament and of the Council of 20 June 2019 on open data and the re-use of public sector information (the Open Data Directive) mandates the release of public sector data in free and open formats in order to encourage strengthening of the EU data economy by increasing the quantity of public sector data available for re-use, thus promoting fair competition and enhancing cross-border innovation based on that data.

The European Union (Open Data and Re-use of Public Sector Information) Regulations 2021, SI No 376/2021 (the Regulations) gives effect to the Open Data Directive in Irish law.

Section 3(2)(j) states that the Regulations do not apply to documents held by cultural establishments other than libraries, museums and archives, so it would appear that documents held by publicly funded galleries are exempt from the Open Data Directive.

At s 2(1) of the Regulations, a document is defined as all or part of any form of document, record or data, whether in physical, electronic or other form, and includes (a) any memorandum, book, plan, map, drawing, diagram, pictorial or graphic work, (b) any photograph, and (c) any sound, visual or audio-visual recording.

Re-use is defined at s 2(1) of the Regulations as:

(a) in relation to a document held by a public sector body, the use of the document by an individual or legal entity for commercial or non-commercial purposes other than the initial purpose within the public task for which the document was produced, but does not include the exchange of that document between public sector bodies solely for the purpose of performing their public tasks, or

(b) in relation to a document held by a public undertaking, the use of the document by an individual or legal entity for commercial or non-commercial purposes other than the initial purpose of providing services in the general interest for which the document was produced, but does not include the exchange of that document between public undertakings and public sector bodies solely for the purpose of the performance of the public tasks of the public sector bodies.

The requirement to make documents available for re-use in respect of a document in which a library, museum or archive holds intellectual property rights is set out at s 5 of the Regulations which states simply that it shall be made available for re-use where the re-use of such a document is allowed.

Section 6(5)(c) of the Regulations exempts libraries, museums and archives from the requirement, if refusing a request for re-use where the refusal is based on the intellectual property rights of a third party, for the public sector body concerned to include in the communication of the refusal to the requester a reference to the third party, where known, or alternatively to the licensor from which the public sector body has obtained the relevant material.

Section 8(3)(b) of the Regulations allows libraries, museums and archives to charge for the re-use of documents, as long as the total income of the library, museum or archive concerned from supplying and allowing the re-use of documents over the appropriate accounting period shall not exceed (i) the sum of the cost of collection, production, reproduction, dissemination, data storage, preservation and rights clearance, (ii) a reasonable return on investment, and (iii) where applicable, the cost of anonymisation of personal data and measures taken to protect commercially confidential information. The charges are to be calculated in accordance with the accounting principles applicable to the library, museum or archive concerned.

Section 14(3)(b) of the Regulations exempts high-value datasets held by libraries, museums and archives from the requirement to be made available free of charge.

"High-value datasets" are defined within the Regulations as documents the re-use of which is associated with important benefits for society, the environment and the economy, in particular because of their suitability for the creation of value-added services, applications and new, high-quality and decent jobs, and the number of potential beneficiaries of the value-added services and applications based on those datasets

Case Study: FOI Section 35 Exemptions

In *John Burns, The Sunday Times and The Arts Council*[10] the requester had submitted an FOI request, seeking access to all correspondence exchanged between the Arts Council and the Abbey Theatre in 2021. The Arts Council responded on 21 January 2022, with a belated decision partially granting the request. The Arts Council identified 103 pertinent records, releasing 42 in their entirety. However, the Arts Council declined to disclose the remaining records, either in full or partially, citing ss 35, 36, and 37 of the 2014 Act (see 'Refusal of access requests' above).

Subsequently, on 22 January 2022, the requester asked for an internal review specifically challenging the decision to withhold 24 specified records. On 21 February 2022, following an internal review, the Arts Council upheld its original decision for 23 out of the 24 records. However, regarding one record (record 48), they modified their stance, releasing a partial version to the requester.

On 23 February 2022, dissatisfied with the Arts Council's decision, the requester lodged an appeal with the Office of the Information Commissioner (OIC), seeking a review of the handling of his FOI request.

In its review of the FOI request the OIC reviewed the exemptions allowable under s 35 of the 2014 Act which mandates the withholding of records containing information provided to an FOI body in confidence. Section 35(1)(b) also imposes a mandatory exemption for records where disclosure would breach a duty of confidence specified by an agreement, enactment, or legal provision. The Arts Council and the Abbey Theatre contended that the records fell under both ss 35(1)(a) and 35(1)(b) of the 2014 Act.

The Arts Council argued that maintaining positive relationships with funded organisations is crucial for fulfilling its mandate. It asserted that confidential information is shared to inform budgetary decisions, especially in discussions with the Abbey Theatre about financial, governance and HR matters. The Arts Council emphasised the importance of organisations freely engaging with them and disclosing information under the expectation of confidentiality.

Regarding s 35(1)(b), the Arts Council pointed to clause 16(b) of their 2021 funding agreement with the Abbey Theatre, imposing a duty of confidence. It also claimed an equitable duty of confidence, asserting that

---

[10] *John Burns, The Sunday Times and the Arts Council* [2022] OIC-119922-V5G3G9.

records contained HR investigation details and settlement information, imparted with the implicit understanding of confidentiality. The Arts Council contended that disclosure would constitute unauthorised use to the detriment of the parties involved.

The Arts Council further argued that disclosure could prejudice future information-sharing by organisations if subjected to public scrutiny, impacting on the Arts Council's ability to fulfil its statutory functions.

Considering public interest, the Arts Council contended that the balance favoured withholding the records to maintain effective functioning, protect the relationship with the Abbey Theatre, and avoid unwarranted scrutiny and criticism. The Abbey Theatre supported these arguments, asserting concerns about the release of confidential information affecting not only them but also potentially causing apprehension among other arts organisations.

In its ruling the OIC acknowledged s 35(1)(b) and the duty of confidence provided for 'otherwise by law' to include an equitable duty. The three elements for a breach of equitable duty of confidence being the information's confidentiality, its communication in circumstances imposing an obligation of confidence, and its wrongful use to the detriment of the communicating party.

Examining the withheld records which involved correspondence between the Arts Council and the Abbey Theatre regarding an HR investigation and settlement, the OIC held it to be evident that the information was confidential and communicated under an obligation of confidence. The Abbey Theatre's refusal to consent to release indicated potential detriment, satisfying the requirements for an equitable duty of confidence.

The OIC held that while public curiosity may be piqued by certain information, this does not necessarily equate to a public interest in disclosure. The Abbey Theatre, despite receiving substantial funding, is not a public body under the FOI Act. The lack of evidence supporting allegations of financial irregularities or wrongdoing diminishes any potential public interest defence.

In its conclusion the OIC confirmed that s 35(1)(b) of the 2014 Act applied to all 23 records withheld, as they fell under an equitable duty of confidence owed by the Arts Council to the Abbey Theatre.

Chapter 3

Title and Provenance

What is Title?

The word 'title,' as it is used in art and cultural heritage law, refers to ownership of a thing that is capable of being owned to the exclusion of all others. The proper owner of an object is said to have title to the object. An interest in an object refers to a possible equitable or legal claim, an expectation or an aspiration in regard to an object. Title is therefore a measure of the strength of the interest in which person or institution claims in an object, with proprietary title — consisting of documentary proof of title — being the strongest form of title and therefore the strongest form of interest in an object.

Anyone purchasing a house will be familiar with the concept of title deeds, which are papers that describe how a house or lands have changed hands over time and are used as the basis for demonstrating that the vendor has good title, thus allowing them to sell the property — and if a mortgage is involved reassuring the lender that they will acquire good title in the property in the event of a default on the loan.[1]

Possessory title is a lesser form of title which allows for the use or enjoyment of an object — for instance under the terms of a loan — and is often referred to in land law as the basis under which adverse possession can be claimed over a property.

Some of the ways in which a gallery, library, archive or museum might acquire title in an object are through: the Taxes Consolidation Act 1997 s 1003 donation; gift; loan; acquisition by purchase; transfer from another institution; or ownership of an archaeological object where such object has no known owner being vested in the state under s 96 of the Historic and Archaeological Heritage and Miscellaneous Provisions Act 2023.[2] The Copyright and Related Rights Act 2000 at s 330A(6) defines a 'work' as

---

[1] This system has been replaced in Ireland by Tailte Éireann, which issues a certificate of title having examined all prior title deeds — this single certificate is now all that is required to demonstrate good title in property and provides a state guarantee.

[2] Not yet commenced at the time of writing.

being permanently in the collections of a cultural heritage institution where it is

> "owned or permanently held by that institution, for example as a result of a transfer of ownership or a licence agreement, legal deposit obligations or permanent custody arrangements."

Provenance

Depending on the source from which an object enters the collections of a gallery, library, archive or museum, it is incumbent on that institution to carry out sufficient research on the object to satisfy itself of the provenance of the item and ensure that good title is held. Institutions should also satisfy themselves that the description provided of an object or work is accurate and true, particularly where assumptions might be made based on usual practice; such as a date referring to the date of creation of a work, not the date of the inception of the concept upon which it is based. An example of this issue recently came to prominence in relation to the Damien Hirst artwork titled 'Myth Explored, Explained, Exploded 1993-1999' which was in fact made in 2017.[3] Furthermore, the failure to carry out sufficient research into an object's provenance arguably demonstrates recklessness as to whether an object may be stolen.

Section 16(2) of the Criminal Justice (Theft and Fraud Offences) Act 2001 states that

> "For the purposes of this Part, a person is reckless if he or she disregards a substantial risk that the property handled is stolen, and for those purposes "substantial risk" means a risk of such a nature and degree that, having regard to the circumstances in which the person acquired the property and the extent of the information then available to him or her, its disregard involves culpability of a high degree."

Section 17 of the Criminal Justice (Theft and Fraud Offences) Act 2001 addresses the question of handling stolen property. A person is guilty of handling stolen property if (otherwise than in the course of the stealing) he or she, knowing that the property was stolen or being reckless as to whether it was stolen, dishonestly receives or arranges to receive it, or undertakes, or assists in, its retention, removal, disposal or realisation by or for the benefit

---

[3] Maeve McClenaghan, 'Damien Hirst formaldehyde animal works dated to 1990s were made in 2017' *The Guardian* <https://www.theguardian.com/artanddesign/2024/mar/19/damien-hirst-formaldehyde-animal-works-dated-to-1990s-were-made-in-2017> accessed 21 August 2024.

of another person, or arranges to do so. Similarly, where a person receives or arranges to receive property, or undertakes, or assists in, its retention, removal, disposal or realisation by or for the benefit of another person, or arranges to do so, in such circumstances that it is reasonable to conclude that the person either knew that the property was stolen or was reckless as to whether it was stolen, he or she shall be taken to have so known or to have been so reckless, unless the court or the jury, as the case may be, is satisfied having regard to all the evidence that there is a reasonable doubt as to whether he or she so knew or was so reckless.

A person to whom s 17 applies may be tried and convicted whether the principal offender has or has not been previously convicted or is not able to be tried. A person guilty of handling stolen property is liable on conviction on indictment to a fine or imprisonment for a term not exceeding 10 years or both, but is not liable to a higher fine or longer term of imprisonment than that which applies to the principal offence.

Section 18 of the Criminal Justice (Theft and Fraud Offences) Act 2001 deals with the issue of possessing stolen property. A person who, without lawful authority or excuse, possesses stolen property (otherwise than in the course of the stealing), knowing that the property was stolen or being reckless as to whether it was stolen, is guilty of an offence. Where a person has in his or her possession stolen property in indicative circumstances, such as through purchase of the property at a price below its market value, that it is reasonable to conclude that the person either knew that the property was stolen or was reckless as to whether it was stolen, he or she shall be taken for the purposes of this section to have so known or to have been so reckless, unless the court or the jury, as the case may be, is satisfied having regard to all the evidence that there is a reasonable doubt as to whether he or she so knew or was so reckless.

A person to whom s 18 applies may be tried and convicted whether or not the principal offender has been previously convicted or is not able to be tried. A person guilty of handling stolen property is liable on conviction on indictment to a fine or imprisonment for a term not exceeding five years or both, but is not liable to a higher fine or longer term of imprisonment than that which applies to the principal offence. Section 56 of the Criminal Justice (Theft and Fraud Offences) Act 2001 states that where property has been stolen and a person is convicted of an offence the court may order the restoration of a stolen object to any person entitled to recover it from the convicted person.

The basic rule in relation to the transfer of title is *Nemo Dat Quod Non Habet*, that the person transferring an interest in goods can only transfer such title as they have and no more. Section 21 of the Sale of Goods Act 1893 states that

> "Subject to the provisions of this Act, where goods are sold by a person who is not the owner thereof, and who does not sell them under the authority or with the consent of the owner, the buyer acquires no better title to the goods than the seller had, unless the owner of the goods is by his conduct precluded from denying the seller's authority to sell."

The Historic and Archaeological Heritage and Miscellaneous Provisions Act 2023[4] further states at s 131 that:

> "(1) Where an archaeological object, historic object, or object removed from a monument to which general protection applies or special protection applies, is sold without the relevant authorisation, section 22(1) or 23 of the Sale of Goods Act 1893, or any rule of law relating to sale in market overt or sale under voidable title, shall not apply to the sale of that object so as to give good title to the purchaser of that object.
>
> (2) Subsection (1) is in addition to, and not in substitution for, section 56 of the Criminal Justice (Theft and Fraud Offences) Act 2001.
>
> (3) In this section, "relevant authorisation", in relation to the sale of an object referred to in subsection (1), means a sale of the object pursuant to an authorisation given—
> (a) by the owner of the object or another person entitled to authorise the sale, and
> (b) freely and without fraud, deception, misrepresentation, duress or undue influence."

Gifts and Loans

Bailment

A bailment arises when goods which belong to one person or institution are delivered into the custody of another for a specific period or purpose. A bailment can be initiated by either the owner or another individual in possession of the goods, termed as the bailor. The recipient of the goods,

---

[4] At the time of writing this has not yet been commenced.

to whom they are given, is known as the bailee. The bailee assumes custody or physical possession of the goods, which may be facilitated through a third party like an employee.

As a result, the goods of the bailor are held by the bailee with the bailor's consent, whether express or implied. In the context of galleries, libraries, archives and museums a bailment is most commonly created through a loan, an agreement to store an object, carriage or transport of an object or when an item is consigned to an auction house for sale.

A bailment arises when the bailor delivers the object to the bailee. The bailor maintains their title and the bailee obtains the object by consent. The common features of a bailment are that the bailee has a special interest in the goods — for instance they are enabled to insure them — but must account to the bailor. The bailee has a duty to take reasonable care of the object while in their possession, and the burden of proof to demonstrate such care has been taken rests with the bailee.

The elements of a bailment are broadly the intent to create the bailment, delivery of possession of the bailed items and acceptance of the bailed items by the bailee. The transfer of goods in a bailment is distinct from a sale or exchange as it implies an obligation to return the same goods. However, if the goods undergo significant alteration in the process, the arrangement ceases to be a bailment.

Bailments can be categorised based on whether they benefit the bailor or the bailee, and whether payment is involved. For instance, a hiring arrangement involves payment from the bailee to the bailor, while a loan may not entail any monetary exchange, constituting a gratuitous bailment. A contractual bailment may include specific terms, for instance those contained in a loan agreement, a contract for storage or carriage, or consignment for auction. An 'attornment' occurs when a bailee in possession of goods on behalf of one person acknowledges that he will hold the goods on behalf of another person — for instance if an object is sold or changes hands, but continues to be stored by the bailee.

In cases of loss or damage to the goods, both the bailor and bailee may have recourse to legal action against third parties, with the nature of their claims influenced by the bailment's contractual specifics.

The question of what comprises a bailment was examined in some detail in

Webb v Ireland and the Attorney General,[5] which was an action by the finders of the Derrynaflan hoard to recover possession of the hoard from the National Museum of Ireland (NMI). See the Case Study at the end of this chapter.

Gifts

The National Cultural Institutions Act 1997 states at s 28 that:

> "(1) A Board may accept gifts of money, land (subject to the consent of the Minister) or other property, upon such trusts or conditions, if any, as may be specified by the donor.
>
> (2) A Board shall not accept a gift if the trusts or conditions attached to it would be inconsistent with its functions.
>
> (3) Any funds of a Board which are a gift or the proceeds of a gift to it may, subject to any terms or conditions of the gift, be invested by the Board in any manner in which a trustee is empowered by law to invest trust funds."

Institutions that are not scheduled institutions under s 42 of the National Cultural Institutions Act 1997 are of course free to accept gifts as they see fit according to any strictures imposed by their founding articles, board of directors or conditions of a trust.

When describing gifts there are effectively two categories of property that may be gifted: real property and movable property. Real property such as lands or buildings must be transferred subject to contract law principles, namely there must be consideration in order for a contract to be enforceable — whoever wishes to enforce a contract must prove that they have provided consideration, albeit nominal, which means that the promisor must receive a benefit, and the promisee must be at a detriment. This is normally achieved by way of a voluntary conveyance under which the normal rules applying to the transfer of deeds apply.

Real property can also be gifted by way of a trust. The most usual form of trust is an express trust which must comply with certain formalities, foremost of which are the 'three certainties.' Certainty of intention is the requirement that it must be obvious from the wording of the trust that the donee intended to create a trust. This is achieved by explicit use of imperative words which show an intention to create legally binding obligations in exchange for property. Certainty of subject matter requires

---

[5] *Webb v Ireland and the Attorney General* [1987] IESC 2.

that it be certain exactly what property is subject to the trust. Certainty of object requires that there be beneficiaries in whose favour a trust can be enforced by the courts. The certainties are cumulative and if any certainty is missing then the trust will be void *ab initio*. A further formality that must be complied with is at s 4 of the Statute of Frauds (Ireland) 1695, which stipulates for land (whether freehold or leasehold), the trust must be evidenced in writing, signed by someone capable of declaring the trust. Alternatively, the donor can establish a trust through their will. It is not mandatory for the declaration of a trust to be in writing, but there must be written proof of its declaration. When a trust is outlined in a will, it must adhere to the requirements of s 78 of the Succession Act 1965.

Movable property, such as cultural heritage objects, can be transferred by trust as above, or by delivery. Where a gift is made by delivery it is governed by common law principles and requires no specific written instructions or other formalities, but in order for a gift to be perfected at law, three elements must be present — delivery, acceptance and donative intent.

Delivery as the term implies requires a physical transfer of the object being gifted and is deemed to affect a transfer of possession. The delivery does not need to have been carried out specifically for the purposes of making a gift, and can precede the existence of donative intent — a decision to donate can occur at any stage after physical delivery. Acceptance need not be expressly indicated and is presumed from an absence of refusal, even if the donee is not aware of the existence of the gift and even in circumstances where accepting the gift is onerous. A donee cannot however be forced to accept a gift, so can always repudiate it once they have become aware of its existence, but this can create its own issues (See Chapter 5). A gift once given by the donor cannot be revoked on the basis that the donee was unaware of it. Donative intent is determined on the balance of probabilities, rather than a requirement to demonstrate specific or irrefutable evidence of intention to donate, and can be demonstrated by the acts of the donor or by the circumstances that accompanied the donation. It should however be noted that in case of dispute the onus is on the donee to demonstrate the existence of a gift, so the more unmistakable evidence of donative intent that can be gathered at the point of donation the better.

Some of the types of appropriate evidence that might be used to distinguish between a loan and a gift include

> "credible statements made by one party to the transaction to a reliable third party, identifying or indicating the nature of the transaction; one party's acquiescence in, or failure to take obvious steps to contest, statements made or

procured by a third party that support the other party's version of the identity of the transaction; conduct by one or both parties indicating a perception of the relationship more convincingly explicable by reference to one possible version of the relationship than by reference to the alternative; a denial of ownership by the recipient, when the cost of some past conservation of the object, or some other inconvenient question, is raised with him."[6]

Gifts can also be made *donatio mortis causa* — a gift made in contemplation of death, or a deathbed gift. In this instance the gift must be made by the donor in anticipation of their death, the gift is contingent on the death of the donor and there must be delivery before death. Gifts may also be made by testamentary disposition (being left in a will) in which case the will must meet the requirements for a valid will as set out in s 78 of the Succession Act 1965.

For tax implications and/or benefits of gifts for donors and donees, see Chapter 8.

Loans

Loans are created either explicitly through the terms of a loan agreement which may state duration, storage and transport conditions, exhibition conditions, insurance requirements and other relevant terms, or through the failure of a donee to demonstrate the existence of a gift (see above).

The Heritage Council Museum Standards Programme sets out the documentation requirements for loans as follows:

"(i) Applicants must have written procedures for borrowing and lending;
(ii) All objects on loan must be recorded... Files for loans should be created to contain all relevant information, (e.g. relevant correspondence, loan agreements, receipts).
(iii) Applicants must designate the authority for all loans.
(iv) All loans must be for a fixed period. Long term loans may be renewed on a regular basis. This allows for regular checks on condition etc. and enables the museum to keep details of the lenders and borrowers up to date.
(v) All loans must be formalised with a loan agreement between both parties. The purpose of a loan should be recorded on the loan agreement. Applicants must submit a generic loan agreement for different types of loans (e.g. loans to the museum's collection, temporary loans for exhibition)."[7]

---

[6] Norman Palmer, *Palmer on Bailment* (3rd edn, Sweet & Maxwell 2009), 3-014.
[7] Heritage Council, 'Museum Standards Programme for Ireland: Loan Agreement and Records' <https://www.heritagecouncil.ie/content/files/28._4.10__4.11__4.12_Loan_Agreement_and_Records.pdf> accessed 21 August 2024.

For an example of a loan policy see the National Museum of Ireland Loans Policy 2020-2023 which is available online.[8]

For institutions scheduled under the second schedule of the National Cultural Institutions Act 1997, the making or receiving of loans is governed by s 11(2) of the National Cultural Institutions Act 1997 which states that:

> "The Board [of a scheduled institution] shall have all such powers as it considers necessary or expedient for the performance of its functions under this Act including, but without prejudice to the foregoing, the following powers: … (d) to lend, subject to the provisions of this Act, museum heritage objects in the collection of the Museum; … (m) to acquire, borrow or accept a donation or bequest of museum heritage objects."

Loans made to institutions scheduled under the second schedule may be indemnified by the state under s 43(1) of the National Cultural Institutions Act 1997:

> "Subject to the subsequent provisions of this section, the Minister may, with the consent of the Minister for Finance, in such cases and to such extent as the Minister may determine, undertake to indemnify any person for the loss of, or damage to, a cultural object kept outside the State while that object is on loan to an institution specified in the Second Schedule from a person resident outside the State for the purpose of public exhibition in an authorised area of the institution" to a sum not exceeding £150,000,000."

Institutions that are not scheduled institutions under s 42 of the National Cultural Institutions Act 1997 are of course free to make and accept loans as they see fit according to any strictures imposed by their founding articles, board of directors or conditions of a trust.

Civil Recovery of Objects

Owners of cultural objects seeking their return in circumstances where that return is refused and the object is the subject of a bailment, for instance where an object has been subject to a loan which the institution holding that object believes to be a gift, or where an object has come into the collections of an institution without good title having been obtained can bring an action in tort for detinue or conversion.

---

[8] National Museum of Ireland, 'Loans Policy' <https://www.museum.ie/en-IE/About/Corporate-Information/Policies-Guidelines/Loans-Policy> accessed 21 August 2024.

Detinue arises when a party wrongfully withholds possession of goods, and a plaintiff can seek recovery of the goods or their equivalent value. In such cases, the plaintiff may also seek damages for the wrongful retention of the goods. The court has discretionary power to order the return of the goods. Where a bailee fails to return goods at the end of a bailment contract an action in detinue cannot be pursued.

For a successful detinue claim, the plaintiff must demonstrate an immediate right to possess the goods and have previously demanded their return from the defendant, who then refused. Moreover, the defendant's actions must be adverse to the plaintiff's right to possession.

For instance, merely holding onto a chattel for safekeeping until the owner is identified doesn't constitute detinue, as established in *Poole v Burns*[9] which related to the retention of a horse while ownership was being investigated. However, in that particular case, the defendant was held liable for detinue due to an unreasonable retention period of five weeks.

In *Webb v Ireland*,[10] the finders of the Derrynaflan Hoard initially succeeded in a detinue claim against the state in the High Court. However, this decision was overturned by the Supreme Court, which determined that the land occupiers' rights to possession of the chattels were transferred to the state upon conveyance of their interests in the land. For more see, Case Study: The Derrynaflan Hoard, at the end of this chapter.

Conversion is the "wrongful taking possession of goods, abusing possession already acquired, or otherwise denying the title of the other person to them, whether or not possession has been acquired."[11] The basic features of conversion were set out by Lord Nicholls in *Kuwait Airways Corporation v Iraqi Airways Company*:

> "In general, the basic features of the tort are threefold. First, the defendant's conduct was inconsistent with the rights of the owner (or other person entitled to possession). Second, the conduct was deliberate, not accidental. Third, the conduct was so extensive an encroachment on the rights of the owner as to exclude him from use and possession of the goods. The contrast is with lesser acts of interference. If these cause damage they may give rise to claims for trespass or in negligence, but they do not constitute conversion ... Whether the owner is excluded from possession may sometimes depend upon whether the

---

[9] *Poole v Burns* [1944] Ir Jur Rep 20.
[10] *Webb v Ireland* [1988] IR 353.
[11] Bryan ME McMahon and William Binchy, *Law of Torts* (4th edn, Bloomsbury Professional 2013), para 30.01.

wrongdoer exercised dominion over the goods. Then the intention with which acts were done may be material."[12]

While there is a requirement for deliberate action to deny the plaintiff use and access to the goods, this does not necessarily mean that the institution in whose custody the object may be must be aware of the fact that they are denying the plaintiff's rights. In general terms the voluntary acceptance of an object without the owner's authority constitutes conversion.[13]

It is important to note that in order for a claim in conversion to succeed the goods in dispute must be chattels, rather than fixtures. That is, properly, that they comprise personal property and are identifiable and movable, rather than being fixed to or installed in a property thus becoming fixtures.

The judgment in *Hollins v Fowler* puts the position in relation to conversion succinctly that "the liability under it is founded upon what has been regarded as a salutary rule for the protection of property, namely, that persons deal with the property in chattels or exercise acts of ownership over them at their peril"[14] — advice that galleries, libraries, archives and museums would be well advised to follow.

Where Can Claims be Brought?

In claims for cultural objects brought in common law countries the principle of *lex situs* applies, which means that the law of the country in which the object is located or where the transfer that is being challenged applies, with some exceptions.

Winkworth v Christie Manson and Woods Ltd[15] was a significant legal ruling by the English High Court concerning the applicable law for determining the transfer of ownership when stolen goods are sold to a third party in a foreign jurisdiction.

The case involved stolen paintings originating from England, later sold by the thief to an unsuspecting buyer in Italy. The court ruled that the determination of whether title to the property was effectively transferred

---

[12] *Kuwait Airways Corporation v Iraqi Airways Company* (Nos 4&5) [2002] AC 883, paras 39–42.
[13] Bryan ME McMahon and William Binchy, *Law of Torts* (4th edn, Bloomsbury Professional 2013), para 30.03.
[14] *Hollins v Fowler* (1875) LR 7 HL 757, 765.
[15] *Winkworth v Christie Manson and Woods Ltd* [1980] 1 Ch 496.

should be based on the law of the location where the property was situated at the time of the purported transfer. Under Italian law, a buyer in good faith without knowledge of the theft acquired valid title. Consequently, the Italian legal principle prevailed over the *nemo dat quod non habet* rule, as it aligned with the location of the paintings at the time of the transfer.

In contrast in *New Zealand v Ortiz*[16] a Maori artefact, consisting of a pair of intricately carved door panels, was exported from New Zealand, allegedly breaching New Zealand laws, and subsequently sold to a collector in Europe. Eventually, it appeared for sale at an auction house in London. The New Zealand government initiated legal action to reclaim ownership, contending that under New Zealand legislation it held title to the artefact. The court upheld the claimant's argument. However, the Court of Appeal ruled against the claimant, determining that they hadn't acquired legal title automatically upon illegal export, and expressed doubts regarding the enforceability of New Zealand legal provisions in the United Kingdom.

International Cultural Object Protection Laws

The Egyptian Law No 117 was enacted in 1983, which marked a significant shift in Egypt's antiquities regulations. This law effectively prohibited the export of all antiquities from Egypt. Article 9 of the law specified that any disposal of antiquities within Egypt required written consent from the Antiquities Authority, with the condition that the object remained within the country. Moreover, the law imposed stricter penalties, including fines and imprisonment, for violators. Subsequent to its enactment, licensed trading in antiquities was completely abolished. In 2010, the law underwent amendments, further prohibiting all antiquities trading and revoking the 10 percent ownership granted to foreign excavation missions upon discovery.

In the case of *United States v Schultz*,[17] the US Court of Appeals for the Second Circuit ruled that the National Stolen Property Act (NSPA) applied to artefacts taken from countries with patrimony laws asserting ownership over all archaeological resources found within their borders. Frederick Schultz, a prominent art dealer based in New York City, had been involved in smuggling Egyptian antiquities into the United States for nearly a decade. Schultz collaborated with Jonathan Tokeley Parry. Parry and Schultz concocted a fictitious collection, claiming that a man named

---

[16] *New Zealand v Ortiz* [1984] AC 1.
[17] *United States v Frederick Schultz*, 178 F.Supp. 2d 445 (SDNY 2002), aff'd, 333 F.3d 393 (2d Cir 2003) (New York, United States).

Thomas Alcock had assembled the artefacts in the 1920s and that they had remained in the collection since then. In 2001, Schultz was charged with conspiring to receive stolen Egyptian antiquities that had been transported across state lines and internationally in violation of the NSPA. According to Egyptian patrimony law, all artefacts discovered after 1983 are considered the property of the Egyptian government. The court ruled that the NSPA applies to any stolen property, irrespective of the true owner's title, and since Schultz conspired to smuggle the artefacts from Egypt, he was found guilty of theft from Egypt in violation of the NSPA.

Turkish Law no 2863 of 1983 on the Protection of Cultural and Natural Property, article 5 states:

> "Immovable property belonging to the state, public institutions and organisations and movable and immovable cultural and natural property to be protected that is known to exist or will be discovered on an immovable property owned by real and legal persons subject to civil law shall have the quality of state property."

In the Iranian Legal Bill of 1979 Regarding Prevention of Unauthorised Excavations and Digging, article 1 sets out that

> "Undertaking any excavation and digging intended to obtain antiquities and historical relics is absolutely forbidden and the offender shall be sentenced to six months to three years correctional imprisonment and seizure [in Farsi "zabt"] of the discovered items and excavation equipment in favour of the public treasury. If the excavation takes place in historical places that have been registered in the National Heritage List, the offender shall be sentenced to the maximum punishment provided (in this Section)."[18]

In 2006, the Islamic Republic of Iran (Iran) initiated legal action in an English court against The Barakat Galleries Limited,[19] seeking the return of a collection of carved jars, bowls, and cups made from chlorite. Iran alleged that these artefacts were unlawfully excavated from the historical Iranian region of Jiroft and were the rightful property of the Iranian state. Barakat, a gallery based in London specializing in ancient antiquities, disputed Iran's claim to ownership of the collection. Barakat claimed to have obtained legal title to the antiquities under the laws of certain countries where they were acquired, namely France, Germany, and Switzerland.

In 2007, the High Court of Justice in London ruled that Iran did not have legal ownership of the antiquities. The court also agreed with Barakat's argument that Iran's claim could not be pursued in English courts because

---

[18] Cited in *Republic of Iran v Barakat Galleries* [2007] EWCA Civ 1374 at 41.
[19] *Republic of Iran v Barakat Galleries* [2007] EWCA Civ 1374.

the referenced laws were related to Iranian criminal law, which English courts could not enforce on behalf of a foreign state. Iran appealed this decision, and in December 2007, the Court of Appeal concluded that Iran had indeed demonstrated ownership of the antiquities under Iranian law. Furthermore, the Court of Appeal ruled that English courts could consider Iranian ownership laws in resolving the dispute, thus affirming Iran's right to seek the return of the artefacts.

UNIDROIT Model Provisions on State Ownership of Undiscovered Cultural Objects (2011), model provision 3 states that "[u]ndiscovered cultural objects are owned by the State, provided there is no prior existing ownership."[20]

In Ireland the Historic and Archaeological Heritage and Miscellaneous Provisions Act 2023 addresses the issue of state ownership of archaeological items as follows at s 96 (which at the time of writing has yet to be commenced):

> "(1) Without prejudice to any other rights of the State arising in relation to any archaeological object found before 21 November 1994 but subject to section 4(4)(a), there shall, by virtue of this subsection, be vested in the State the ownership of any archaeological object where such object has no known owner.
>
> (2) The ownership of an archaeological object vested in the State by virtue of subsection (1) is an absolute and immediate right to possession of the object.
>
> (3) An owner or owner exception of land, not being the State, is deemed not to acquire any rights of ownership to an archaeological object found on, in or under the land.
>
> (4) A finder of an archaeological object is deemed not to acquire any rights of ownership to the object."

Compulsory Acquisition

The National Cultural Heritage Institutions Act 1997 at s 52 allows compulsory acquisition of cultural objects under certain circumstances, namely that it is

> "entered on a register and for an uninterrupted period of 5 years before the

---

[20] UNESCO, 'UNIDROIT Model Legislative Provisions on State Ownership oF Undiscovered Cultural Objects' <https://www.unidroit.org/instruments/cultural-property/2012-model-provisions/> accessed 21 August 2024.

commencement of this section was in the care of an institution specified in the Second Schedule or in any other institution owned or funded wholly or substantially by the State or by any public or local authority."

Section 53(1) states that

"Whenever the owner of a cultural object to which this Part applies requests the return of the object from an institution referred to in section 52, then, if it appears to the Minister that the common good requires that the object should be in the ownership, care and control of the State, the Minister may, with the consent of the Minister for Finance, acquire the object by agreement with the owner thereof or, in default of agreement, compulsorily by order made by the Minister... acquire the object."

Section 53(2) sets out that when the owner of a cultural object requests its return, the minister must write to the owner of the object within two weeks from the date of the request stating that they shall decide within six weeks whether they propose to acquire the object. Where the minister acquires a cultural object the object shall vest in the minister for the benefit of the State, the price or compensation payable on the acquisition shall be paid out of moneys provided by the Oireachtas.

Any person claiming to be the owner of a cultural object thus acquired may apply to the minister for compensation in respect of the object, which application for compensation under this s 57 shall be made to the minister within three months (or such longer period, not exceeding six months, as the minister may in any particular case allow) from the date upon which the notice of the proposal to acquire the cultural object the subject of the application was published in Iris Oifigiúil pursuant to this section.

Section 58 details that within three months receipt of such an application the minister may either make an offer in writing to the applicant specifying a sum of compensation, or declining to offer any compensation. If the applicant either refuses the compensation offered or is offered no compensation they may make an application to the High Court for compensation in respect of the object, under s 59(1), within three months of either the refusal of the offer or the notice of no offer of compensation being made. Section 59(3) gives the High Court powers to make an award of compensation, fix the amount of compensation and order payment of compensation to the applicant by the minister. However, s 59(7) allows the minister to apply for an order overturning an order made under s 59(3) instead and direct the return of the object to the applicant. In other words, if the compensation awarded is deemed too high, the minister may elect to simply return the object in question instead.

Section 98 of the Historic and Archaeological Heritage and Miscellaneous Provisions Act 2023 (at the time of writing yet to be commenced) allows for the acquisition of archaeological objects for the state by the minister.[21] Such acquisition can occur (whether or not for valuable consideration) by agreement or

> "subject to subsection (3), compulsorily an archaeological object from the owner of the object or a person purporting to be such, or (b) accept, on behalf of the State, a gift, bequest or devise of an archaeological object where the conditions (if any) to which the gift, bequest or devise, as the case may be, is subject are not inconsistent with the provisions of this Act."

Section 98(3) states that

> "An archaeological object shall not be compulsorily acquired under this section if— (a) a person has lawfully brought it into the State, and (b) there is an agreement in writing between that person and the Minister or Board that the object will not be so acquired if the conditions (if any) specified in the agreement relating to the object are complied with."

In other words, the state will not be able to seize items brought into the state lawfully, for instance subject to the terms of a loan agreement.

Section 98(4) sets out that a person (not being the minister or the Board) shall not initiate legal proceedings seeking the recovery, on behalf of the State, of an archaeological object lawfully brought into the state subject to an agreement that it not be compulsorily acquired except with the consent of the minister.

Limitation Periods

In Irish law, the primary legislation determining the limitation periods within which an action may be brought is the Statute of Limitations 1957 (the Statute). The Statute sets out a set of broad limitation periods for common causes of action, such as in contract and tort, for the recovery of land, in relation to tenancies, actions against trustees and actions against the estate of deceased persons, which are set out in Part II of the Statute.

---

[21] While the Minister for Housing, Local Government and Heritage has overall responsibility for the provisions of the Historic and Archaeological Heritage and Miscellaneous Provisions Act 2023, according to the letter of 5 March 2024 received by the author from the office of the Malcolm Noonan TD, Minister of State for Nature, Heritage and Electoral Reform, the Minister for Tourism, Culture, Arts, Gaeltacht, Sport and Media has responsibility for moveable cultural property.

For instance, the limitation period for simple actions in contract or tort is six years, unless specific limitation periods apply. Generally, limitation periods apply from "the date on which the cause of action accrued."[22]

From the perspective of galleries, libraries, archives and museums it is important to note the specific provisions in relation to detinue and conversion set out at s 12 of the statute which states that where

> "(1) (a) any cause of action in respect of the conversion or wrongful detention of a chattel has accrued to any person, and
> (b) before he recovers possession of the chattel, a further conversion or wrongful detention takes place, then, subject to section 26, no action shall be brought in respect of the further conversion or wrongful detention after the expiration of six years from the accrual of the cause of action in respect of the original conversion or wrongful detention."

Furthermore, at s 12(2) where

> "(a) any cause of action in respect of the conversion or wrongful detention of a chattel has accrued to any person, and
> (b) the period fixed for bringing that action and for bringing any action in respect of such a further conversion or wrongful detention as is mentioned in subsection (1) of this section has expired, and
> (c) he has not during that period recovered possession of the chattel, then, subject to section 26, the title of that person to the chattel shall be extinguished."

What this means is if a detinue or conversion of an object has occurred, and a further conversion or detinue occurs before the object is recovered by the claimant then a limitation period of six years applies from the accrual of the original cause of action, after which the claimant's title is extinguished.

An example of this principle in action from English law was case of *The London Borough of Tower Hamlets v The London Borough of Bromley*,[23] the ownership of the Henry Moore sculpture "Draped Seated Woman" was examined. One of six casts of the sculpture was purchased by the London County Council in 1962 and installed on the newly built Stifford Estate in Stepney, London which later became part of the London Borough of Tower Hamlets. Owing to a financial shortfall, Tower Hamlets decided to sell the sculpture, but the London Borough of Bromley challenged the decision.

---

[22] Statute of Limitations 1957, s 11(2)(a).
[23] *The London Borough of Tower Hamlets v The London Borough of Bromley* [2015] EWHC 1954 (Ch).

The courts first examined the question of whether the sculpture was a chattel or a fixture. Two aspects of the sculpture's history were compelling in deciding that it was a chattel: first, it had been purchased from an art fund rather than a buildings fund; secondly the sculpture could be, and had been, moved previously — including a loan to the Yorkshire Sculpture Park, so it was not affixed to the land. Following from this decision it was held that the sculpture did not transfer to Tower Hamlets along with the Stifford Estate by virtue of s 62 of the Law of Property Act 1925, but instead remained the property of Greater London Council, whose assets were vested in the London Residuary Body from 1985 to 1996 when the remaining assets were transferred to the London Borough of Bromley.

However, Tower Hamlets now argued that the sculpture had passed to it by the tort of conversion, as it had openly converted the sculpture to its use and that as a result Bromley could no longer assert any rights to it. Tower Hamlets had treated the sculpture as if it were the legal owner of same, including the aforementioned loan to Yorkshire Sculpture Park and commissioning and paying for a programme of conservation.

These actions were held by the court as assertions of rights by Tower Hamlets which met the *Kuwait Airways* test in that: first, the defendant's conduct was inconsistent with the rights of the owner (or other person entitled to possession). Secondly, the conduct was deliberate, not accidental. Thirdly, the conduct was so extensive an encroachment on the rights of the owner as to exclude him from use and possession of the goods.

Bromley furthermore failed to assert any rights over the sculpture in the intervening period and as a result following s 3(2) of the UK Limitation Act 1980 the title of Bromley over the statue had been extinguished. The negative publicity generated by the case was however sufficient to ensure that Tower Hamlets reversed its decision.

Limitation periods can also be defined by separate legislation. For instance, the Historic and Archaeological Heritage and Miscellaneous Provisions Act 2023 sets out at s 97(1) (at the time of writing yet to be commenced) that

> "The Statute of Limitations 1957 shall not— (a) apply to an action for recovery by the State of an archaeological object, whether such action is made under this Act or another enactment, or (b) extinguish a title of the State to, or any other interest of the State in, an archaeological object."

Title and Provenance

The UNESCO 1954 Convention

Following the destruction wrought during the second world war, the UNESCO 1954 Convention for the Protection of Cultural Property in the Event of Armed Conflict, commonly known as the 1954 Hague Convention, was adopted to lessen "large-scale destruction of cultural heritage, weakening the foundations of communities, lasting peace and prospects of reconciliation."[24]

The 1954 Hague Convention built on the Hague Conference of 1899, officially titled the 'Laws and Customs of War on Land, July 29, 1899' that established regulations governing land warfare for its signatories. These regulations encompassed protocols for the treatment of prisoners of war and wounded soldiers on the battlefield, building upon the precedents set by the Geneva Convention of 1864. The regulations also safeguarded cultural sites and artefacts. It explicitly prohibited the looting or destruction of private property, including art and historical landmarks, by military occupiers and nations. The provisions of the Hague Convention were supplemented by two protocols, in 1954 and 1999.

The primary objective of the 1954 Hague Convention is to preserve cultural property, including architectural monuments, artworks, archaeological sites, historical artefacts, manuscripts, books, and other items of artistic, historical, or archaeological significance, along with scientific collections of any nature, regardless of their origins or ownership.

The commitments made by the states parties to the Convention serve to preserve cultural heritage through adopting preventive measures such as preparing inventories, planning emergency measures to protect property against the risk of fire or the collapse of buildings, and preparing the removal of cultural property to places of safety.

State Parties must also develop initiatives which guarantee respect for cultural property situated on their own territory or on the territory of other states parties. This involves refraining from using such property in any manner that might expose it to destruction or deterioration in the event of armed conflict, and by refraining from all acts of hostility directed against it.

---

[24] UNESCO, 'Convention for the Protection of Cultural Property in the Event of Armed Conflict with Regulations for the Execution of the Convention' <https://www.unesco.org/en/heritage-armed-conflicts/convention-and-protocols/1954-convention> accessed 21 August 2024.

Other commitments include registering cultural property of very high importance on the International Register of Cultural Property under Special Protection; marking certain important buildings and monuments with a distinctive emblem of the Convention; providing a place for eventual refuge to shelter movable cultural property; establishing special units within the military forces responsible for the protection of cultural property; setting sanctions for breaches of the Convention; and promoting the Convention among the general public and through target groups such as cultural heritage professionals, and military or law-enforcement agencies.

Case Study: The Derrynaflan Hoard

Dr Michael Ryan, Keeper at the NMI described the Derrynaflan hoard in the following terms:

> "The Derrynaflan hoard is one of the most significant discoveries of early Christian art ever made. The chalice dates to the early ninth century and preliminary study has revealed the extremely important break-through which analysis of its decoration and technology will have for later Irish and, probably also Viking studies. The Paten stands close comparison with the Ardagh Chalice in style, technique and range of motifs—it is a superb piece and like the chalice is an immensely important contribution to knowledge. The strainer is also a first class objet d'art unique in many respects—while the covering basin, although severely corroded, is likewise a significant and valuable find in its own right."[25]

The collection comprising the hoard was discovered by Michael Webb, and his son also named Michael, on 17 February 1980 using metal detectors. Derrynaflan spans approximately 73 acres and contains remnants of a church and other structures associated with an abbey, including a tomb believed to belong to Guban Saor. A Preservation Order, issued on 8 June 1935 by the Minister for Finance under s 8 of the National Monuments Act 1930, safeguards the buildings and tomb referred to as "Derrynaflan Abbey or Guban's Church and grave." At the time of discovery, a notice from Bord Fáilte was posted on a church wall, providing brief information about the site, along with a notice from the Board of Works warning against any damage or interference with a national monument.

The hoard was unearthed from a pit partially dug into a bank and partially into the side of a ditch, which, at the time of depositing the hoard, had either filled with sediment or been backfilled. It is evident that the hoard was deliberately buried in the pit with the intention of concealment (for

---

[25] Michael Ryan, 'The Derrynaflan Hoard and Early Irish Art', *Speculum*, Vol 72 No 4 (October 1997), p 995.

more on the importance of concealment and intention to retrieve see Chapter 7).

It was determined that while the Webbs had implied permission from the landowners to visit the island and its church and tomb, which were subject to the Preservation Order, they lacked any express or implied permission to conduct excavation on the land.

Following the discovery, the Webbs removed the hoard and the following day, Mr Webb delivered the hoard to the National Museum and entrusted it to Dr Brendán Ó Ríordáin, the Museum's Director. Concurrently, Mr Webb presented Dr Ó Ríordáin with a letter from his solicitor which stated *inter alia*

> "… our client is advised that these articles should, with the minimum possible delay and handling, be delivered to the care and custody of experts who have the facilities for examination and preserving same. We have accordingly advised our client that he should deliver these articles to your care for the present and pending determination of the legal ownership or status thereof…"[26]

In response Dr Ó Ríordáin told Mr Webb that he thought that the articles making up the hoard were treasure trove (see Chapter 7), but that he would have to be guided by the Attorney General's Office. He told Mr Webb that he would be honourably treated. In June 1981 the Chief State Solicitor wrote to the plaintiffs offering £10,000 in respect of their interest in the hoard, which the plaintiffs rejected and subsequently requested the return of the hoard. In 1982, the Chief State Solicitor again wrote to the Webbs informing them that the hoard was the property of the state.

Separately the state concluded negotiations with the landowners upon whose land the hoard had been discovered by the Webbs, both of whom accepted payments of £25,000 and signed statements conveying all rights, property or interest that they had in the hoard and in the possession of the National Museum of Ireland to the Minister for Education.

The Webbs brought a suit for detinue, which comprises the wrongful withholding, retention or detention of goods by the defendant, in respect of which the claimant has a better title. The person detaining the chattel must do so adversely to the claimant's rights.

The trial judge found that that the state should return the hoard or pay the

---

[26] *Webb v Ireland and the Attorney General* [1987] IESC 2.

plaintiffs £5.5m (a sum arrived at by independent valuation), on the basis that the former royal prerogative of treasure trove was not carried over into Irish law by either of the Constitutions of 1922 or 1937, that the state had received the hoard in the capacity of bailees and was estopped from denying the title of the plaintiffs, as bailors, to the hoard. The judge did not examine the question of ownership, as the requirement to return the hoard under the principle of bailment had been established.

The State appealed this decision, and the court found that, relying on the contents of the 1980 solicitors letter which stated that the hoard was placed in the NMI's care pending determination of the legal status of the objects, that the express terms of the letter precluded a bailment from being formed. The Supreme Court found that

> "where a bailee asserts and establishes a title in himself to the goods is that he establishes the termination of the bailment and that by reason of that termination any estoppel which would otherwise arise between a bailee and a bailor ceases to operate."[27]

The court next examined the question of whether the state had acquired a good title to the hoard prior to the institution of proceedings. The state asserted title to the goods through the landowners on the basis of two criteria:

> "Firstly, they allege that the landowner had a title to any chattel found in the land against any finder of it, under any circumstances. Secondly, they allege that the Plaintiffs, having found the chattels and obtained possession of them by an act of trespass as found by the learned trial Judge, namely, the digging in the land, and/or being guilty, as it is alleged, of an offence under Section 14 of the National Monuments Act 1930, cannot derive any lawful title to the goods thus acquired."[28]

The court concluded that the owners of the land on which the hoard had been found had a right to possession of the hoard, superior to the plaintiffs who were finders of it, and that by the agreements made between the state and those two landowners these rights had become vested in the State, and further that even if the right of ownership of the hoard as between the owners of the land and the finders were different from what the court had stated it to be, that the fact that the plaintiffs are finders by an act of trespass would disentitle them to any rights in the objects found, certainly as between them and the owners of the land.

---

[27] ibid.
[28] ibid.

The court next proceeded to examine the question of treasure trove. After examining the history and development of treasure trove, including its original purpose as a means of enriching the royal mint – including the practice of melting down gold and silver finds (see Chapter 7) the court held that the royal prerogative of treasure trove had not been carried over into Irish law by either of the Constitutions of 1922 or 1937. However, Article 10.1 of the Constitution states:

> "All natural resources, including the air and all forms of potential energy, within the jurisdiction of the Parliament and Government established by this Constitution and all royalties and franchises within that jurisdiction belong to the State subject to all estates and interests therein for the time being lawfully vested in any person or body."

It was found by the Court that the term 'royalty' must be widely construed and must include the sovereignty or sovereign rule of the state. In his judgment Finlay CJ stated that:

> "It would, I think, now be universally accepted, certainly by the People of Ireland, and by the people of most modern States, that one of the most important national assets belonging to the people is their heritage and knowledge of its true origins and the buildings and objects which constitute keys to their ancient history. If this be so, then it would appear to me to follow that a necessary ingredient of sovereignty in a modern State and certainly in this State, having regard to the terms of the Constitution, with an emphasis on its historical origins and a constant concern for the common good is and should be an ownership by the State of objects which constitute antiquities of importance which are discovered and which have no known owner. It would appear to me to be inconsistent with the framework of the society sought to be created and sought to be protected by the Constitution that such objects should become the exclusive property of those who by chance may find them.
>
> The existence of such a general ingredient of the sovereignty of the State, does, however, seem to me to lead to the conclusion that the much more limited right of the prerogative of treasure trove known to the common law should be upheld not as a right derived from the Crown but rather as an inherent attribute of the sovereignty of the State which was recognised and declared by Article 11 of the 1922 Constitution.
>
> For the purpose of determining the issues in this case, therefore, I would conclude that there does exist in the State a right or prerogative of treasure trove, the characteristics of which are the characteristics of the prerogative of treasure trove at common law which I have already outlined in this judgment as they stood in 1922."

Accordingly, it was held that the state had good title in the hoard on the basis of contract with the landowners, and by the existence of a common law prerogative of treasure trove created under Article 11 of the Constitution, and the plaintiffs' proceedings for payment of £5m or the return of the hoard were denied.

The position in relation to state ownership of archaeological items was clarified by the National Monuments (Amendment) Act 1994 at s 4(1): "No person shall have in his possession or under his control an archaeological object which has been found in the State after the coming into operation of this section." The Historic and Archaeological Heritage and Miscellaneous Provisions Act 2023 further clarifies at s 96 which will vest absolute ownership of all such finds in the state. This section had not yet been commenced at the time of writing.

Chapter 4

Art Crime and Acquisitions

Introduction

What is the difference between a criminal act and one which carries the possibility of resolution by civil action? At its most basic level, a criminal act is one that can be punished by the state. In Ireland, criminal acts are expressly prohibited by statute. In addition there are offences recognised by the common law and a smaller number of offences which are provided for under the Constitution. Civil law concerns the infringement of the rights of one private entity by another.

In civil law matters, cases are heard between a plaintiff and a defendant. In criminal matters they are heard between the state/the Director of Public Prosecutions (DPP) and a defendant. In civil law matters, the standard of proof is 'on the balance of probabilities' and the burden of meeting this standard of proof rests with the plaintiff. In criminal matters, the standard of proof is 'beyond all reasonable doubt' and the burden of proof rests with the prosecution, with limited exceptions, for instance some defences to murder charges, but these are beyond the scope of this book.

A key question in relation to criminal matters, as they relate to art and cultural heritage law is that of jurisdiction — the authority of a court to hear and make determinations in cases. As a rule, criminal matters are heard and punished in the country in which they were committed. However, international provisions exist for some criminal activities. For instance at s 45 of the Criminal Justice (Theft and Fraud Offences) Act 2001 provision is made for a person who has been ordinarily resident in Ireland for the previous 12 months or a company registered in Ireland to be guilty of an offence at Irish law if they commit fraud affecting the financial interests of the European Union, or misappropriation of public funds.

In Ireland, criminal matters are tried in courts with varying jurisdictions, or ability to hear different matters. The District Court is a court of limited and summary jurisdiction — this means it can hear minor matters that do not require a jury trial. Where an offence is detailed at statute it will indicate whether the offence is capable of being tried summarily, whether it must be tried on indictment (trial by jury) or whether it is an indictable offence which may be tried summarily with the agreement of the defendant and the DPP.

The Circuit Court hears all indictable offences except murder, rape, aggravated sexual assault, treason, piracy and related offences which may only be tried before the Central Criminal Court. The Circuit Court sits with a judge and jury. The Circuit Court also hears appeals from the District Court, in which case the appeal is held as a *de novo* hearing (heard again from scratch) and there is no further appeal from that decision.

The High Court is imbued with its powers by the Constitution at Article 34.3.1° which states that the High Court has "full original jurisdiction in and power to determine all matters and questions whether of law or fact, civil or criminal." When hearing criminal matters, the High Court is known as the Central Criminal Court and sits with a judge and jury. The High Court hears murder, rape, aggravated sexual assault, treason, piracy and related offences as well as offences under the Offences against the State Acts 1939-1998 and offences under the Genocide Act 1973, the Geneva Conventions Act 1962 and the Criminal Justice (United Nations Convention against Torture) Act 2000. The High Court can also hear questions sent to it on a 'case stated' basis whereby questions of law can be referred by the District Court.

The Special Criminal Court was founded under Part V of the Offences against the State Act 1939 and hears cases relating to offences against the state and offences related to criminal organisations as detailed under the Criminal Justice (Amendment) Act 2009 in a court with three judges and no jury.

The Court of Appeal was established in 2014, sits with three judges and can hear appeals against convictions from the Circuit, Central and Special Criminal Courts. The Court of Appeal can hear both appeals against conviction and appeals against sentencing, where a convicted person believes their sentence to be unduly harsh or where the prosecution believes a sentence is unduly lenient. The Court of Appeal can also hear 'cases stated' from the Circuit Court.

The Supreme Court is a court of appeal and hears only two types of appeal: an appeal from the Court of Appeal in cases where the Supreme Court is satisfied that it is a matter of general public importance or the interests of justice require that the appeal be heard, or in exceptional circumstances a decision of the High Court can be appealed where the Supreme Court is satisfied that it is a matter of general public importance or the interests of justice require that the appeal be heard. The Supreme Court sits with either three or five judges and makes its decisions based on transcripts and documentation which had been before the original trial court.

Elements of a Crime

In order for a defendant to be convicted a crime there are normally two elements which are required to be present. An *actus reus* and a *mens rea*. The *actus reus* is the element of the offence which relates to an action on the behalf of the accused, but can also comprise inaction or omission on their behalf, including recklessness as to the result of their actions. The type of offence of which a defendant is accused is also of relevance. Result offences (e.g. murder) require that the defendants actions had a demonstrable specific result; conduct offences assign liability based on the defendant engaging in specific conduct rather than this conduct having any particular result. There must be an *actus reus* in order for an offence to have occurred.

Criminal liability might also arise through omission. Omission arises where the accused is under a duty to act but fails to do so. This duty can be based on a statutory duty, that is defined at law under statute; a contractual duty where by virtue of a contract or by holding a particular office a duty or duties are imposed on an individual — though the neglect of duty in this instance is normally held to be required to be wilful rather than inadvertent;[1] where the accused creates a danger and does nothing to mitigate it, and;[2] a voluntary assumption of duty. In the case of R *v Gibbins and Proctor*,[3] the first defendant abandoned his wife and took their children to live with the second defendant. Despite not being related to the deceased, the second defendant acted as her mother. The second defendant deprived one of the children of food, leading to her death from starvation. Both defendants were convicted of murder, as the second defendant, by assuming a maternal role, was found to owe the child a duty of care.

Mens rea is the element of an offence which relates to intention or the state

---

[1] See: *DPP v Bartley* (HC, 13 June 1997) (Carney J).
[2] See: R *v Miller* [1983] 1 All ER 978.
[3] R *v Gibbins and Proctor* [1918] 13 Cr App Rep 134.

of mind of the accused in relation to the offence. Intention is not motive, but rather an understanding of the desired outcome of the defendant's actions, or the probable outcome of their actions. In R v Moloney,[4] a two-part test was set out to determine intention: was the outcome a natural consequence of the voluntary act of the accused?; and, was this result foreseen by the accused as being a natural consequence of their actions? If so, a jury may be entitled to infer that the accused intended to bring about that result. In Ireland, the Criminal Justice Act 1964 states at s 4(2), in relation to the *mens rea* for murder, that "the accused person shall be presumed to have intended the natural and probable consequences of his conduct; but this presumption may be rebutted," but this presumption applies to all offences.

Recklessness is another form of *mens rea* and occurs where the accused has taken a course of action which either subjectively involves risk, in cases where the accused was aware of the risk but took it anyway; or objective recklessness where the accused denies awareness of the risk but that risk would have been obvious to a reasonable person.

In Irish law there appears to be a preference for use of the subjective test, for instance in *DPP v Murray*,[5] in which it was held that one of the accused who fired the fatal shot in a capital murder case could not be convicted of capital murder as they could not have known an off-duty Guard not in uniform was a Guard, and therefore could not be guilty of capital murder — being convicted instead for common murder and spared a death sentence.

Section 16(2) of the Criminal Law (Theft and Fraud Offences) Act 2001 also demonstrates a preference for the subjective test for recklessness by stating that

> "a person is reckless if he or she disregards a substantial risk that the property handled is stolen, and for those purposes 'substantial risk; means a risk of such a nature and degree that, having regard to the circumstances in which the person acquired the property and the extent of the information then available to him or her, its disregard involves culpability of a high degree."

Negligence in the context of criminal law — as opposed to the law of tort — arises exclusively in the case of manslaughter and arises in instances where the accused either failed to discharge a duty or breached a duty imposed by statute.

---

[4] *R v Moloney* [1985] 1 All ER 1025.
[5] *DPP v Murray* [1977] IR 360.

Strict liability offences, such as statutory rape, are such that a conviction can be obtained without a requirement for *mens rea*. These offences are usually designated as strict liability offences in order to discourage risk-taking behaviour or undesirable conduct.

Fraud and Theft Offences

In Ireland, the Criminal Justice (Fraud and Theft Offences) Act 2001 states at s 4(1) that a person is "guilty of theft if he or she dishonestly appropriates property without the consent of its owner and with the intention of depriving its owner of it."

The *actus reus* of theft is the appropriation of someone else's property without their consent. Section 4(5) of the 2001 Act states that "'appropriates', in relation to property, means usurps or adversely interferes with the proprietary rights of the owner of the property." Proprietary rights in relation to property include the right to enjoyment of that property, the right to transfer ownership of the property and the right to prevent anyone from interfering with either of the previous rights. Section 2(1) of the 2001 Act defines 'property' as "money and all other property, real or personal, including things in action and other intangible property."

Consent is an essential element of a theft offence — it must be proven that the owner did not consent to appropriation of their property. Section 2(4)(a) of the 2001 Act states that a person owns property if he possesses it. A person possesses something if he enjoys actual or constructive control over that thing and is aware of the fact that they can exercise such control. Under s 4(2) of the 2001 Act, a person does not appropriate property without consent if they believe that they have consent, they believe that the owner would consent if they knew of the appropriation and lastly if the owner cannot be identified by following reasonable steps. Section 4(2) confirms that consent obtained by deception or intimidation does not meet the threshold for consent presented by the previous three criteria.

The *mens rea* of theft is that the accused intended to deprive the owner of their property. Section 4(5) of the 2001 Act states that "'depriving' means temporarily or permanently depriving." It must also be proven that the non-consensual appropriation of the property was dishonest. Section 2(1) of the 2001 Act defines 'dishonestly' as "without a claim of right made in good faith." Dishonesty is a common aspect to all offences under the 2001 Act, except possessing stolen property.

The requirement for an absence of consent in the appropriation of the property in question can be informed by a number of criteria — for instance an absence of capacity to consent, use of force or threats in obtaining consent and most commonly in the case of art crime, fraud. There are traditionally two types of fraud that may serve to vitiate consent: fraud as to identity, whereby consent is obtained by means of a deliberate misrepresentation as to whom is seeking the consent; and fraud as to the nature of the transaction to which consent is given — commonly in relation to the nature of the object in question.

Theft is an indictable offence which carries a maximum sentence of ten years imprisonment and/or an unlimited fine.

Under s 96(5) of the Historic and Archaeological Heritage and Miscellaneous Provisions Act 2023 (not yet commenced at the time of writing), despite the vesting in the state of ownership of any archaeological object where such object has no known owner, and the clarification that neither landowners upon whose land such objects are found, nor the persons who find such objects acquire any rights of ownership over such objects (see Chapter 7),

> "the landowner on whose land an archaeological object is found, or the finder of an archaeological object, shall, if the object is taken from him or her other than in accordance with this Act or another enactment, or if he or she is induced to relinquish possession of the object by dishonesty, be deemed to be the owner of the object for the purposes of any offences under the Criminal Justice (Theft and Fraud Offences) Act 2001."

Handling Stolen Property

Section 17 of the 2001 Act provides that the offence of handling is committed where a person, knowing that property is stolen, or is reckless as to that fact, dishonestly receives it or arranges to receive it, or undertakes to assist in its retention, removal, disposal or realisation by or for the benefit of another person.

The *actus reus* of handling is receiving or arranging to receive, or assisting in the removal, disposal or realisation of stolen property. The *mens rea* of handling is to have carried out the above acts while reckless to the fact of whether an object is stolen or not. Handling stolen property is an indictable offence which carries a maximum sentence of ten years imprisonment and/or an unlimited fine.

Possession of Stolen Property

Section 18 of the 2001 Act details the offence of possession of stolen property. The offence is committed where a person, without lawful authority or excuse, possesses stolen property, knowing that the property has been stolen, or is reckless as to whether it has been stolen.

The *actus reus* is being in possession of stolen property. The *mens rea* is knowledge that the property is stolen, or recklessness as to whether the property is stolen. A person possesses something if he enjoys actual or constructive control over that thing and is aware of the fact that they can exercise such control.

Section 18(2) of the 2001 Act provides that where a person possesses stolen property such that it is reasonable to conclude that the person knew the property to be stolen or was reckless as to the fact, it will be presumed that they knew it to be stolen. It is possible to rebut this presumption where there is a reasonable doubt as regards such knowledge or recklessness on the part of the person who has possession of the property. Possession of stolen property is triable on indictment and carries a maximum prison sentence of five years and/or an unlimited fine.

Money Laundering

Money laundering refers to the various methods used to hide the fact that assets or property are the proceeds of criminal activity. This offence is detailed in Part 2 of the Criminal Justice (Money Laundering and Terrorist Financing) Act 2010. The global nature of money laundering has prompted numerous initiatives aimed at coordinating an international response. One purpose of the 2010 Act was to transpose the EU Third Money Laundering Directive (Directive 2005/60) into Irish law. The 2010 Act repealed earlier statutory measures on money laundering contained in the Criminal Justice Act 1994. The 2010 Act was later amended by the Criminal Justice (Money Laundering and Terrorist Financing) Act 2013 and in 2021 the Criminal Justice (Money Laundering and Terrorist Financing) (Amendment) Act 2021 entered into force transposing the EU's Fifth Anti-Money Laundering Directive into Irish law.

Section 7 of the 2010 Act provides that a person commits the offence of money laundering by

> "Concealing or disguising the true nature, source, location, disposition, movement or ownership of the property, or any rights relating to the property;

> converting, transferring, handling, acquiring, possessing or using the property; or, removing the property from, or bringing the property into, the State."

The accused must know or believe that the property has been obtained as a result of criminal activity or that it probably has been so obtained, or be reckless as to whether this is the case.

The subjective test for recklessness is set out at s 7(5) of the 2010 Act, where a

> "person is reckless as to whether or not the property is the proceeds of criminal conduct if the person disregards, in relation to the property, a risk of such a nature and degree that, considering the circumstances in which the person carries out any act referred to in [the preceding subsections), the disregard of that risk involves culpability of a high degree."

Section 7 relates to offences carried out within the state. Section 8 provides that under certain circumstances, the 2010 Act will have extra-territorial effect and in that event, a person whose conduct would constitute an offence under s 7 of the 2010 Act if any of the following the following apply:

(a) The conduct in question takes place on board an Irish-registered ship or aircraft;
(b) The conduct is an offence in the place where it is carried out and the person is an Irish citizen or is ordinarily resident in the State, or is a body corporate registered under the Companies Acts;
(c) The surrender of the person had been sought under the Extradition Act 1965 and the request has been finally refused;
(d) The person had been the subject of a European Arrest Warrant but a determination had been made not to hand him over to the requesting authorities.

Under any of these circumstances the person may be tried as if the offence had been committed within the state. On summary conviction, the maximum penalty is a fine of €5,000 and/or twelve months imprisonment. On conviction on indictment, the maximum penalty is an unlimited fine and/or fourteen years' imprisonment. Any prosecutions in respect of offences committed outside the state require the consent of the DPP.

Proceeds of Crime

A civil non-conviction based model for the confiscation of the proceeds of crime was introduced in Ireland under the Proceeds of Crime Act 1996.

The same year, the Criminal Assets Bureau Act 1996, establishing the Criminal Assets Bureau (CAB), was enacted.

Section 4 of the CAB Act sets out the objectives of the Bureau as:

> "(a) the identification of the assets, wherever situated, of persons which derive or are suspected to derive, directly or indirectly, from F3[criminal conduct],
> (b) the taking of appropriate action under the law to deprive or to deny those persons of the assets or the benefit of such assets, in whole or in part, as may be appropriate, and
> (c) the pursuit of any investigation or the doing of any other preparatory work in relation to any proceedings arising from the objectives mentioned in paragraphs (a) and (b)."

Importantly, the Proceeds of Crime (Amendment) Act of 2005 sets out at s 10 that:

> "for the avoidance of doubt, it is hereby declared that section 11(7) of the Statute of Limitations 1957 does not apply in relation to proceedings under the Principal Act. Section 11 (7) states that "an action to recover any penalty or forfeiture, or sum by way of penalty or forfeiture, recoverable by virtue of any enactment shall not be brought after the expiration of two years from the date on which the cause of action accrued."

The disapplication of this section means that, in theory, the proceeds of crime can be seized regardless of the date at which the cause of action accrued — in this case when the crime was committed or the assets acquired.

Ethics of Acquisition — International Conventions

Ethical considerations in relation to the acquisition of cultural objects by galleries, libraries, museums and archives are bounded and defined by a mixture of international legal conventions, and codes of ethics which are made available by professional organisations.

The primary international conventions that relate to ethical considerations are the UNESCO Convention on the Means of Prohibiting and Preventing the Illicit Import, Export and Transfer of Cultural Property 1970; the Hague Convention for the Protection of Cultural Property in the Event of Armed Conflict 1954; the UNIDROIT Convention on Stolen or Illegally Exported Cultural Objects 1995 (see Chapter 5); the UNESCO 2001 Convention for the Protection of Underwater Heritage; The UNESCO 2003 Convention for the Safeguarding of Intangible Cultural Heritage; the Convention on

International Trade in Endangered Species of Wild Fauna and Flora 1973; and the UN Declaration on the Rights of Indigenous Peoples 2007.

The 1970 UNESCO Convention "urges States Parties to take measures to prohibit and prevent the import, export and transfer of cultural property" and "provides a common framework for the States Parties on the measures to be taken to prohibit and prevent the import, export and transfer of cultural property."[6]

The primary objective of the 1954 Hague Convention is to preserve cultural property, including architectural monuments, artworks, archaeological sites, historical artefacts, manuscripts, books, and other items of artistic, historical, or archaeological significance, along with scientific collections of any nature, regardless of their origins or ownership (see Chapter 3).

In 1984, UNIDROIT was asked to examine the issues of private law applicable to illicit traffic in cultural objects. In 1995, a final text as prepared by UNIDROIT was adopted at the Diplomatic Conference in Rome. A clear distinction is the requirement under the UNESCO Convention 1970 for a cultural object to have been designated as such by any state requesting return, whereas the UNIDROIT Convention 1995 allows for private individuals to seek the return of objects stolen from private ownership without a requirement for them to have been included on an official register. The UNIDROIT Convention states quite distinctly in Article 3(1) that "the possessor of a cultural object which has been stolen shall return it."[7] (see Chapter 5).

The UNESCO 2001 Convention for the Protection of Underwater Heritage defines underwater cultural heritage as

"all traces of human existence of a cultural, historical or archaeological nature which, for at least 100 years, have been partially or totally immersed, periodically or permanently, under the oceans and in lakes and rivers."[8]

States that are party to the 2001 Convention "shall, individually or

---

[6] UNESCO, 'Fight Illicit Trafficking (1970 Convention)' <https://www.unesco.org/en/fight-illicit-trafficking> accessed 21 August 2024.
[7] UNIDROIT, 'UNIDROIT Convention on Stolen or Illegally Exported Cultural Objects' <https://www.unidroit.org/instruments/cultural-property/1995-convention/> accessed 21 August 2024.
[8] UNESCO, 'Convention on the Protection of the Underwater Cultural Heritage', <https://www.unesco.org/en/underwater-heritage/2001-convention> accessed 21 August 2024.

jointly as appropriate, take all appropriate measures in conformity with this Convention and with international law that are necessary to protect underwater cultural heritage, using for this purpose the best practicable means at their disposal and in accordance with their capabilities."[9] Ireland has not ratified the 2001 Convention (see Chapter 7).

The UNESCO 2003 Convention for the Safeguarding of Intangible Cultural Heritage describes how:

> "the term 'cultural heritage' has changed content considerably in recent decades, partially owing to the instruments developed by UNESCO. Cultural heritage does not end at monuments and collections of objects. It also includes traditions or living expressions inherited from our ancestors and passed on to our descendants, such as oral traditions, performing arts, social practices, rituals, festive events, knowledge and practices concerning nature and the universe or the knowledge and skills to produce traditional crafts. While fragile, intangible cultural heritage is an important factor in maintaining cultural diversity in the face of growing globalization. An understanding of the intangible cultural heritage of different communities helps with intercultural dialogue, and encourages mutual respect for other ways of life. The importance of intangible cultural heritage is not the cultural manifestation itself but rather the wealth of knowledge and skills that is transmitted through it from one generation to the next. The social and economic value of this transmission of knowledge is relevant for minority groups and for mainstream social groups within a State, and is as important for developing States as for developed ones."[10]

This does, of course, beg the question 'how does one go about safeguarding something that is intangible?' UNESCO themselves have answered this question:

> "Not in the same way that you safeguard other cultural heritage. The safeguarding measures of a living heritage aim to strengthen the diverse tangible and intangible conditions that are necessary for its continuous evolution and interpretation by the holding community, as well as for its transmission to future generations. That is why the safeguarding measures shall always gravitate around the community and meet its needs. Also central is the adaptation to changing realities of the socioeconomic contexts in which the communities live."

Ireland ratified the UNESCO 2003 Convention in 2015. Under the terms of the convention ratifying parties must define and create an inventory

---

[9] UNESCO, 'Convention on the Protection of the Underwater Cultural Heritage', <https://www.unesco.org/en/underwater-heritage/2001-convention> accessed 21 August 2024.

[10] UNESCO, '2003 Convention for the Safeguarding of the Intangible Cultural Heritage' <https://ich.unesco.org/doc/src/18440-EN.pdf> accessed 21 August 2024.

of intangible cultural heritage with the participation of the communities concerned; adopt policies and establish institutions to monitor and promote it; encourage research; and take other appropriate safeguarding measures, always with the full consent and participation of the concerned communities. Six years after ratifying the Convention, each state party must submit a report to the Committee in regards to both the measures it has taken for the implementation of the Convention at the national level and the status of the elements inscribed by its country on the Representative List.

In order to develop Ireland's National Inventory of Intangible Cultural Heritage, an open call for expressions of interest was held and over 80 submissions were received in response. In 2019, Ireland officially launched its National Inventory of Intangible Cultural Heritage (ICH),[11] which to date comprises some 91 inscribed ICH practices drawn from all categories of intangible cultural heritage. The National Inventory aims to safeguard and raise awareness of Ireland's intangible cultural heritage locally, nationally, and internationally. Ireland has also had three elements of intangible cultural heritage inscribed on the UNESCO Representative List of the Intangible Cultural Heritage of Humanity — Uileann Piping, Hurling and Harping.[12]

The Convention on International Trade in Endangered Species of Wild Fauna and Flora (CITES) 1973[13] is an international agreement that aims to ensure that international trade in specimens of wild animals and plants does not threaten the survival of the species. This trade is diverse, ranging from live animals, such as pets, and live ornamental plants to a vast array of wildlife products derived from them, including food products, exotic leather goods, wooden musical instruments, timber, tourist curios and medicines. Levels of exploitation of some animal and plant species are high, and the trade in them, together with other factors such as habitat loss, is capable of heavily depleting their populations and even bringing some species close to extinction. Specimens include live, dead, parts, derivatives and final products, as well as specimens produced through biotechnology.

---

[11] 'Ireland's National Inventory of Cultural Heritage', <https://nationalinventoryich.tcagsm.gov.ie/about/> accessed 21 August 2024.

[12] Permanent Representation of Ireland to the OECD and UNESCO, 'Intangible Cultural Heritage', <https://www.ireland.ie/en/oecd-unesco/paris/ireland-and-unesco/intangible-cultural-heritage/> accessed 21 August 2024.

[13] CITES, 'Convention on International Trade in Endangered Species of Wild Fauna and Flora', <https://www.wto.org/english/res_e/booksp_e/int_exp_regs_part1_1_e.pdf> accessed 21 August 2024.

Article 10(6) sets out the exemption that the requirements for import, export or re-export licences

> "shall not apply to the non-commercial loan, donation or exchange between scientists or scientific institutions registered by a Management Authority of their State, of herbarium specimens, other preserved, dried or embedded museum specimens, and live plant material which carry a label issued or approved by a Management Authority."[14] (See Chapter 9)

The UN Declaration on the Rights of Indigenous Peoples 2007 (see Chapter 5) sets out at Article 12 that:

> "1. Indigenous peoples have the right to manifest, practice, develop and teach their spiritual and religious traditions, customs and ceremonies; the right to maintain, protect, and have access in privacy to their religious and cultural sites; the right to the use and control of their ceremonial objects; and the right to the repatriation of their human remains.
>
> 2. States shall seek to enable the access and/or repatriation of ceremonial objects and human remains in their possession through fair, transparent and effective mechanisms developed in conjunction with indigenous peoples concerned."[15]

Ethics of Acquisition — Codes of Ethics

The International Council of Museums (ICOM) has prepared and made available a Code of Ethics for Museums. It is the statement of ethics for museums referred to in the ICOM Statutes. The Code reflects principles generally accepted by the international museum community. The Code of Ethics states that

> "Museums have the duty to acquire, preserve and promote their collections as a contribution to safeguarding the natural, cultural and scientific heritage. Their collections are a significant public inheritance, have a special position in law and are protected by international legislation. Inherent in this public trust is the notion of stewardship that includes rightful ownership, permanence, documentation, accessibility and responsible disposal."[16]

---

[14] CITES, 'Convention on International Trade in Endangered Species of Wild Fauna and Flora', <https://cites.org/sites/default/files/eng/disc/CITES-Convention-EN.pdf> accessed 21 August 2024.

[15] United Nations, 'United Nations Declaration on the Rights of Indigenous Peoples' <https://www.un.org/development/desa/indigenouspeoples/wp-content/uploads/sites/19/2018/11/UNDRIP_E_web.pdf> accessed 21 August 2024.

[16] International Council of Museums, 'Code of Ethics' <https://icom.museum/wp-content/uploads/2018/07/ICOM-code-En-web.pdf > accessed 21 August 2024.

The Code of Ethics specifically addresses the issues of ethical acquisition at 2.1:

> "Museums have the duty to acquire, preserve and promote their collections as a contribution to safeguarding the natural, cultural and scientific heritage. Their collections are a significant public inheritance, have a special position in law and are protected by international legislation. Inherent in this public trust is the notion of stewardship that includes rightful ownership, permanence, documentation, accessibility and responsible disposal. The governing body for each museum should adopt and publish a written collections policy that addresses the acquisition, care and use of collections. The policy should clarify the position of any material that will not be catalogued, conserved, or exhibited."

At 2.2 the Code of Ethics states that

> "No object or specimen should be acquired by purchase, gift, loan, bequest, or exchange unless the acquiring museum is satisfied that a valid title is held. Evidence of lawful ownership in a country is not necessarily valid title."[17]

At 2.3 that

> "Every effort must be made before acquisition to ensure that any object or specimen offered for purchase, gift, loan, bequest, or exchange has not been illegally obtained in, or exported from its country of origin or any intermediate country in which it might have been owned legally (including the museum's own country). Due diligence in this regard should establish the full history of the item since discovery or production."[18]

For those working commercially in the trade of cultural objects UNESCO adopted an 'International Code of Ethics for Dealers in Cultural Property' in 1999 which states at Article 1 that:

> "[p]rofessional traders in cultural property will not import, export or transfer the ownership of this property when they have reasonable cause to believe it has been stolen, illegally alienated, clandestinely excavated or illegally exported."[19]

and at Article 4 that:

> "A trader who has reasonable cause to believe that an item of cultural property has been illegally exported will not assist in any further transaction with that item, except with the agreement of the country of export. A trader who is in possession of the item, where the country of export seeks its return within a

---

[17] ibid.
[18] ibid.
[19] UNESCO, 'International Code of Ethics for Dealers in Cultural Property' <https://unesdoc.unesco.org/ark:/48223/pf0000121320> accessed 21 August 2024.

reasonable period of time, will take all legally permissible steps to co-operate in the return of that object to the country of export."[20]

The UNESCO ethical guidance is reiterated in the Professional Guidelines established by International Association of Dealers in Ancient Art (IADAA) which states at Annex 1 paragraph 2 that

"[t]he Members of IADAA undertake not to purchase or sell objects until they have established to the best of their ability that such objects were not stolen from excavations, architectural monuments, public institutions or private property."[21]

Case Study: *Qatar Investment & Projects Development Holdings Co v Eskenazi*

In the case of *Qatar Investment & Projects Development Holdings Co v Eskenazi*,[22] the English High Court found that several ancient objects sold in private transactions were modern forgeries. Consequently, it ordered the repayment of the US $4.99 million purchase price. Crucially, however, the court ruled that the dealer's director was not fraudulent.

John Eskenazi was widely regarded as a leading dealer of Eastern art and whose

"reputation as a scholar is such that he has been able to cross the dealer/curator line, as with his exhibition on the court arts of Safavid Iran at the Asia Society in New York and the Museo Poldi Pezzoli and Palazzo Reale in Milan (2003-04) and the show of Chola bronzes at the Royal Academy of Arts in London (RA) in 2007."[23]

Eskenazi had previously complained that

"the rigid application of the Unesco Convention 1970 cut-off date excludes many works of art that came out of their countries of origin much earlier, but

---

[20] ibid.
[21] International Foundation for Art Research, 'Professional Guidelines established by International Association of Dealers in Ancient Art (IADAA)' <https://www.ifar.org/professional_guideline_item.php?docid=1226949426> accessed 21 August 2024.
[22] *Qatar Investment & Projects Development Holdings Co & His Highness Sheikh Hamad Bin Abdullah Al Thani v John Eskenazi Limited & Mr John Eskenazi* [2022] EWHC.
[23] Ana Somers Cocks, 'Johnny Eskenazi: from wannabe theatre director to leading Eastern art dealer who rescued stolen Afghan ivories' *The Art Newspaper* <https://www.theartnewspaper.com/2020/12/21/johnny-eskenazi-from-wannabe-theatre-director-to-leading-eastern-art-dealer-who-rescued-stolen-afghan-ivories> accessed 21 August 2024.

whose owners may not be able to prove it. These works have now become almost unsaleable. The consequence, says Eskenazi, is that a whole generation of orphan works of art now exists, owned by elderly collectors who can neither sell them, nor bequeath or even lend them to a museum, which is to no one's benefit."[24]

For each of the seven objects in question in *Qatar Investment & Projects Development Holdings Co v Eskenazi*, each sale invoice contained a note saying: "I declare that to the best of my knowledge and belief the item detailed on this invoice is antique and therefore over one hundred years of age."[25] The Court was not convinced that there was a reasonable basis for the descriptions and ultimately concluded that "no reasonable leading specialist antique dealer would have expressed an unqualified opinion" that the objects in question were ancient.[26] Key evidence supporting this conclusion included the "immaculate"[27] condition of some items, which would be highly unusual for genuinely ancient artefacts, the survival of certain objects, such as the Head of Krodha, an unfired clay object purportedly 1500 years old with no known comparator, described as "so remote as to be fanciful,"[28] testimony of expert witnesses that described fake patination, the presence of plastics and fibres and use of chemicals to age the surfaces of the objects; and the lack of proper provenance — Eskenazi at one point explaining that one of the pieces "had been in a European collection for a significant time, but that he could not give [the purchaser] details of its previous ownership for reasons of discretion."[29]

The court determined that the dealer had been negligent in attributing seven objects as ancient, acting without reasonable care when asserting their authenticity.

A fraud allegation against the dealer's director, related to one of the seven objects, did not meet the legal test for fraud. In the English courts it had long been the case that to prove that someone had acted dishonestly in theft or fraud cases, the jury had to find that the defendant's conduct was dishonest by the standards of ordinary, reasonable people; and the defendant appreciated that what he or she did was dishonest by the standards of those ordinary, reasonable people. The 2020 Court of Appeal

---

[24] ibid.
[25] *Qatar Investment & Projects Development Holdings Co & His Highness Sheikh Hamad Bin Abdullah Al Thani v John Eskenazi Limited & Mr. John Eskenazi* [2022] EWHC at 8.
[26] ibid, at 692.
[27] ibid, at 701.
[28] ibid, at 607.
[29] ibid, at 49.

case of *Barton & Booth v R* clarified that "[there was no possibility that] the jury could have been in any doubt that, when applying the objective standard of dishonesty, they should do so by reference to their findings about the state of the knowledge or belief of [the accused] regarding the circumstances."[30]

The judge concluded that the director genuinely believed, albeit wrongly and without reasonable grounds, that the Hari Hara statue was an outstanding treasure from Vietnam, this conclusion being based in part on the fact that Eskenazi had paid $85,000 for the piece. A spokesperson for Eskenazi stated that in its judgment the court had merely accepted "the view of one group of experts over another."[31]

This judgment reaffirms the necessity on behalf of those acquiring works for

> "systematic, assiduous and painstaking research when contemplating acquisitions. It pays to read the small print and challenge opaque assurances or evasive responses. Reliance on documents taken at face value, on assumed expertise and on uncorroborated provenance is a risky business. For public institutions, these obligations are more pertinent, given the exacting ethical standards to which they are held. The lessons from these recent cases are a reminder that vigilance is critical."[32]

Following the ruling, Eskenazi called in administrators for his business John Eskenazi Ltd, while only ever accepting that one of the seven pieces was a fake. At the time of writing John Eskenazi Ltd was in an extended period of Administration. The Administrator's progress report of January 2024 noted that "[a]s set out in the Directors' Statement of Affairs as at 20 December 2022, the Company holds stock with an estimated book value of £8,960,659. The estimated realisable value as per the Statement of Affairs is uncertain. This Stock comprises assorted antiques and antiquities of varying value and provenance."[33]

---

[30] *Barton & Booth v R* [2020] EWCA Crim 575 at 116.
[31] Jon Yeomans, 'Art dealer who sold fake goods to Qatari sheikh calls in administrators' *The Times*, <https://www.thetimes.com/business-money/article/art-dealer-who-sold-fake-goods-to-qatari-sheikh-calls-in-administrators-66msqd83d> accessed 21 August 2024.
[32] Emily Gould, 'A series of recent lawsuits could change the way UK museums acquire works for their collections', *The Art Newspaper* <https://www.theartnewspaper.com/2023/04/05/a-series-of-recent-lawsuits-could-change-the-way-uk-museums-acquire-works-for-their-collection> accessed 21 August 2024.
[33] Simon James Bonney, 'Notice of Administrator's Progress Report., available via < https://find-and-update.company-information.service.gov.uk/company/02840297/filing-history> accessed, 21 August 2024, direct link to

The website eskenazi.co.uk was still live at the time of writing, including a list of some 83 'Museums and Institutions'[34] in 20 countries who had purchased objects from Eskenazi, including, for instance the British Museum, the Victoria and Albert Museum, the Metropolitan Museum of Art and the Museum of Islamic Art.

---

document too long to reproduce here.

[34] Eskenazi Ltd website <https://www.eskenazi.co.uk/en-gb/about/museums> accessed 21 August 2024.

Chapter 5

Restitution, Repatriation and Deaccession

The phrase 'To the Victor belong the spoils' was originally coined by New York Senator William L Marcy in 1828, referring to Andrew Jackson's election victory of that year. However, it is a maxim of warfare which, until the Hague Conference of 1899 (see Chapter 3), was more or less tolerated as common practice between hostile nations.

In 1422, the Ottoman Sultan Murad II, in anticipation of laying siege to Constantinople,

> "dispatched heralds to proclaim to all the ends of the earth that the emir promised to deliver all the riches and people of the city to the Muslims… some came to buy prisoners, some women, other came to take the men and still others, the infants; others came to seize the animals, and others goods; and the Turkish monks came to get our nuns and free booty from the despot of the Turks."[1]

Of course, Constantinople did not eventually fall until 1453, partially through the assistance of the Imperial Cannon designed by the Hungarian engineer Orban — formerly an employee of the Byzantine Court. Constantinople was comprehensively looted by the Ottoman troops — except for items which had already been looted following the sack of Constantinople by crusader forces during the Fourth Crusade in 1204. An example of such looted objects are the four ancient classical bronze horses which were originally brought to Constantinople by the Emperor Theodosius from the island of Chios and set up on the Hippodrome.

'The Horses of Saint Mark,' also known as the 'Triumphal Quadriga' or 'Horses of the Hippodrome of Constantinople' were originally part of a monument showcasing a quadriga —a four-horse carriage used for chariot racing. The horses were brought to Venice in 1204 following the sack of Constantinople and adorned the facade of St Mark's Basilica, positioned

---

[1] Judith Herrin, *Byzantium: The Surprising Life of a Medieval City* (Penguin Books 2007) p 317.

on the loggia above the porch. They were seized by Napoleon in 1797 and eventually returned to Venice in 1815. To preserve them, the sculptures have been moved from the facade to the interior of St Mark's, with replicas now occupying their former position on the loggia.

In 1801, Thomas Bruce, 7th Earl of Elgin, and his team, stripped 15 *metopes* and 247 feet of the then surviving frieze of the Parthenon in Athens from the fabric of the building. This material was loaded into 200 boxes and shipped to England. Elgin's justification was that he was acting legally under a *firmen*, or permission, from the Ottoman Sultan Selim III which stated "when they wish to take away some pieces of stone with old inscriptions and figures, no opposition be made." This document is problematic as the original is lost, the surviving Italian translation appears not to follow standard Ottoman 'diplomatic' (or formal structure of official documents) and to have been granted by a regional governor rather than the then owner of the monuments, Selim III. It also appears to be absent from Ottoman archives. Having said that, Elgin's men spent 11 years removing material from the Parthenon, so the work was carried out without concealment. Two hundred and twenty years later, in October 2021, the UNESCO Advisory Board urged for the return of the Elgin Marbles to Greece. The UK Government responded with a statement that the marbles had been acquired legally in accordance with the law at the time and that repatriation would not occur.

Restitution and repatriation are separate but linked concepts; restitution occurs when a cultural object is returned to an individual or community, repatriation when cultural objects are returned to a nation or state at the request of the government of that nation or state.

Ethical and Legal Considerations of Deaccession

A useful definition of a cultural object is contained in the 1995 UNIDROIT Convention on Stolen or Illegally Exported Cultural Objects, which states that "cultural objects are those which, on religious or secular grounds, are of importance for archaeology, prehistory, history, literature, art or science."

Restitution or repatriation normally occur on foot of a request. The owner or owners of a cultural object make their case for return of the object either on the basis that it is held illegally, in contravention of an existing national or international law or treaty, or they request its return on broader ethical grounds.

However, there is an increasing movement towards cultural institutions being proactive in offering restitution or repatriation. Pressures on resources can make the prospect of restitution or repatriation attractive as an avenue for deaccessioning of collection items, without the opprobrium which often accompanies attempts to sell or otherwise dispose of unwanted material. Northampton Borough Council's sale of the 4500 year old Egyptian *Sekhemka* sculpture may have resulted in a £7m windfall, but it also resulted in the expulsion of its Museums Service from the UK Museums Association and loss of accreditation for five years.

The International Council of Museums (ICOM) has published 'Guidelines on Deaccessioning of the International Council of Museums'[2] which contains a list of reasons whereby a museum might consider deaccession of an object from its collection — "where the law does not prohibit a museum from de-accessioning." This list includes poor condition, duplicates, inability of the museum to care for the object, lack of aesthetic, historical or scientific quality and, notably, "the museum's possession of the object is inconsistent with applicable law or ethical principles, e.g., the object was, or may have been, stolen or illegally exported or imported, or the object may be subject to other legal claims for return or restitution". The ICOM guidelines also set out steps to review the legal status of an object before deaccessioning, to include examining its authenticity, the legal status of ownership (see Chapter 3), restrictions made by the donor, all available provenance and any conditions or restrictions made at time of acquisition.

Famously, the British Museum Act 1963 states at s 3(4) that "Objects vested in the Trustees as part of the collections of the Museum shall not be disposed of by them", which is frequently cited as justification for the apparent impossibility of the return of the Parthenon Marbles to Greece. A similar provision at s 6(3) of the National Heritage Act 1993 states that the boards of the Victoria and Albert Museum, Science Museum, Royal Armouries, Royal Botanic Gardens, Kew, the Armed Forces Museums and the Royal Naval College "may not dispose of an object the property in which is vested in them." It is worth noting, however, that under the terms of the Holocaust (Return of Cultural Objects) Act 2009 restitution of pieces that were spoliated during the Nazi-era is permissible from named institutions, despite the prohibitions listed above.

---

[2] International Council of Museums, 'Guidelines on Deaccessioning of the International Council of Museums' <https://icom.museum/wp-content/uploads/2019/10/Guidelines-on-Deaccessioning-of-the-International-Council-of-Museums.pdf> accessed 21 August 2024.

In Ireland, state ownership of cultural objects is provided for under the terms of statutes including, but not restricted to, the National Monuments Acts 1930 to 2014 and the National Cultural Institutions Act 1997 (the 1997 Act).

Under s 68 of the 1997 Act, the Director of the National Museum of Ireland (NMI) may dispose of archaeological objects.

Section 47 of the 1997 Act allows for the transfer or exchange of cultural objects between designated cultural institutions. Section 18(2) of the 1997 Act allows the disposal by sale, exchange or gift of any library material by the National Library under conditions similar to those imposed under the UK Museums and Galleries Act 1992.

There are clearly some lacunae in the statutes — for instance no provision is made for how the NMI might dispose of items which are not archaeological.

Sale and Disposal

The NMI has produced a 'Collections Disposal Policy' which outlines principles in relation to deaccession based on best international practice. The basic tenet of this policy is that the NMI will retain all cultural objects until there are exceptional reasons put forward in a written proposal for their de-accession.

Section 3 of the Policy states *inter alia* that:

> "Reasons for de-accession of a Museum Heritage Object may include:
>
>> 3.1. Legal: Lack of title or other legal reasons where the holding of an object in the core collection is brought into question.
>>
>> 3.2. Repatriation: Response to a request to repatriate an object."

Section 5.5 of the Policy states that "Objects will not be disposed of in any way that results in financial or commercial gain."

The ICOM 'Guidelines on Deaccessioning of the International Council of Museums' makes some observations on sale and disposal as follows, referencing the ICOM 'Code of Ethics for Museums':

> "Once an object has been deaccessioned from a museum's collection, it is still the property of the museum until ownership of the object is transferred legally

and the object leaves the custody of the museum that has deaccessioned the object. After an object has been deaccessioned, the museum must determine the means for disposing of the object (e.g. donation to another cultural or educational institution, transfer, exchange, sale, auction or if more appropriate by private sale, return or restitution to its rightful private owner or the country of origin). If none of the above is possible, disposition might also include the destruction of the object. After having made the decision to de-accession, there is a strong presumption that a deaccessioned object should first be offered to another museum or public collecting institution except in cases where the object is fraudulent or where it's provenance is suspect. Funds realized from the deaccessioning and disposal of an object should be used solely for the benefit of the museum's collection, that is, acquisitions to and care that same museum's collection. By no means, however, should the funds be used for the costs of regular museum administration or maintenance."[3]

Human Remains and Ethnological Items

One problematic category of cultural object as contained under the UNIDROIT definition is human remains. Human remains are captured under the definitions of cultural objects as "anatomy" or "products of archaeological excavations" or, indeed, from the perspective of their original collectors "objects of ethnological interest." The UNESCO-UNIDROIT Model Legislative Provisions on State Ownership of Undiscovered Cultural Objects of 2011 specify that states are also free to interpret more broadly than the strict definition given for cultural objects and therefore can apply it to human remains.

The balancing of ethical considerations with scientific rationale for retention are often called into play when dealing with anatomical or archaeological human remains, as distinct from the ethnological category which are addressed further below in light of the United Nations Declaration on the Rights of Indigenous Peoples (UNDRIP) 2007.

One prominent example is the case of the 'Irish Giant' Charles Byrne, who grew to a height of 7'7" before his death in 1783. Byrne had requested a burial at sea to prevent his remains from being put on show, but they were purchased and eventually exhibited in the Hunterian Museum at the Royal College of Surgeons. The RCS decided to remove the remains from display following a refit, but opted to retain them for future scientific analysis.

In 1890, thirteen human skulls were removed by academics from Inishbofin,

---

[3] International Council of Museums, 'ICOM Code of Ethics for Museums' <https://icom.museum/wp-content/uploads/2018/07/ICOM-code-En-web.pdf> accessed 21 August 2024.

off the coast of Galway and subsequently gifted to Trinity College Dublin. In 2022, TCD set up a Legacies Review Working Group (LRWG) to "review the university's complex historical legacies since its foundation in 1592." One of the first decisions of the LRWG was to "work with the community to ensure that the (Inishbofin) remains are returned in a respectful manner and in accordance with the community's wishes."[4] The skulls were returned to Inishbofin on 16 July 2023.

In English law, the Human Tissue Act 2004 s 47(2) empowers the trustees and boards of named museums to

> "transfer from their collection any human remains which they reasonably believe to be remains of a person who died less than one thousand years before the day on which this section comes into force if it appears to them to be appropriate to do so for any reason, whether or not relating to their other functions."

UNDRIP sets out at Article 12 that:

> "1. Indigenous peoples have the right to manifest, practice, develop and teach their spiritual and religious traditions, customs and ceremonies; the right to maintain, protect, and have access in privacy to their religious and cultural sites; the right to the use and control of their ceremonial objects; and the right to the repatriation of their human remains.
>
> 2. States shall seek to enable the access and/or repatriation of ceremonial objects and human remains in their possession through fair, transparent and effective mechanisms developed in conjunction with indigenous peoples concerned."

The very diversity that is implicit in the term 'indigenous' itself opens up questions about the application of UNDRIP. According to the UN Permanent Forum on Indigenous Peoples,

> "an official definition of 'indigenous' has not been adopted by any UN-system body. Instead the system has developed a modern understanding of this term based on... Self- identification as indigenous peoples at the individual level and accepted by the community as their member."

These issues are complicated by the nature of Ireland's relationship with Britain and with its close involvement in the administration of the British Empire during the period 1860 to 1914. In 1860, 40% of recruits to the British Army were Irish and "were drawn in particular to serve in the European regiments of Britain's Indian Armies and played an important

---

[4] Trinity College Dublin, 'Trinity College Launches Legacies Review Working Group' < https://www.tcd.ie/news_events/articles/trinity-college-dublin-launches-legacies-review-working-group-/> accessed 21 August 2024.

role in the building of the British Empire."[5] A direct result of this involvement was the collection and acquisition of c. 11,000 ethnographic cultural objects which made their way back to Ireland via the Royal Dublin Society and TCD into the collections of the NMI from 1877 to 1922, including some materials sent back from the Congo by Sir Roger Casement.

In the words of Abdulqawi Ahmed Yusuf, Judge of the International Court of Justice:

> "The pillage and plundering of African art and artefacts by the colonial powers was mostly done to erase African culture in support of the colonial project and the claim that African nations had no history, statehood, or civilization. But, if that was the case, why steal their worthless artefacts or build museums in Europe to preserve them? The attempts at cultural erasure and denial of the history and civilization of African societies' continues today as European museums and their states hang on to stolen African cultural heritage and refuse to return it to Africa. However, the African nations were not the only ones who suffered from such injustice. Other colonized and oppressed peoples in Asia, the Pacific, and Latin America had to endure similar deprivation of their cultural heritage."[6]

A recent article in 'Foreign Policy' magazine claimed that 'Belgium's Royal Museum for Central Africa alone has 180,000 objects, Germany's Ethnological Museum has 75,000, France's Quai Branly Museum has almost 70,000, the British Museum has 73,000, and the Netherlands National Museum of World Cultures has 66,000.[7]

Following the establishment of the Irish Free State in 1922, a movement to "accumulate, preserve and display such objects as may serve to increase and define the knowledge of Irish Civilisations, of the National History of Ireland"[8] resulted in ethnographic and colonial exhibits being de-emphasised. This change of focus met with public approval as "Imperial war medals and uniforms [and] . . . the disgusting spectacle of a dead or

---

[5] Rachel Hand, 'From Empire to Independence: The Ethnographic Collections of the National Museum of Ireland', *Exhibit Ireland: Ethnographic Collections in Ireland*, edited by Séamas Ó Síocháin, Pauline Garvey & Adam Drazin (2012).

[6] Ana Filipa Vrdoljak, Andrezj Jakubowski and Alessandro Chechi, *The 1970 UNESCO and 1995 UNIDROIT Conventions on Stolen or Illegally Transferred Cultural Property* (1st edn, OUP 2024) xi.

[7] Nosmot Gbadamosi, 'Africa's Stolen Art Debate is Frozen in Time', *Foreign Policy Magazine*, https://foreignpolicy.com/2022/05/15/africa-art-museum-europe-restitution-debate-book-colonialism-artifacts/ accessed 21 August 2024.

[8] Mairéad Carew, 'The Glamour of Ancient Greatness', *Archaeology Ireland*, Spring 2008 https://www.academia.edu/20173041/The_Glamour_of_Ancient_Greatness_the_importance_of_the_1927_Lithberg_Report_to_Irish_archaeology accessed 21 August 2024.

dying sepoy at the feet of a British Officer was removed from our offended eyes."[9]

Other Irish institutions have similar holdings; the Ulster Museum repatriated ancestral Hawaiian human remains and sacred objects that were removed by collectors from burial caves in 1840. According to Dan Hicks, author of *The Brutish Museums*,[10] the Hunt Museum in Limerick holds material looted during the destruction of Benin City, Nigeria in 1897 — also known as Benin Bronzes. In 2022, University College Cork announced its intention to repatriate a collection of mummified human remains dating from 100AD to about 975BC on foot of enquiries from the Egyptian Embassy in Dublin.

Recent developments in Ireland include the Historic and Archaeological Heritage Act 2023 which enables the Irish State to accede to the 1995 UNIDROIT Convention. The state will also be enabled to ratify the 1970 UNESCO Convention on the Means of Prohibiting and Preventing the Illicit Import, Export and Transfer of Ownership of Cultural Property.

The UNESCO 1970 Convention

The 1970 UNESCO Convention on the Means of Prohibiting and Preventing the Illicit Import, Export, and Transfer of Ownership of Cultural Property is an international treaty designed to combat the illicit trafficking of cultural property. The convention "urges States Parties to take measures to prohibit and prevent the import, export and transfer of cultural property" and "provides a common framework for the States Parties on the measures to be taken to prohibit and prevent the import, export and transfer of cultural property."[11]

The 1970 Convention assigns a central role to prevention in tackling the illicit trafficking of cultural property, to be achieved through the establishment of inventories, the establishment of export certificates, the application of controls and approval of traders, the application of criminal

---

[9] Rachel Hand, 'From Empire to Independence: The Ethnographic Collections of the National Museum of Ireland', *Exhibit Ireland: Ethnographic Collections in Ireland*, edited by Séamas Ó Síocháin, Pauline Garvey & Adam Drazin (2012).
[10] Dan Hicks, *The Brutish Museums: The Benin Bronzes, Colonial Violence and Cultural Restitution* (Pluto Press 2020).
[11] UNESCO, 'Fight Illicit Trafficking (1970 Convention)' < https://www.unesco.org/en/fight-illicit-trafficking> accessed 21 August 2024.

and administrative sanctions and the organisation of information and education campaigns.

Issues relating to the ability of the 1970 Convention to prevent illicit trafficking in cultural property became apparent through differences in national law in relation to the level of protection afforded to purchasers in good faith and systems which more strictly adhered to the *nemo dat quod non habet* principle. The reach of the 1970 Convention was further hindered by difficulties of implementation created by, for instance, "impoverished local populations looting their heritage, corruption in administrations, or the involvement of organised criminal elements."[12]

The UNESCO Convention is not retroactive, so no proceedings for return of artefacts that were removed before the entry into force of the instruments in 1970 can be brought, which unlike the US Holocaust Expropriated Art Recovery Act 2016 for instance, severely restricts the rights of those whose cultural property has been misappropriated prior to those dates.

The UNIDROIT 1995 Convention

Resulting from these identified issues UNESCO commissioned consultants, starting in 1982, to examine ways in which the shortcomings of the 1970 Convention could be addressed and, in 1984, UNIDROIT being asked to examine the issues of private law applicable to illicit traffic in cultural objects. In 1995, a final text as prepared by UNIDROIT was adopted at the Diplomatic Conference in Rome.

Both the UNESCO and UNIDROIT Conventions share a definition of cultural objects. A clear distinction is the requirement under the UNESCO Convention 1970 for a cultural object to have been designated as such by any state requesting return, whereas the UNIDROIT Convention 1995 allows for private individuals to seek the return of objects stolen from private ownership without a requirement for them to have been included on an official register. The UNIDROIT Convention states quite distinctly in Article 3(1) that "the possessor of a cultural object which has been stolen shall return it."

The UNIDROIT Convention 1995 is not retroactive, so no proceedings

---

[12] Lyndel V Prott, *UNESCO AND UNIDROIT: A Partnership against Trafficking in Cultural Objects* (RDU 1996-1) 60.

for return of artefacts that were removed before the entry into force of the instruments can be pursued "and thus would not directly apply to claims during the Nazi era, colonial administrations, or other major periods that witnessed mass theft and misappropriation of cultural objects."[13]

Article 10 of the convention states at (1) that:

> "The provisions of Chapter II shall apply only in respect of a cultural object that is stolen after this Convention enters into force in respect of the State where the claim is brought, provided that: (a) the object was stolen from the territory of a Contracting State after the entry into force of this Convention for that State; or (b) the object is located in a Contracting State after the entry into force of the Convention for that State."

Chapter III Article 5 sets out that "[a] Contracting State may request the court or other competent authority of another Contracting State to order the return of a cultural object illegally exported from the territory of the requesting State," but Article 10(2) sets out that "the provisions of Chapter III shall apply only in respect of a cultural object that is illegally exported after this Convention enters into force for the requesting State as well as the State where the request is brought."

Article 10(3) clarifies that:

> "This Convention does not in any way legitimise any illegal transaction of whatever nature which has taken place before the entry into force of this Convention or which is excluded under paragraphs (1) or (2) of this article, nor limit any right of a State or other person to make a claim under remedies available outside the framework of this Convention for the restitution or return of a cultural object stolen or illegally exported before the entry into force of this Convention."

Chapter II sets out limitation periods for the bringing of a claim as follow:

> "(3) Any claim for restitution shall be brought within a period of three years from the time when the claimant knew the location of the cultural object and the identity of its possessor, and in any case within a period of fifty years from the time of the theft.
>
> (4) However, a claim for restitution of a cultural object forming an integral part of an identified monument or archaeological site, or belonging to a public collection, shall not be subject to time limitations other than a period of three

---

[13] Ana Filipa Vrdoljak, Andrezj Jakubowski and Alessandro Chechi, *The 1970 UNESCO and 1995 UNIDROIT Conventions on Stolen or Illegally Transferred Cultural Property* (1st edn, OUP 2024) p 551.

years from the time when the claimant knew the location of the cultural object and the identity of its possessor.

(5) Notwithstanding the provisions of the preceding paragraph, any Contracting State may declare that a claim is subject to a time limitation of 75 years or such longer period as is provided in its law. A claim made in another Contracting State for restitution of a cultural object displaced from a monument, archaeological site or public collection in a Contracting State making such a declaration shall also be subject to that time limitation.

(6) A declaration referred to in the preceding paragraph shall be made at the time of signature, ratification, acceptance, approval or accession."

What this means in brief is that a claim must be brought after the provisions of the Convention enter into force in the state in which the claim is brought, within three years of the claimant knowing the location of the cultural object and within 50 years of the theft, except if the object formed part of an identifiable monument or archaeological site or belonged to a public collection in which case there is no limitation period save the three year period from knowing the location of the object.

Section 3(8) of the Convention extends the same time limit to claims "for restitution of a sacred or communally important cultural object belonging to and used by a tribal or indigenous community in a contracting state as part of that community's traditional or ritual use."

A contracting state may declare that claims under s 3(4) are subject to a time period of 75 years or longer, but in the event they make such a declaration they are bound by this timeframe if attempting to make a claim for return of an object from another state which has made no such declaration.

The Law Reform Commission Report on the UNIDROIT Convention on Stolen or Illegally Exported Cultural Objects recommends that:

> "On balance, we are of the view that Ireland should not enter an Article 3(5) declaration, but instead should impose no limitation period in respect of the objects described in Article 3(4). We have pointed out that the practical benefit for Ireland in doing so is at present unpredictable, depending as it does on whether other States adopt a similar view. It is worth noting in this regard that of the 22 States which signed the Convention, only one – the Netherlands – entered a time limiting declaration. We are of the view that to adopt a position which favours maximum return is consistent with the ideological precepts underlying the Convention. States should not seek to benefit from the acquisition in dubious

circumstances of objects from States which may not, for political or economic reasons, be in a position to adequately protect their national heritage."[14]

The Historic and Archaeological Heritage and Miscellaneous Provisions Act 2023 states at s 1(7) that

> "This Act… shall come into operation on such day or days as the Minister may by order or orders appoint either generally or with reference to any particular purpose or provision and different days may be so appointed for different purposes and different provisions."[15]

Chapter 9 of the Act, "Acceptance into the law of the State of rules established under the UNIDROIT Convention on Stolen or Illegally Exported Cultural Objects," is addressed at ss 117-124; and Chapter 10 addresses "Measures to assist the State in ratifying UNESCO Convention on the Means of Prohibiting and Preventing the Illicit Import, Export and Transfer of Ownership of Cultural Property 1970" which is addressed at ss 125-130.

A letter to the author of 5 March 2024 from the office of the Michael Noonan TD, Minister of State for Nature, Heritage and Electoral Reform states:

> "As the 1970 UNESCO Convention and the 1995 UNIDROIT Convention both concern moveable cultural property, (rather than immoveable cultural property, which is the remit of The Minister for Housing, Local Government and Heritage), responsibility for progressing the ratification of such Conventions rests with The Minister for Tourism, Culture, Arts, Gaeltacht, Sport and Media (TCAGSM).
>
> Since this legislation was enacted in October 2023, I understand work is underway in the Department of Tourism, Culture, Arts, Gaeltacht, Sport and Media to explore the implementation of the sections to which you refer, in addition to the other aspects of Part 4 of the Act.
>
> At present, this Department is unable to provide an exact timeline for the commencement of these provisions however, going forward I understand that officials from this Department and officials from Department TCAGSM will be liaising with regard to a timescale for the commencement of Part 4 of the Act."

It will be interesting to see if and when Ireland ratifies UNESCO

---

[14] The Law Reform Commission, *The UNIDROIT Convention on Stolen or Illegally Exported Cultural Objects* (LRC 55-1997) 3.65.
[15] Some sections of the Act are omitted from this commencement section.

1970 and accedes to UNIDROIT 1995, and when it does, whether the recommendations of the Law Reform Commission are followed.

On 20 June 2023, the Irish Government announced the formation of an advisory committee on the restitution and repatriation of cultural heritage.

> "Membership of the committee will be drawn from the museum, archives and gallery sector, the civil service, and legal and ethical expertise, as well as representation from claimant communities."[16]

While the UNESCO Convention and UNIDROIT Convention have had notable successes — for instance, the 2008 return to China of pottery figurines of the Tang Dynasty as well as some rare items dating back to the Xia, Shang, Yuan and Ming dynasties that had been illegally imported into Denmark, or the eventual return of the Boğazköy Sphinx along with 7,400 cuneiform tablets from Germany to Turkey — it should be noted that the claims of owners of cultural property will be frustrated in instances where countries involved have not signed or ratified either Convention. For instance the UK is currently not a party to either Convention.

If Ireland accedes to the 1995 UNIDROIT convention it will be possible for private individuals to seek the return of stolen or illegally exported objects through the Irish courts, subject to the limitation periods discussed in Chapter 3 — most importantly that the convention is not retroactive. Claims under the Convention will be brought in the Circuit Court which will be conferred with the necessary jurisdiction. Article 4 of the convention places the burden on the possessor of the item to demonstrate that it "exercised due diligence when acquiring the object." Article 4(4) of the convention states:

> "In determining whether the possessor exercised due diligence, regard shall be had to all the circumstances of the acquisition, including the character of the parties, the price paid, whether the possessor consulted any reasonably accessible register of stolen cultural objects, and any other relevant information and documentation which it could reasonably have obtained, and whether the possessor consulted accessible agencies or took any other step that a reasonable person would have taken in the circumstances."

To quote Abdulqawi Ahmed Yusuf again:

---

[16] Department of Tourism, Culture, Arts, Gaeltacht, Sport and Media, 'New advisory committee on the restitution and repatriation of cultural heritage <https://www.gov.ie/en/press-release/49f4d-new-advisory-committee-on-the-restitution-and-repatriation-of-cultural-heritage/ > accessed 21 August 2024.

"The looting of African works of art and artefacts by the colonial powers was indeed aimed at depriving African societies of their historical records, their memory, and their identity. Those who are still resisting the return of this cultural heritage to the African countries are clearly not in favour of reviving those memories or resuscitating their lost identities. They prefer to keep the works of art in their museums as commodities and objects of curiosity, instead of returning them so that they can regain their status as objects of profound cultural and historical significance to the peoples from whom they were stolen or taken by force."[17]

Nazi-Era Spoliation

During the Second World War, an estimated 600,000 artworks were either confiscated by the National Socialist Party or sold at less than market value by members of the Jewish community attempting to flee Nazi Germany. Of these 600,000 artworks, some 100,000 are estimated to still be missing or unaccounted for.[18] In the words of Ronald S Lauder to a Senate Judiciary Committee in 2016

"What makes this particular crime even more despicable is that this art theft, probably the greatest in history, was continued by governments, museums and many knowing collectors in the decades following the war. This was the dirty secret of the post-war art world, and people who should have known better were part of it."[19]

Advances in the quality and availability of family history and online archival and ancestral resources have resulted in increased ability to track down lost family members and connections, and as a result to connect cultural property to family members and survivors.

In US law, where a chattel has been stolen and resold to a good faith purchaser, then the original owner has a cause of action in replevin, which originates in common law.

Replevin can take the form of a suit for return of property and damages,

---

[17] Ana Filipa Vrdoljak, Andrezj Jakubowski and Alessandro Chechi *The 1970 UNESCO and 1995 UNIDROIT Conventions on Stolen or Illegally Transferred Cultural Property* (1st edn, OUP 2024) x.

[18] Fallon S Sheridan, 'The Sunset of the Holocaust Expropriated Art Recovery Act of 2016 and the Rise of the Demand and Refusal Rule' (2022) 89(6) Fordham Law Review 2841, 2841.

[19] 'Ronald Lauder, Helen Mirren testify before US Senate committee on Nazi-looted art' World Jewish Congress <https://www.worldjewishcongress.org/en/news/ronald-lauder-helen-mirren-testify-before-us-senate-committee-on-nazi-looted-art-6-3-2016> accessed 21 August 2024.

or can be a provisional remedy seeking possession of the property prior to a judgment on the action. Traditionally replevin was subject to limitation under the discovery rule — whereby the limitation period was held to run from the time that the original owner knew, or ought to have known, that circumstances existed (e.g. an artwork had been stolen) which might lead to the accrual of a cause of action. It is worth noting that some states, such as New York, operate the 'demand and refusal rule' which states that the cause of action for replevin accrues from the moment that an owner makes demand for the return of a chattel and the possessor refuses.

The Washington Principles

Following a Congressional hearing in February 1998, the Association of Art Museum Directors established a set of standards for American museums to research, identify, and return Nazi-looted art. These standards comprised 11 principles to be adopted by European nations, the first of which was Austria which pledged the enactment of legislation allowing for the return of Nazi-looted art in Austrian museums to their rightful owners.

While voluntary, the Washington Principles have created a moral and ethical imperative for holders of Nazi-looted art, prompting many to return such artworks to their rightful owners or devise other equitable solutions, including compensation, long-term loans, and negotiated agreements. Thousands of artworks, books, and Jewish cultural objects have been returned and claims have been successfully resolved.

Five nations — Austria, Germany, France, the Netherlands, and the United Kingdom — established claims commissions to facilitate the recovery of art confiscated from families. These commissions publish their decisions and, in recent years, have formed a network to exchange expertise and guide best practices.

In the UK, the Holocaust (Return of Cultural Objects) Act 2009 allows for the transfer of objects from a schedule of museums and galleries if their return has been recommended by an Advisory Panel appointed by the Secretary of State to consider claims made in respect of objects, and which relate to events occurring during the Nazi-era which is defined as beginning on 1 January 1933 and ending on 31 December 1945.

In June 2009, the Washington Principles were reinforced by the Terezin Declaration at the Prague Holocaust Era Assets Conference organised by the Czech Republic. In November 2022, with the leadership of the Czech government, the Terezin II conference reaffirmed the Terezin declaration which recognised the State of Israel's special moral role as a home for the largest number of survivors of the Holocaust.

The Washington Principles underscore several fundamental ideals: first, that artwork confiscated by the Nazis should be identified and publicised; secondly, that pre-war owners and their heirs should be prompted and encouraged to assert their claims; and thirdly, that endeavours should be undertaken to reach a just and fair solution regarding these claims. Additionally, the Principles advocate for open and accessible records and archives, the establishment of a central registry for confiscated art, and the development of national processes by countries to implement these Principles. Furthermore, they emphasised the importance of alternative dispute resolution mechanisms to address ownership disputes efficiently and avoid protracted and expensive litigation.

In March 2024 on the 25th anniversary of the Washington Principles a set of legally non-binding but morally important best practices were issued to clarify and improve the practical implementation of the Principles. As was the case with the Principles, the best practices were drafted with an awareness of differing legal systems and that states must act within the context of their own laws, therefore countries will implement the best practices in accordance with their own national laws.

Included are recommendations that

> "the sale of art and cultural property by a persecuted person during the Holocaust era between 1933-45 can be considered equivalent to an involuntary transfer of property based on the circumstances of the sale";

> "All pre-War owners who are identified through provenance research or their heirs should be proactively sought by the current possessors for the purpose of restitution";

> "Governments should encourage provenance research and projects to catalogue, digitise and make available on the internet public and private archives, including dealer records. Public and private collections should be encouraged to publish their inventories";

> "Provenance researchers should have access to all relevant archives and source documents. Provenance research carried out by public or private bodies should be made publicly available on the internet";

> "countries should consider making exceptions to barriers such as regulations against deaccessioning from state collections, statutes of limitations, market

overt, usucapion (mode of acquiring title to property by uninterrupted possession of it for a definite period), good faith acquisition, and export bans" and;

> "Art and cultural property that is determined to have been the property of Jewish communities should be returned to an existing successor community, institution, or organization, and/or a successor organization for the Jewish people as a whole. The objects should not be seen as collection items but as part of the collective memory of the Jewish people. As yet unreturned items that exist in textual form, such as manuscripts, archives, scrolls, and books, should be digitised and made easily accessible over the internet."[20]

Holocaust Expropriated Art Recovery Act (2016)

The US Holocaust Expropriated Art Recovery Act of 2016 (HEAR Act) supplanted state statutes of limitations with a national six year statute of limitations, to accrue from the point of 'actual discovery' by the owner of a claim against the current possessor for artwork or other property lost during the period 1 January 1933 to 31 December 1945 on foot of Nazi persecution. The HEAR Act defines "actual discovery" as "having actual knowledge of a fact or circumstance or sufficient information with regard to a relevant fact or circumstance to amount to actual knowledge thereof."[21]

In *Reif, Fraenkel and Vavra v Nagy and Richard Nagy Ltd*,[22] a case was brought under the HEAR Act for the return of two paintings by Egon Schiele which had been disposed of, *inter alia*, on foot of a power of attorney signed by the original owner in Dachau concentration camp in 1938. The court found that the Schiele paintings in dispute belonged to the original owner, partially on the basis of a Nazi inventory compiled at the time of the signing of the power of attorney and that the defendants could not have good title to the artworks as they were unable to demonstrate anyone holding good title had transferred such to them at any stage between 1938 and 2015, when the artworks were seized after being exhibited in New York. A third artwork by Schiele, 'Russian War Prisoner', remains in dispute with the Art Institute of Chicago claiming that it had legally acquired title.

---

[20] 'Best Practices for the Washington Conference Principles on Nazi-Confiscated Art', Office of the Special Envoy for Holocaust Issues <https://www.state.gov/best-practices-for-the-washington-conference-principles-on-nazi-confiscated-art/> accessed 21 August 2024.
[21] Holocaust Expropriated Art Recovery Act of 2016, s 4.
[22] *Reif, Fraenkel and Vavra v Nagy and Richard Nagy Ltd* [2018] 175 AD 3d 107.

It is, however, worth noting that a claim can be frustrated by delay under the doctrine of laches, as the HEAR Act does not preclude equitable defences.

In *Zuckerman v Metropolitan Museum of Art*[23] a claim by the estate of the Leffman family, who had sold a Picasso originally purchased in 1912 for a nominal sum before fleeing Nazi Germany, was dismissed on the basis of laches. It was held that the Leffman family's failure to seek out the painting for some 70 years constituted an unreasonable delay and that the passage of time had resulted in the decease of witnesses and disappearance of documentary evidence which resulted in a prejudice to the Met Museum.

The HEAR Act also applies retrospectively under s 5(c), in that the six year limitation period runs from the date of enactment of the HEAR Act in instances where either the claimant already had knowledge of the accrual of a cause of action before the enactment of the HEAR Act but was precluded from bringing an action by a pre-existing limitation period, or, in instances where the claimant had knowledge of the accrual of a cause of action, but was not precluded from bringing an action by a pre-existing limitation period. Under s 5(d), the HEAR Act applies to cases pending in court as of the date of enactment. Section 5(e), states that the HEAR Act does not apply to cases barred on a date before enactment if: (1) the claimant had knowledge on or after January 1999 and (2) six or more years have passed since the claimant acquired knowledge.

The HEAR Act therefore has significant shortcomings in addressing that which it set out to resolve — namely that claims brought are not frustrated by the passage of time and limitation periods. The ruling in *Zuckerman,* that the HEAR Act does not preclude defences at equity, such as laches, was based on a narrow interpretation of the wording of the Act — that states its limitation period allows claims "regardless of any defence at law." The positive absence of the words "or at equity" was deemed to be indicative of an intention that these defences continue to be available to defendants.

Finally, and significantly, the HEAR Act contains a sunset provision, such that the Act expires on 1 January 2027. At this point the accrual of a cause of action for recovery of artwork confiscated under the Nazi regime will revert back to the rule of the respective state under which the claim is brought — in other words discovery, or demand and refusal. However, it has been observed that many claims under the HEAR Act expired in 2022 on the basis that if a claimant had knowledge of their claim before

---

[23] *Zuckerman v Metropolitan Museum of Art* 928 F.3d 186 (2d Cir 2019).

the enactment of the HEAR Act then the six year period runs from the enactment date (see s 5(c) above).

Foreign Sovereign Immunities Act

The US Foreign Sovereign Immunities Act (FSIA) passed in 1976 and outlined in sections 1602 to 1611 of Title 28 of the United States Code, formalises the principle of sovereign immunity. It stipulates that a foreign state, which includes its political subdivisions, agencies, or instrumentalities, is generally considered immune from the jurisdiction of US courts.

Exceptions to this immunity exist, but a foreign state cannot be compelled to submit to US court jurisdiction unless one of these exceptions, outlined in sections 1605 to 1607 of the Act, applies. The most significant of these exceptions from an art and cultural heritage law perspective is s 1605(a)(3) which provides for an exception to sovereign immunity for "property taken in violation of international law." It is worth noting that the taking of property belonging to a foreign national by a state, but not the taking of property by a state from one of its own citizens, can be classified as a breach of international law, as was held in the US Supreme Court ruling in *Federal Republic of Germany v Philipp*.[24]

The case in *Philipp* related to a consortium of Jewish-owned art firms in Frankfurt who had purchased a collection of medieval relics known as the *Welfenschatz* during the inter-war years. In 2015, three descendants of consortium members sued in the US district court, alleging that, in 1935, a Nazi official used political persecution and physical threats to coerce the consortium into selling collection pieces to Prussia for one-third of their value. The descendants sought $250 million in compensation from Germany and the Prussian Cultural Heritage Foundation invoking the FSIA's exception to sovereign immunity for property taken in violation of international law.

The district court and the DC Circuit ruled for the heirs on jurisdiction, holding that the exception to immunity for property taken in violation of international law was satisfied because "genocide perpetrated by a state even against its own nationals is a violation of international law."[25]

The Supreme Court reversed this decision unanimously. The court explained

---

[24] *Federal Republic of Germany v Philipp*, No. 19-351, 592 US (2021).
[25] *Philipp v Federal Republic of Germany*, 894 F.3d 406, 410-11 (DC Cir 2018).

that, historically, a sovereign's taking of a foreigner's property breached international law, whereas a sovereign's taking of its own citizens' property did not. That is because international law regulates relations between states. Thus, a sovereign's taking of a foreigner's property historically breached the international legal system only to the extent that it constituted an injury to the foreign national's state. By contrast, a domestic taking did not interfere with inter-state relations.

Case Study: Rue Saint-Honoré in the Afternoon—Effect of Rain

'Rue Saint-Honoré in the Afternoon—Effect of Rain' is part of a collection of fifteen paintings created by Camille Pissarro in Paris. Painted during the winter of 1897 and 1898, Pissarro captured scenes from the window of his hotel overlooking the *Place du Théâtre Français*.

In 1939, Lilly Cassirer Neubauer, the owner of the painting sold it to Jakob Scheidwimmer, an art dealer affiliated with the Nazi party, at a price below its market value. She did so to secure a visa and escape Germany, thus avoiding internment in a concentration camp. Following this transaction, the painting came into the possession of Julius Sulzbacher, only to be later seized by the Gestapo. In 1954, an Allied tribunal affirmed the Cassirer family's rightful ownership of the painting. The family, believing the artwork to have been lost during the war, accepted $13,000 in compensation from the German government. In 1976, Baron Hans Heinrich Thyssen-Bornemisza acquired the painting from the Hahn Gallery in New York, allegedly unaware of its origin. The museum Thyssen-Bornemisza later obtained the artwork in 1993.

Claude Cassirer, Lilly's grandson, discovered the painting on display in Madrid and initiated legal action in 2002, forty-four years after Lilly Cassirer Neubauer's compensation agreement with the German government. The foundation Thyssen-Bornemisza promptly dismissed this claim. In 2005, Claude Cassirer initiated legal action in California under the Foreign Sovereign Immunities Act 1976. Following Claude's death in 2010, his children David and Ana continued the suit, backed by the United Jewish Federation of San Diego County.

In 2012, the Central District Court of California dismissed the 2005 claim due to prescription, a US legal concept similar to adverse possession in Irish law, whereby it is possible to acquire an easement over the property of another (also colloquially known as 'squatters rights'). However, in July

2014, the California Court of Appeals reversed this decision on procedural grounds and returned the case to the district court, without prejudicing its central issue.

In 2015, the district court ruled against the Cassirer family, stating that the Foundation acquired the painting through 'usucapion' under Spanish law. The concept of usucapion is again similar to adverse possession, whereby title is acquired over time. The requirements of usucapion are possession without attempt to conceal possession; a good faith purchase or transfer combined with good title in the object; absence of violence in the acquisition of the item by the party claiming usucapion; and continuous possession not interrupted by any legal claim or private agreement, for a usual term of three years.

The Cassirer heirs appealed to the United States Court of Appeals for the Ninth Circuit, introducing the argument that if Baron Thyssen-Bornemisza lacked valid title to sell, the Foundation could not acquire title through usucapion. The court overturned the previous ruling in July 2017 and remanded the case to the district court to determine if the Foundation was complicit in a crime against property. In September 2017, the Thyssen-Bornemisza Foundation requested reconsideration, supported by the Solicitor General's Office, but their appeal was rejected in December. In 2018, with the support of the Solicitor General's Office, the Foundation brought the case before the United States Supreme Court, but the court declined jurisdiction in May.

In December 2018, the district judge ruled in favour of the Foundation, affirming its legitimate ownership. The Cassirer family's case was dismissed. The Court of Appeals upheld this decision in August 2020, confirming that Spanish law applied to the core issue of the case, making the Foundation the rightful owner of the painting.

In January 2022, the Supreme Court instructed the Court of Appeals to verify if California law would support the conclusion that Spanish law applies. In January 2024, the Court of Appeals confirmed that, according to California's conflict of law rule, Spanish law is indeed applicable, thereby establishing the Foundation as the legitimate owner of the painting.[26]

This case highlights the complexities of international property disputes and the challenge of balancing competing legal interests. Despite growing sensitivity to cultural heritage and wartime atrocities, traditional legal

---

[26] See https://law.justia.com/cases/federal/appellate-courts/ca9/19-55616/19-55616-2024-01-09.html> accessed 30 September 2024.

conflict rules as they relate to international claims continue to guide such cases.

Chapter 6

Contracts

Introduction to Contract Law

Contract law addresses the rights and duties that arise out of the making of agreements and generally applies to obligations that are freely assumed by the parties involved in making such an agreement. Combined with title (see Chapter 3), contract provides the backbone of the legal functioning of trade, whereby goods or services are exchanged. Contract law is of itself a large and complicated practice area, beyond the scope of this book. However we will very briefly address some of the elements that are required to be present in a contract, how a contract might be enforced, and what remedies are available for a breach of contract.

First, there must be an offer which sets out the terms of what is to be contracted for, there must be an acceptance of that offer and there must be an intention to create legal relations (based on among other elements, a presumption that agreements between family members are presumed not to intend to create legal relations and agreements of a commercial variety are presumed to do so). Secondly, there must be consideration (unless a contract is made as a deed under seal which has been signed by both parties). Consideration broadly means that a contract will only be enforceable where the person to whom something has been promised has given something of tangible value in exchange.

Contracts without consideration may be enforceable under promissory estoppel, whereby if one party promises not to enforce a particular term or terms of a contract and the other party relies on this promise then the first party can be prevented from reneging on their promise. In general terms, contracts are only enforceable between the parties that have entered into that contract — the principle known as privity of contract; a third party cannot sue or be sued on the basis of a contract to which they are not a party.

Persons entering into a contract must be capable of doing so in order for it to be enforceable. Incapacity to enter into a contract can be on the basis of age, mental illness, intoxication or an incorporated body (such as a limited company) acting beyond the powers set out in its memorandum and articles of association.

Contracts for the sale of goods are required to be in writing, under s 4 of the Sale of Goods Act 1893, for any goods with a value of more than €12. Exceptions to this rule include instances where the buyer has accepted delivery of the goods which form the basis of the contract, if a deposit has been paid or if payment has been made in full and accepted by the seller.

The Statute of Frauds (Ir) 1695 s 2 places a requirement for a contract to which it applies to be evidenced in writing. These contracts include: sureties or guarantees, whereby one person undertakes to pay the debt of another should they default on that debt; contracts for marriage; contracts where the obligations therein are liable to continue for more than one year — such as loan agreements; contracts for the sale or lease of land (unless an oral contract has been performed in full or in part — e.g. where a party has already moved into a property). Broadly speaking a written memorandum of such a contract must include at a minimum the parties; the price or consideration; the subject matter of the contract and the essential details of the contract stated in an accurate manner.

Essential Terms

Among the most common forms of contract for galleries, libraries, archives and museums are deposit, gift, licence, loan agreements and sale agreements (see Chapter 9), which essentially all deal with the transfer of objects on a temporary or permanent basis from one institution to another, or from an individual to an institution. It is essential to include certain elements in these agreements, both as dictated by the Sale of Goods Act 1893 and the Statute of Frauds (Ir) 1695, and from the perspective of outlining the expectations of the parties involved, outlining all obligations in full and ensuring that the rights of both parties are adequately protected.

The nature of the contract must be set out; is it a loan? Is it a sale? The parties must be set out, ensuring that the correct legal entities are detailed and enumerated; is the owner of the object an individual, a company or a trust? Is the item being sold by a gallery that owns the work, or on behalf of an individual who has consigned the work for sale? What is the object or collections of objects that are the subject of the contract? Is there a schedule that lists these items that can be appended and referred to? When the contract is to be performed; what dates will the object be delivered or returned? What costs are associated with the contract; what is the sale price? Which taxes are applicable? Title; what evidence of provenance, ownership and title are being advanced? Who assumes responsibility for any risk associated with bad title?

At this stage it might be appropriate to briefly explain the difference between terms, conditions, warranties and indemnities. Every contract has terms, but not every term is a condition. A condition of a contract is a term that is essential to the functioning of the contract and is one that if breached allows the party that is the recipient of the breach to treat the contract as repudiated. A warranty is a secondary term, that is not central to the fundamental aspects of the contract. The key difference being that if a warranty is breached the party against whom the breach occurs is still bound by the terms of the contract and can only seek an award of damages. An indemnity might also be sought whereby one party indemnifies the other in the event that an issue comes to light in relation to title, or a claim is brought by a third party seeking restitution of the object. Indemnities can either be narrowly drafted to cover direct losses (for instance in the event of another party proving title over an object) or more broadly to include costs, reputational damage, damages and legal fees.

It is possible to indicate in writing within a contract that certain terms are conditions. For instance it could be specified that the seller of an object have good title and have carried out adequate provenance research to assure themselves that the object is not the subject of a current dispute nor is likely to be the subject of a dispute in future and that that item is exactly as described, or that the date included in the title of the object is the date that it was actually made (see 'Case Study' below). Other warranties might include that the item was not stolen or illegally exported, that there are no extant ownership claims over the item and that the item does not infringe any third party IP rights. For instance, a US Supreme Court ruling in 2023 against the estate of Andy Warhol found that a series of silkscreens based on a photograph of the musician Prince by photographer Lynn Goldsmith was not sufficiently transformative not to present a breach of copyright, nor was a fair use (see Chapter 1) derogation possible as both the photograph and prints were of a commercial nature.[1]

Other Terms

Copyright, moral rights or IP might also be considerations depending on the subject matter of the contract. If so, there may be a requirement for

---

[1] *Andy Warhol Foundation for the Visual Arts Inc v Goldsmith et al*, (2023) No 21-869.

these rights to be assigned or licensed for a set period to allow full use of the object for the purposes under which the contract was undertaken. For instance, a collection of letters on loan from the estate of a famous literary figure may still be in copyright, which means that in order to digitise them and then use the images in a catalogue a licence will be required.

Extension clauses are normal for a contract with a set time period, such as allowing a set number of time extensions each of a set time period. Contracts for services may also allow an extension up to a certain value, or a certain amount of work to be completed.

Confidentiality clauses may place an onus on all parties to hold confidential all information, documentation and other material received, provided or obtained arising from their participation in the contract and shall not disclose same to any third party except, unless as required by law.

A key personnel clause places an obligation on one of the parties to ensure that persons assigned responsibility for a particular aspect of performance of a contract are available to perform that role, or that at a minimum a suitably qualified replacement be available. Obligations might also be placed on one or both parties to comply with international regulations, such as the International Council of Museums *(ICOM) Code of Ethics*,[2] or the *Archives and Records Association Code of Ethics*,[3] and to act with due care, skill and diligence in carrying out their obligations.

Termination clauses within a contract set out the circumstances under which either party may terminate the agreement; the ways in which they must notify the other party of any breach; the timeframes that are allowed for the party in breach to rectify that breach and those circumstances that will lead to immediate termination of the contract. Termination clauses are frequently reciprocal, but there is no requirement for both parties to enjoy the same rights to notice or compensation as all contractual obligations are freely assumed by the parties involved. For this reason contracts for services are often heavily skewed towards the contracting party at the expense of the contractor, for instance including 'no fault' cancellation clauses allowing a contract to be cancelled by one party at any time on the giving of a set period of notice.

---

[2] International Council of Museums, 'ICOM Code of Ethics for Museums' <https://icom.museum/wp-content/uploads/2018/07/ICOM-code-En-web.pdf> accessed 21 August 2024.

[3] Archives and Records Association, 'ARA Code of Ethics' <https://www.archives.org.uk/ara-code-of-ethics> accessed 21 August 2024.

Contracts will normally include a section addressing steps to be taken in the event of a dispute, for instance naming individuals nominated by both parties to resolve any dispute, or a period after which a dispute might be referred to mediation. Similarly, it is usual to include the governing law under which the contract be governed and construed, as well as the choice of jurisdiction for the hearing of any disputes that might arise from the contract.

The circumstances under which any aspect of the contract might be assigned or subcontracted may be set out, or in the contrary a clause expressly prohibiting any assignment or subcontracting.

Force majeure clauses will frequently be included so that an event or circumstance not within the reasonable control of the affected parties which has the effect of delaying or preventing that party from complying with its obligations under the contract allows for termination of the contract after a set period of time without responsibility for loss or damage. The types of events covered under a force majeure clause might include acts of God, war, out-break of disease, insurrection, riot, civil disturbance, rebellion, acts of terrorism, government regulations, embargoes, explosions, fires, floods, tempests, or failures of supply of electrical power, or public telecommunications equipment or lines, excluding industrial action of whatever nature or cause (strikes, lockouts and similar). Interestingly, an exclusion from force majeure clauses that is being seen in contracts, following Brexit, is the departure of a country from the European Union. Definitions of 'out-break of disease' may also need careful drafting in a post-COVID-19 environment where government-mandated lockdowns are arguably now foreseeable in the event of future pandemics.

An entire agreement clause will usually set out the understanding of the parties that all terms to which the contract is subject are contained within the contract and that any previous agreements, understandings or contracts are superseded by that contract.

Loan Agreements

Loan agreements will often contain specific conditions and obligations, in addition to the essential terms outlined above. Loan agreements will include the lender's undertakings, for instance to lend the object in question for a set period of time or to grant certain rights to the institution receiving the loan, such as licensing of copyright, rights to publicise the loan, rights to use imagery in publicity materials or merchandising rights to images of the object during the duration of a loan. Borrowers' undertakings will outline what is agreed in terms of ensuring the safekeeping of the object and may also guarantee it being available for public viewing for set periods of time, may set out ticket pricing or restrictions, for instance prohibition of photography or flash photography.

A condition check will normally be included in a loan agreement, to include a conservator's report at the time of despatch of the object, a conservators report at the time of receipt of the object and vice versa on the object's return. This ensures that in the event of any damage it is possible to ascertain which party, if any, is at fault.

Specific conditions might be applied to how the object is to be installed. For instance limitations on the amount of lux to which an object is exposed, the temperature and relative humidity of the display space and how this is to be monitored and the control of dust and pollutants might all be specified. The British Association of Paintings Conservator-Restorers recommends 18-24° C, 40-60% relative humidity with no more than 10% variation in any 24 hour period, no more than 200 lux of light exposure and keeping paintings away from open windows, pets and known dusty areas.[4]

But, as with all non-essential terms in a contract, all obligations are negotiable and freely undertaken. In the case of the *David Bowie Is* exhibition for instance, the author asked the curator from the Victoria and Albert Museum what obligations had been imposed by the David Bowie archive to display costumes, instruments and documents. Climate and light controlled vitrines to display costume items were originally requested but the Victoria and Albert Museum insisted that items be put on open display on mannequins in order to allow maximum impact and proper interpretative display, or they could not mount a proper exhibition. The Bowie archive relented and agreed to open display.

Loan agreements will typically specify insurance requirements, to include any and all circumstances of loss or damage, specify how materials are to be transported and by whom, security precautions to be taken, responsibility for costs; detail indemnities to be given by the borrowing institution and address any requirements on the borrowing institution to apply for immunity from seizure for the duration of the loan (see Chapter 9).

---

[4] 'Care for your Paintings', British Association of Paintings Conservator-Restorers https://www.bapcr.org.uk/advice/care-for-your-paintings/ accessed 21 August 2024.

The UK Museums Association has produced a guide to *Simple Loans Administration* detailing suggested core terms, additional terms and sample loan documents and agreements which is available online.[5] Similarly, ICOM issued a *Guidelines for Loans* document in 1974 which addresses key terms in a loan agreement which is also available freely online.[6]

The Heritage Council Museum Standards Programme requires that participating institutions submit copies of their loan-in agreement procedures, loan-out agreement procedures and sets out requirements that should be included in such agreements and system and procedures for recording loans as part of a *Documentation Procedure Manual*.[7]

Digitisation and Cataloguing Contracts

A contract between an institution and a third-party service provider for digitisation work might contain a term stating that all IP rights in the digitised images remain with the owner of the materials being digitised, but as we have seen in Chapter 1 it is unlikely that the act of digitisation is sufficient to meet the CRRA requirement that copyright subsists in "original literary, dramatic, musical or artistic works" and the DSM statement that "any material resulting from an act of reproduction of that work is not subject to copyright or related rights."

Contracts for cataloguing or inventories might typically also contain a term that stipulates that all IP title and interest in all reports, data manuals and/ or other materials (including without limitation all and any audio or audio-visual recordings, transcripts, books, papers, records, notes, illustrations, photographs, diagrams) produced for the purposes of the contract shall vest in the client. Section 23(1) of the CRRA states that

> "[t]he author of a work shall be the first owner of the copyright unless... the work is made by an employee in the course of employment, in which case the employer is the first owner of any copyright in the work, subject to any agreement to the contrary."

---

[5] 'Simple Loans Administration', UK Museums Association, <https://archive-media.museumsassociation.org/simpleloansadministration_firstedition.pdf> accessed 21 August 2024.

[6] International Council of Museums, 'ICOM Guidelines for Loans' <https://icom.museum/wp-content/uploads/2018/07/Loans1974eng.pdf> accessed 21 August 2024.

[7] Heritage Council, 'Museum Standards Programme for Ireland: Loan Agreement and Records' <https://www.heritagecouncil.ie/content/files/28._4.10__4.11__4.12_Loan_Agreement_and_Records.pdf> accessed 21 August 2024.

Public Procurement

Public service bodies, including but not limited to the National Archives, the National Gallery of Ireland, the National Museum of Ireland, the National Library of Ireland, the Irish Museum of Modern Art and the Crawford Art Gallery Cork Ltd, or any other body wholly or partly funded by the State, public or local authority[8] are required to comply with public procurement regulations, namely SI No 284/2016 EU (Award of Public Authority Contracts) Regulations 2016.

For contracts worth less than €5,000 verbal quotes are sufficient. For work worth more than €5,000 a request for quotes must be sent to three suppliers, which must be evaluated subjectively against stated requirements using a scoring sheet, the most suitable offer selected and all participants informed of the result of the process. Under Circular 05/2023,[9] all contracts for goods or services worth more than €50,000 must be advertised on the e-tenders website[10] where suppliers from across the EU are able to bid. Award criteria must be assigned weighting and tenders must be evaluated according to this weighting with the highest scoring tender being awarded the contract and unsuccessful tenders being provided with sufficient commentary to allow them to understand the basis of selection. A contract notice must then be published to the Official Journal of the European Union (OJEU) via e-tenders.

As the process for tendering is quite cumbersome institutions will frequently contract under framework agreements. A single party framework agreement means that all work of that type (for instance cataloguing or digitisation) for a set period of time will be undertaken by one contractor at an agreed price for the duration of that framework. A multi-party framework will appoint multiple contractors to a framework which then allows for mini-competitions that mirror the requirements for contracts for services of between €5,000 and €50,000 to take place between the contractors placed on the framework agreement, subject to a total value and time period.

---

[8] The Central Statistics Office keeps a record of all public sector bodies at <https://www.cso.ie/en/releasesandpublications/ep/p-rpbi/registerofpublicsectorbodies2022-final/publicsector/> accessed 21 August 2024.

[9] Circular 05-2023, 'Initiatives to assist SMEs in Public Procurement', Department of Public Expenditure, NDP Delivery and Reform (2023).

[10] Office of Government Procurement, 'eTenders' <https://www.etenders.gov.ie/> accessed 21 August 2024.

Auctions

Auctioneers are classified as property service providers (PSPs) and as such are governed by the Property Services Regulatory Authority (PSRA). All PSPs must hold a PSRA licence which is valid for one year. Type A licences allow the auction of property other than land, for example fine arts, antiquities or livestock.

The PSRA provides a sample agreement[11] to be used for the consignment to auction of property other than land, such as 'fine arts' and any other item that is not considered land under the definition of land contained in s 3 of the Land and Conveyancing Law Reform Act 2009.

For a purchaser at an auction, a binding contract is entered into from the moment that the auctioneer bangs their gavel. The information that is contained in the auction catalogue is the basis of the agreement that is entered into, for instance the terms attributed to, from the studio of or even the date in the title may mean different things than what the purchaser expects (see 'Case Study' below).

For instance 'Damien Hirst' means this is an original work by Damien Hirst. 'Damien Hirst. Replica' means Damien Hirst made this work himself as a replica of a previous work he himself made. 'Attributed to Damien Hirst' denotes that the auctioneer believes this work to be by Damien Hirst but is not prepared to guarantee this fact. 'Damien Hirst. His Studio' is a work made in Damien Hirst's studio, potentially under their supervision, but by another person. 'Damien Hirst. His Circle' means another person made the work during Damien Hirst's lifetime and in a similar manner to Damien Hirst, possibly a collaborator or contemporary. 'Damien Hirst. Follower of' means the work was made in the style of Damien Hirst, after Damien Hirst's death. 'Damien Hirst. After' means a work by another artist in the style of Damien Hirst.

Auction catalogues may contain symbols beside the entry that may indicate a reserve selling price, a guarantee to sell at a certain price (in which case the auction house must pay that price to the seller, regardless of whether bidding reaches this level) or legal restrictions around importing or exporting the work. Similarly use of capitals or bold may be indicative of whether a warranty or guarantee by the auction house applies to that item.

---

[11] Property Services Regulation Authority, 'Property Services Agreements' <https://www.psr.ie/licensees/letters-of-engagement/auction/> accessed 21 August 2024.

Any buyer at auction should at a minimum have inspected the item physically, checked its previous exhibition history (as this can impact on value), looked for the provenance of the item, if it is a painting checked that it features in a catalogue raisonné[12] of the artist's work, looked for a condition report from a conservator and carefully checked the conditions of sale. The conditions will include reasonable limits to any warranties or indemnities offered by the auctioneer, so it is important to understand these. Buyers should also be careful to check import and export restrictions that may apply to the object (see Chapter 9).

In Ireland in 2021, the Criminal Justice (Money Laundering and Terrorist Financing) (Amendment) Act 2021 entered into force transposing the EU's Fifth Anti-Money Laundering Directive into Irish Law. Under s 25 of the 2021 Act persons trading or acting as an intermediary in the trade of works of art in respect of transactions of a total value of at least €10,000, or persons storing, trading or acting as an intermediary in the trade of works of art when this is carried out in a free port in respect of transactions of a total value of at least €10,000 are designated persons required to take measures to ensure their business is not being used for money laundering and/or terrorist financing.

As a result some 234 identified businesses in Ireland are obliged to take measures prior to carrying out any service for any customer as outlined in s 33 of the Criminal Justice (Money Laundering and Terrorist Financing) Act 2010 to include verifying identity of individuals on the basis of documents and identifying any beneficial owners of businesses involved in potential transactions. These businesses trading or acting as intermediaries in the trade of works of art also have a mandatory obligation under the Act of 2021 to report any unusual patterns of transactions which appear to have no obvious economic purpose, as this can be symptomatic of an attempt at 'layering', or attempting to create layers of transactions to create confusion and introduce distance between funds and their initial criminal origin.

The Anti-Money Laundering Compliance Unit is now responsible for the supervision of art traders and intermediaries to ensure compliance with their obligations under the 2023 Act.

---

[12] An annotated listing of all known art works by a particular artist designed to assist in authentication.

Case Study: Dating Damien Hirst

In March 2024, it came to light that at least three Damien Hirst artworks were created at a later date than their titles might suggest.

Hirst had previously risen to fame as one of the Young British Artists (YBA) group during the 1990s, with some of his most famous works including dead animals, sometimes dissected, preserved in formaldehyde. In 1991, Charles Saatchi offered to fund whatever art Hirst wished to make and the result was *The Physical Impossibility of Death in the Mind of Someone Living* which features a 4.3m long tiger shark in a clear vitrine, which sold at the Young British Artists exhibition at Saatchi Gallery for £50,000. In 2004, the same work was reportedly[13] purchased for $8m by a hedge fund billionaire named Steven Cohen.

In 1993, Hirst exhibited *Mother and Child Divided* comprising a dissected cow and calf in separate vitrines and in 1994 *Away from the Flock*, a sheep in a vitrine filled with formaldehyde. *Away from the Flock* was subsequently vandalised by Mark Bridger who poured black ink into the vitrine and retitled the work *Black Sheep*. Bridger was prosecuted for criminal damage on Hirst's request, found guilty and was conditionally discharged for two years. Hirst featured *Away from the Flock* in a 1997 book with a black card that could be drawn down to cover the tank. Bridger subsequently sued Hirst for breach of his copyright in *Black Sheep*.

Hirst during his career has been no stranger to copyright claims, for instance in 2000 Hirst made an out of court settlement with Norman Emms, who was the designer of a children's anatomy toy, Humbrol's 'Young Scientist Anatomy Set.' Hirst scaled up the toy to around 6 metres in height and used bronze, silver and gold to make the various internal organs that were plastic in the original toy. The anatomy set retailed for £14.99, Hirst's work, entitled *Hymn*, sold for £1m. The settlement made with Emms is estimated to have been £100-150,000. Hirst was similarly accused of plagiarism by fellow-artist John Le Kay who had been making skulls covered in crystals since 1993; Hirst made a work called *For the Love of God*, a platinum sculpture of a skull covered in diamonds modelled on an 18th century human skull and featuring the original human teeth. It reportedly cost £14m to make, and was sold to a group of collectors for $100m in 2007. Hirst subsequently sued a 16-year-old artist who had used an image of *For the Love of God* in

---

[13] Eileen Kinsella, 'Damien Hirst Backdated Signature Formaldehyde Sculptures, U.K. Paper Reports', Artnet, <https://news.artnet.com/art-world/damien-hirst-backdated-signature-formaldehyde-sculptures-u-k-paper-reports-2455123> accessed 21 August 2024.

a collage, demanding repayment of the £195 the minor had made in sales of his prints.

In 2017, three formaldehyde vitrine pieces that had never been seen in public before were exhibited in Hong Kong; *Cain and Abel (1994)*, *Dove (1999)* and *Myth Explored, Explained, Exploded (1993-99)*. According to an investigation by the *Guardian*,[14] the three works which have been exhibited in galleries in Hong Kong, New York, Munich, London and Oxford as examples of Hirst's 1990s work were actually created by employees of Hirst's company, Science Ltd, at a workshop in Dudbridge, Gloucestershire, in 2017 and employees were instructed to artificially age the pieces to make them look like they were made in the 1990s.

Representatives at Science Ltd confirmed the sculptures were made in 2017, stating that the dates in the titles refer to when the works were conceived, rather than made, stating that Hirst "has been clear over the years when asked what is important in conceptual art; it is not the physical making of the object or the renewal of its parts, but rather the intention and the idea behind the artwork."[15] Hirst's lawyers subsequently stated that "the dating of artworks, and particularly conceptual artworks, is not controlled by any industry standard... Artists are perfectly entitled to be (and often are) inconsistent in their dating of works."[16]

In a subsequent report by the *Guardian*[17] it was revealed that potentially thousands of works signed by Hirst from his series *The Currency* were actually manufactured later than claimed. The works were put on sale in 2021, whereby buyers could purchase an NFT (see Chapter 8) of one of

---

[14] Maeve McClenaghan, 'Damien Hirst formaldehyde animal works dated to 1990s were made in 2017' *The Guardian* <https://webstories.theguardian.com/stories/2024/mar/20/damien-hirst-formaldehyde-animal-works-dated-to-1990s-were-made-in-2017/> accessed 21 August 2024.

[15] Riah Pryor, 'Major discrepancy in dates of Damien Hirst formaldehyde works revealed in Guardian investigation' *The Art Newspaper* <https://www.theartnewspaper.com/2024/03/23/discrepancy-dates-damien-hirst-formaldehyde-works-revealed-guardian-investigation> accessed 21 August 2024.

[16] Maeve McClenaghan, 'Damien Hirst shark that sold for about $8m is fourth 2017 work dated to 1990s' *The Guardian* <https://www.theguardian.com/artanddesign/2024/mar/22/damien-hirst-shark-that-sold-for-about-8m-is-fourth-2017-work-dated-to-1990s> accessed 21 August 2024.

[17] Maeve McClenaghan, 'At least 1,000 Damien Hirst artworks were painted years later than claimed' *The Guardian* <https://www.theguardian.com/artanddesign/article/2024/may/22/damien-hirst-artworks-painted-years-later-currency-artist> accessed 21 August 2024.

the artworks and were marketed as 10,000 NFTs each corresponding to a unique artwork made in 2016. The initial sale of NFTs raised c. $18m.

The *Guardian* reported that many of the paintings were mass produced in 2018-2019 by painters hired by Science Ltd. Hirst's lawyers did not dispute that many of the paintings dated 2016 had in fact been produced later.

In October 2022, Hirst and his team engaged in a livestreamed burning of physical versions of roughly half of the paintings, as purchasers of the works could opt for either the NFT or the physical work. Of 10,000 works made, some 5,149 buyers chose to retain the physical version, 3,851 buyers chose to retain the NFT and Hirst kept 1,000 NFTs personally.

Mark Carney, former governor of the Bank of England, had been recruited by Hirst to appear in a video promoting *The Currency* and stated "Money is based on trust… and at the heart of this is also a sense of trust — trust in the underlying art."[18]

---

[18] ibid.

Chapter 7

Archaeology and Monuments

National Monuments

The Historic and Archaeological Heritage and Miscellaneous Provisions Act 2023 has not been commenced in full. In the words of the Department of Housing, Local Government and Heritage:

> "When fully commenced, the Act will replace the existing National Monuments Act 1930 to 2014, and other related legislation, and introduce a range of new provisions to protect and conserve Ireland's historic heritage. Under the new Act, newly-discovered archaeological sites will be protected and existing sites and structures will be afforded greater legal protection. Innovations include a single, integrated licencing system, and the State will be enabled to ratify important international conventions to protect of historic heritage, should the Government decide to do so."[1]

Part 8 chapter 1 of the 2023 Act has been commenced, which sets out that the minister may carry out or cause to be carried out inventories of or in relation to historic heritage, World Heritage Property or property which is situated in the state that the minister is satisfied may have the potential to become World Heritage Property as he or she considers appropriate. In addition the minister shall establish and maintain, or cause to be established and maintained, inventories in respect of each of the following: (a) relevant things of archaeological interest; (b) architectural heritage; (c) wrecks of archaeological or historic interest, the minister may designate classes of the archaeological or architectural heritage or historic objects to be included in any particular inventory; and, amend, add to or delete from any such inventory. The key point here being that these inventories relate solely to property that may have the potential to become World Heritage Property.

'Relevant things' are defined at s 2(1) of 2023 Act as:

---

[1] Department of Housing, Local Government and Heritage, 'New powers to protect Ireland's valuable historic and archaeological heritage' <https://www.gov.ie/en/press-release/ab826-new-powers-to-protect-irelands-valuable-historic-and-archaeological-heritage/> accessed 21 August 2024.

> "(a) any artificial structure, construction, deposit, feature or layer (including any building and any burial or interment);
> (b) any artificially altered structure, construction, deposit, feature or layer, whether or not natural in origin;
> (c) any wreck;
> (d) any ritual or ceremonial site;
> (e) any site where an historic event took place, including any other site directly associated with that event;
> (f) any battlefield;
> (g) any site with legendary or mythological associations;
> (h) any feature, deposit or layer, whether or not natural in origin and whether or not artificially altered."

Part 2 of the 2023 Act is the section that deals with the powers vested in the minister to prescribe monuments if they are of the opinion that they are of archaeological or other interest. These monuments will then become 'Registered Monuments' and once placed on the register can only be removed on consultation with the Heritage Council. A registered monument may be placed as a burden on a piece of land and may be compulsorily purchased by the minister, which converts the registered monument into a 'National Monument'. A series of offences are also detailed with penalties up to five years in prison, or €10 million, or both.[2]

But since this Part of the Historic and Archaeological Heritage and Miscellaneous Provisions Act 2023 has not been commenced, the situation in regard to National Monuments continues to fall under the auspices of the National Monuments Act 1930 and the amendments to same of 1987, 1994 and 2004.

The National Monuments (Amendment) Act 1987 at s 11 amended the 1930 Act to define a National Monument as:

> "the following, whether above or below the surface of the ground or the water and whether affixed or not affixed to the ground—
> (a) any artificial or partly artificial building, structure or erection or group of such buildings, structures or erections,
> (b) any cave, stone or other natural product, whether or not forming part of the ground, that has been artificially carved, sculptured or worked upon or which (where it does not form part of the place where it is) appears to have been purposely put or arranged in position,
> (c) any, or any part of any, prehistoric or ancient—
>   (i) tomb, grave or burial deposit, or

---

[2] Ronan Bergin, 'The new Historic and Archaeological Heritage and Miscellaneous Provisions Act 2023 in Ireland' <https://www.artlawyersassociation.com/post/the-new-historic-and-archaeological-heritage-and-miscellaneous-provisions-act-2023-in-ireland> accessed 21 August 2024.

> (ii) ritual, industrial or habitation site, and
>
> (d) any place comprising the remains or traces of any such building, structure or erection, any such cave, stone or natural product or any such tomb, grave, burial deposit or ritual, industrial or habitation site, situated on land or in the territorial waters of the State, but does not include any building, or part of any building, that is habitually used for ecclesiastical purposes."

The current position as to who decides what is and what is not a National Monument is unclear.

> "The process of identifying and designating a monument as a national monument is wholly unclear and lacks the indicia of a public consultation or participation process. While the National Monuments Act 1930 defines what a national monument is and the degree of protection afforded to national monuments, it does not set out a formal process for identifying or designating a national monument."[3]

The 1987 Act introduced a 'Historic Monuments Council' at s 4 which states at s 4(2) that

> "It shall be the function of the Council to advise and assist the Commissioners in relation to any matter respecting the carrying into execution of the provisions of the National Monuments Acts, 1930 to 1987, or any other matter affecting historic monuments or other archaeological areas or wrecks, and their protection and preservation and the Council shall, if requested by the Commissioners to do so, advise them in relation to any specified such matter as aforesaid."

The Council is formed of representatives of the Taoiseach, the Minister for the Marine, the Minister for the Environment, the Commissioners of Public Works and representatives from universities, Bord Fáilte, the Royal Irish Academy, the Royal Society of Antiquaries in Ireland, the Royal Institute of Architects of Ireland and the Maritime Institute of Ireland, as well as up to five other persons as determined by the minister.

Section 5(1) of the 1987 Act sets out that "[t]he Commissioners shall cause to be established and maintained a register of historic monuments which shall be known as 'the Register of Historic Monuments' and is referred to in this Act as 'the Register.'" The National Monuments (Amendment) Act 1994 expanded this requirement at s 12(1) which states that

> "The Commissioners shall establish and maintain a record of monuments

---

[3] David Browne, *The Law of Local Government* (2nd edn, Round Hall 2020) para 11-152.

and places where they believe there are monuments and the record shall be comprised of a list of monuments and such places and a map or maps showing each monument and such place in respect of each county in the State."

Section 12(3) of the National Monuments (Amendment) Act 1994 states that:

"When the owner or occupier (not being the Commissioners) of a monument or place which has been recorded under subsection (1) of this section or any person proposes to carry out, or to cause or permit the carrying out of, any work at or in relation to such monument or place, he shall give notice in writing of his proposal to carry out the work to the Commissioners and shall not, except in the case of urgent necessity and with the consent of the Commissioners, commence the work for a period of two months after having given the notice."

Under s 5 of the National Monuments (Amendment) Act 2004, s 14 of the 1930 Act is amended as follows:

"In respect of a national monument of which the Minister or a local authority are the owners or the guardians or in respect of which a preservation order is in force, it shall not be lawful for any person to do any of the following things in relation to such national monument:
(a) to demolish or remove it wholly or in part or to disfigure, deface, alter, or in any manner injure or interfere with it, or
(b) to excavate, dig, plough or otherwise disturb the ground within, around, or in proximity to it, or
(c) to renovate or restore it, or
(d) to sell it or any part of it for exportation or to export it or any part of it,
Without… consent."

It is worth noting however that under the amended s 14(3)(d) of the 1930 Act, the minister may, in the exercise of discretion in granting such consent, consider the public interest in allowing the carrying out of works, even in cases where these result in injury to or interference with the monument or the destruction in whole or in part of the monument. The public interest in question being presumably the construction of infrastructure projects.

Section 11 of the 1994 Act empowers the commissioners of public works to acquire by agreement or compulsorily any monument which is in their opinion a national monument and any land that is in the vicinity of such a monument for the provision of facilities to any persons having access to the monument. The commissioners may also acquire any right, easement, title or interest of any kind in, over or in respect of such a monument or land or any easement over land to allow access to such a monument (such as a right of way).

Under s 7 of the 1987 Act, the commissioners of public works, or a local authority, who are owners of a monument, may remove same to a museum if they can do so without injury to the monument and it is in their opinion desirable to do so to safeguard the monument. If the monument is deposited in a museum, it shall be open to inspection by the public to the like extent and manner as other objects in the museum. Section 8(1) allows for the commissioners of public works to

> "cause such inspections, investigations and reports as they may direct (either generally or particularly) to be made by their officers, servants, agents or other persons duly authorised by them in that behalf in regard to—
> (a) historic monuments and places where the Commissioners have reason to believe that historic monuments exist, and
> (b) restricted areas and sites that the Commissioners have reason to believe to be the sites of wreck or archaeological objects."

Under s 8(2)

> "[t]he Commissioners, their officers, servants or agents, or other persons duly authorised by the Commissioners in that behalf, may for the purpose of performing their functions under this section enter on any lands or premises and there do all such things as may reasonably be necessary for the purposes of those functions."

Section 9 of the 1987 Act allows for the making of byelaws in relation to monuments by the commissioners of public works or a local authority with the approval of the minister and sets out that any person who contravenes such a byelaw shall be guilty of an offence.

Section 2 of the 1987 Act sets out a licensing system for the use of metal detectors, by which their unlicensed use is prohibited at, in or at the site of a monument of which the commissioners of public works or a local authority are owners or guardians in respect of which a preservation order is in force or which is listed on the Register without a consent being granted by the commissioners. The use of metal detectors at any other site for the purpose of searching for archaeological objects is prohibited under s 2(1)(b) and promotion of the sale or use of metal detectors for the purpose of searching for archaeological objects is prohibited at s 2(1)(c).

The position in relation to state ownership of archaeological items following *Webb v Ireland* (see Chapter 3) was clarified by the National Monuments (Amendment) Act 1994 at s 4(1): "[n]o person shall have in his possession or under his control an archaeological object which has been found in the State after the coming into operation of this section." The Historic and

Archaeological Heritage and Miscellaneous Provisions Act 2023 further clarifies at s 96 which will vest absolute ownership of all such finds in the state. This section had not yet been commenced at the time of writing.

Under s 5 of the 1994 Act there is a requirement that:

> "No person shall have in his possession or under his control an archaeological object which has been found in the State after the coming into operation of the Principal Act unless it has been reported under section 23 (as amended by the Act of 1987[4]) of the Principal Act or under this section within three months of the coming into operation of this section."

Section 5(2) sets out that:

> "No person shall purchase or otherwise acquire, sell or otherwise dispose of an archaeological object which has been found in the State after the coming into operation of the Principal Act, unless, at the time of purchase, acquisition, sale or disposal or within 30 days thereof he makes a report… to the Director or a designated person of the purchase, acquisition, sale or disposal."

Section 13 of the 1994 Act sets out penalties for possession, purchase or sale, non-reporting or failure to hand over archaeological objects; obstructing or interfering with a member of An Garda Síochána seizing or detaining detection equipment, impeding the Director of the National Museum from inspecting a site or commencing work on the site of a monument within two months of giving notice to commence works as a fine not exceeding £1,000 or imprisonment for a period not exceeding 12 months, or both, on summary conviction; and, fine not exceeding £50,000 or imprisonment for a period not exceeding 5 years, or both, on conviction on indictment.

"A person who finds an archaeological object shall, within 4 days after the finding, make a report of it to a member of the Garda Síochána on duty in the district in which the object was found or the Director of the National Museum or a servant or agent of his and shall when making the report state his own name and address, the nature or character of the said object and the time and place at which and the circumstances in which it was found, and shall also, and whether he has or has not made such report as aforesaid, and irrespective of the person to whom he has made the report (if any), give to any member of the Garda Síochána or to the said Director or a servant or agent of his on request any information within his knowledge in relation to the object or the finding thereof and shall permit—
(a) any member of the Garda Síochána or the said Director or a servant or agent of his to inspect, examine or photograph the object, and
(b) the said Director or a servant or agent of his to take possession of the object."

Protected Structures and their Contents

In 1985, the Council of Europe published the Convention for the Protection of the Architectural Heritage of Europe, also known as the Grenada Convention, which was ratified by Ireland in 1985 and came into force in 1997, reserving the right not to comply with Article 4(2)(c) of the Convention which "permits public authorities to require the owner of a protected property to carry out work or to carry out such work itself if the owner fails to do so."[5] Under article 3, Ireland agreed to "take statutory measures to protect the architectural heritage" and to "make provision for the protection of monuments, groups of buildings and sites."[6]

Ireland legislated for this requirement under Part IV of the Planning and Development Act 2000 that relates to architectural heritage. Section 51(1) of the 2000 Act states

> "For the purpose of protecting structures, or parts of structures, which form part of the architectural heritage and which are of special architectural, historical, archaeological, artistic, cultural, scientific, social or technical interest, every development plan shall include a record of protected structures (RPS), and shall include in that record every structure which is, in the opinion of the planning authority, of such interest within its functional area."

A structure is defined at s 2 of the 2000 Act as:

> "any building, structure, excavation, or other thing constructed or made on, in or under any land, or any part of a structure so defined, and—
> (a) where the context so admits, includes the land on, in or under which the structure is situate, and
> (b) in relation to a protected structure or proposed protected structure, includes—
>   (i) the interior of the structure,
>   (ii) the land lying within the curtilage of the structure,
>   (iii) any other structures lying within that curtilage and their interiors, and
>   (iv) all fixtures and features which form part of the interior or exterior of any structure or structures referred to in subparagraph (i) or (iii)."

A 'protected structure' is

> "(a) a structure, or (b) a specified part of a structure, which is included in a record of protected structures, and, where that record so indicates, includes

---

[5] Council of Europe, "Convention for the Protection of the Architectural Heritage of Europe" <https://rm.coe.int/168007a087> accessed 21 August 2024.
[6] ibid.

any specified feature which is within the attendant grounds of the structure and which would not otherwise be included in this definition."

In the 2003 case of *Begley & Clarke v An Bord Pleanála*,[7] it was held that the designation of any part of a structure as a protected structure resulted in the designation of the whole structure as a protected structure.

Under s 53(1) of the 2000 Act, the Minister for Arts may make recommendations in writing to a planning authority in relation to the inclusion of particular structures, parts of structures or features in the grounds of structures for inclusion in an RPS. To this end, the National Inventory of Architectural Heritage (NIAH) was formed as a state initiative under the administration of the Department of Arts, Heritage and the Gaeltacht. It was established on a statutory basis under the provisions of the Architectural Heritage (National Inventory) and Historic Monuments (Miscellaneous Provisions) Act 1999.

> "Its purpose is to identify, record, and evaluate the post-1700 architectural heritage of Ireland, uniformly and consistently as an aid in the protection and conservation of the built heritage. It is intended that the NIAH will provide the basis for the recommendations of the Minister for Arts, Heritage and the Gaeltacht to the planning authorities around the country for the inclusion of particular structures in their Record of Protected Structures (RPS)."[8]

The results of the NIAH surveys are available and freely searchable online.[9]

The effects of a structure being registered as a protected structure are fourfold: First, it impacts on the determination in a planning application — as the protected nature of the structure is taken into account in assessing the application. Secondly, an obligation upon the owner is created to ensure that the structure or any part of it that contributes to special architectural, historical, archaeological, cultural, scientific, social or technical interest is not endangered. Thirdly, the planning authority is empowered to acquire the structure and to serve notices requiring that its character be restored. Fourthly, development that would normally be exempt from a requirement for planning permission requires permission for protected structures.[10]

---

[7] [2003] IEHC 137, Ó Caoimh J.
[8] Department of Arts, Heritage and the Gaeltacht, 'NIAH Handbook' July 2012, p 3.
[9] National Built Heritage Service, 'Building and Garden Surveys' https://www.buildingsofireland.ie/buildings-search/ accessed 21 August 2024.
[10] David Browne, *The Law of Local Government* (2nd edn, Round Hall 2020) para 11-152.

This lack of access to usual exemptions is balanced out under s 57 of the 2000 Act, whereby the owner or occupier of a protected structure may make a written request to the local authority for a declaration setting out, in writing, those works it considers would materially affect its character, and therefore require planning permission, and those works which may be carried out as exempted development.

Fixtures and Chattels

We have seen above that "all fixtures and features which form part of the interior or exterior of any structure" are part of the definition of a 'structure' and therefore of a protected structure. This begs the question, 'what is a fixture?' The traditional determinants of whether an object is a fixture (something installed or fixed to a structure thereby becoming part of that structure) or a chattel (an item of personal property that can identified and moved), as examined in England in relation to *The Three Graces, The Time & Life Building* and *The Midland Hotel*,[11] are:

> 1) the 'degree of annexation' of the object to the realty so as to become part of the land, and, if there is some or sufficient annexation, and;
>
> 2) the 'purpose' of the annexation.[12]

In *The Three Graces*, it was held that a statue by Canova of that name, housed in an addition to a gallery space comprising a domed structure known as the 'Temple of the Three Graces', was in fact a chattel. The basis of the decision was a history of the statue having been moved, that there had been prior negotiations with the government for acquisition of the statue and that removal of the statue would not cause the gallery to cease being of architectural or historical interest. The fact that the statue could be lifted from its plinth (the degree of annexation) was also deemed significant.

In *The Time & Life Building*, the degree of annexation of a number of sculptures and paintings was examined at appeal, and where they were found to be 'sufficiently' annexed, the inspector went on to examine the purpose of the annexation. The question of whether a piece had been 'specifically designed' for the space in which it was exhibited was given particular weight.

---

[11] Jeremy Le M Scott, 'Classification of Fixtures Under English Law: An Inspector's Whim?' (2000) 5(4) Art Antiquity and Law, p 319.
[12] ibid.

In *The Midland Hotel* case a sculpture by Eric Gill was held to be a fixture, having been commissioned specifically for the hotel.

In Irish law, a similar case was examined in *RGRE Grafton Ltd v Bewley's Café*.[13] This case related to the question of whether six stained glass windows by Harry Clarke that had been commissioned for the Bewley's Café on Grafton Street, Dublin, in 1928, were in the possession of the tenant or the building owner. The premises had changed hands on a number of occasions from 1987 onwards, with the eventual owners being RGRE, a company belonging to property developer Johnny Ronan. RGRE had leased the property back to Bewley's and a disagreement over the payment of rent during COVID-19 closures had been partially settled with a cash payment. Bewley's proposed to address the remaining arrears by selling the windows to RGRE. Bewley's claimed that the windows were tenants' chattels and that their ownership remained with Bewley's and had not passed with the sale of the premises. RGRE argued that the windows were fixtures. In its ruling the court distinguished between four windows, known as the 'Four Orders Works', which were installed in the exterior of the building and performed the function of ordinary windows, thus forming part of the structure. These windows were ruled to belong to RGRE. Two other windows, known as the 'Swan Yard pair', had been moved internally within the building, eventually being used as fronts for light boxes. These windows were ruled to be chattels on the basis that their removal would not interfere with the convenient use of the café premises, so their ownership remained with Bewley's. A Court of Appeal ruling of 31 July 2024[14] overruled this decision while referring to a 1941 *Irish Times* report suggesting that all six windows should be removed to a place of safety during the Second World War to preclude risk of damage through aerial bombardment, stating that while the Swan Yard windows had been moved and were moveable they were still fixtures that remained the property of the landlord.

An Taisce

In Ireland, An Taisce — the National Trust for Ireland — holds and preserves a range of heritage properties in trust, including historic buildings and nature reserves. A full list is available online.[15]

---

[13] *RGRE Grafton Ltd v Bewley's Café* [2023] IEHC 25.
[14] *RGRE Grafton Ltd v Bewley's Café Grafton Street Ltd & Bewley's Ltd* [2024] IECA 199.
[15] An Taisce, 'Heritage Properties in Trust' <https://www.antaisce.org/Listing/Category/properties> accessed 21 August 2024.

An Taisce also maintain the Buildings at Risk Register,[16] which was developed in response to a concern at the growing number of structures that are vacant and falling into a state of disrepair. The Register provides information on structures of architectural, historical, archaeological, artistic, cultural, scientific, social or technical interest throughout the country that are considered to be at risk.

Battlefield Sites

In 2007, a project was undertaken by the Department of the Environment which produced some 245 reports into Irish Battlefield sites, a battle being defined by the advisory panel to the project as a significant military engagement, excluding sieges and urban warfare, which took place before 1800 AD, and which involved in the order of one thousand or more combatants. One of the remits of the project was to 'assist in identifying the appropriate protection for battlefields.'[17] This remit does not appear to have translated into any legislative change.

Battlefields as we have seen above are defined as 'relevant things' under the Historic and Archaeological Heritage and Miscellaneous Provisions Act 2023, which means that they may be designated. Battlefields are not however included within the definition of 'National Monuments" under the National Monuments (Amendment) Act 1987. Part 2 of the Historic and Archaeological Heritage and Miscellaneous Provisions Act 2023, when commenced, will allow the minister to prescribe battlefields as monuments if they are of archaeological or other interest. These monuments will then become 'Registered Monuments'.

Where a battlefield site comprises a structure or structures, these structures can be added to the Record of Protected Structures, as occurred in the case of No's 10, 12-13, 14-17 and 20-21 Moore Street, Dublin, on foot of their association with the 1916 Rising. Interestingly No's 12 and 13 have in the description on the RPS "[t]wo-storey, historic brick party wall (only) between 12 and 13 Moore Street, with evidence of 'creep holes' from 1916,"[18] which would seem to imply that only the party walls with evidence

---

[16] An Taisce, 'Buildings at Risk Register' <https://www.antaisce.org/buildings-at-risk> accessed 21 August 2024.

[17] Damian Shiels 'The Irish Battlefields Project' Current Archaeology Live (British Museum London 2011).

[18] Dublin City Council, 'Record of Protected Structures'<https://www.dublincity.ie/sites/default/files/2022-12/FINAL%20Dublin%20City%20Development%20Plan%202022-2028%20-%20Volume%204%20RPS.pdf> accessed 21 August 2024.

of 1916 'creep holes' (used to move between the buildings) were included on the register, but as we have seen from *Begley & Clarke v An Bord Pleanála*,[19] the designation of any part of a structure as a protected structure results in the designation of the whole structure as a protected structure.

Wrecks and Underwater Sites

Part 5 Chapter 1 of the Historic and Archaeological Heritage and Miscellaneous Provisions Act 2023 addresses wrecks and other elements of underwater cultural heritage. As we have already seen, 'any wreck' is defined as a 'relevant thing' at s 2(1) of the 2023 Act. A 'relevant wreck' is defined at s 132 as a wreck that is 100 or more years old, or otherwise of archaeological interest. Section 133 clarifies that the same provisions relating to state ownership of archaeological objects as set out in Part 4 apply to relevant wrecks.

Restrictions are placed on the payment of salvage in cases involving a relevant wreck, or any object removed from such a wreck, an archaeological object more than 100 years old and a registered monument including any part removed from such a monument. Special protection is afforded to registered monuments, or prescribed monuments, that are situated on, in or under land covered by water. A licence will be required to dive at, possess or use diving or salvage equipment at, dump or deposit at or interfere, remove or tamper in any way at, on, in, over, under, or in the vicinity of wrecks or underwater monuments.

Part 5, Chapter 2 sets out measures to allow the state to ratify the 2001 UNESCO Convention on the Protection of Underwater Cultural Heritage.

> "Recognising that underwater cultural heritage is largely undervalued, the 2001 Convention provides a common legally binding framework for States Parties on how to better identify, research and protect their underwater heritage while ensuring its preservation and sustainability. Underwater cultural heritage is defined as all traces of human existence of a cultural, historical or archaeological nature which, for at least 100 years, have been partially or totally immersed, periodically or permanently, under the oceans and in lakes and rivers."[20]

Part 5 of the 2023 Act has not yet been commenced so the situation in relation to wrecks and underwater sites continues to fall under the auspices

---

[19] [2003] IEHC 137, Ó Caoimh J.
[20] UNESCO, 'Underwater Cultural Heritage 2001 Convention' <https://www.unesco.org/en/underwater-heritage/2001-convention> accessed 21 August 2024.

of the National Monuments (Amendment) Act 1987 and the National Monuments (Amendment) Act 1994.

Under the terms of s 3(1) of the 1987 Act:

> "Where the Commissioners are satisfied in respect of any place on, in or under the sea bed of the territorial waters of the State or on, in or under the sea bed to which section 2 (1) of the Continental Shelf Act, 1968,[21] applies or on or in land covered by water that—
> (a) it is or may prove to be the site where a wreck or an archaeological object lies or formerly lay, and
> (b) on account of the historical, archaeological or artistic importance of the wreck or the object, the site ought to be protected,
>
> they may by order (in this section referred to as 'an underwater heritage order') designate an area of the sea bed, or land covered by water, around and including the site as a restricted area."

Ireland's territorial waters extend beyond its coastline for some 220 million acres,[22] being comprised of Ireland's current designated continental shelf, which is one of the largest seabed territories in Europe. The continental shelf is the extension of a state's territorial waters, where the natural land extends under the sea to the outer edge of the continental margin beyond 200 nautical miles from the coastline baseline. Ireland enjoys sovereign rights over the continental shelf under the Exclusive Economic Zone provisions of the United Nations Convention on the Law of the Sea to explore and develop its natural resources, according to the Law of the Sea Part VI.

Section 3(3) sets out that tampering, depositing and carrying out

> "diving, survey or salvage operations directed to the detection, location or exploration of a wreck or archaeological object or to recovering it or a part of it from, or from under, the sea bed or from land covered by water, as the case may be, or use equipment constructed or adapted for any purpose of diving, survey or salvage operations are all forbidden at such a restricted area."

Section 3(4) sets out identical restrictions which apply to a wreck which is

---

[21] "Any rights of the State outside territorial waters over the sea bed and subsoil for the purpose of exploring such sea bed and subsoil and exploiting their natural resources are, subject to subsection (2) of this section, hereby vested in the Minister and shall be exercisable by the Minister."

[22] Marine Institute, 'The Real Map of Ireland' <https://www.marine.ie/site-area/irelands-marine-resource/real-map-ireland-0> accessed 21 August 2024.

more than 100 years old or another archaeological object that is "lying on, in or under the sea bed or on or in land covered by water."

Section 3(5) sets out a licensing system for access to wrecks and restricted areas. Section 3(6) as amended by the 1994 Act sets out the requirement to report the finding of a wreck

> "being a wreck which is more than 100 years old... within 4 days after such finding, make a report of the finding to a member of the Garda Síochána or to the Commissioners and shall, when making the report, give to the member or to the Commissioners his name and address, state the nature of the wreck and the time and place at which and the circumstances in which it was found."

An identical requirement is set out at s 3(6)(b) as amended by the 1994 Act for archaeological objects discovered underwater.

Section 49 of the Merchant Shipping (Salvage and Wreck Act) 1993 states that

> "Where no owner establishes a claim to any wreck found in or brought into the State and in the possession of a receiver within one year after it came into the receiver's possession, the receiver shall notify the Director of the National Museum that the wreck is unclaimed and the Director shall, within 30 days, decide whether or not the wreck or any part thereof is of historical, archaeological or artistic importance and shall notify the receiver of the decision. If the Director decides that the wreck or any part thereof is of historical, archaeological or artistic importance, the receiver shall deliver the wreck or that part to the Director."

Case Study: The *SS Gairsoppa* and *SS Mantola*

In 2011, it was reported that a US exploration and salvage company Odyssey Marine had located the wreck of the *SS Gairsoppa*, a 412-foot steel-hulled British cargo ship that sank in February 1941 having been torpedoed by a German U-Boat. The ship was carrying 1,574 silver ingots weighing about 1,100 ounces each or almost 1.8 million troy ounces in total, setting a record for the deepest and largest precious metal recovery from a shipwreck, with a reported value of £150m. The wreck was found in international waters and Odyssey Marine carried out the salvage under a contract with the British government, the owners of the ship, under which it retained 80% of the silver found.

Subsequently it was reported that Odyssey Marine's ship, the *Odyssey Explorer*, had been found surveying 25 miles west of the Blasket Islands, off Ireland's South West Coast. As reported in the *Irish Times*:

> "The Naval Service said it notified the company's research ship Odyssey Explorer that it should inform the Irish authorities when it came across the vessel surveying some 25 miles west of the Blasket Islands, Co Kerry, on August 2nd.
>
> Under international law, a ship undertaking scientific research should inform the relevant state. However, Odyssey has said that searching for wrecks is exempt from this. Wrecks of less than 100 years old are not protected by Ireland's National Monuments Act."[23]

Odyssey Marine may have been correct in the provision they were relying on in relation to marine scientific research not relating to searching for wrecks. Article 56 of the United Nations Convention on the Law of the Sea states that:

> "In the exclusive economic zone, the coastal State has:
> (a) sovereign rights for the purpose of exploring and exploiting, conserving and managing the natural resources, whether living or non-living, of the waters superjacent to the seabed and of the seabed and its subsoil, and with regard to other activities for the economic exploitation and exploration of the zone such as the production of energy from the water, currents and winds."

The wreck that Odyssey Marine found as part of this surveying activity was that of the *SS Mantola,* which had been sunk in 1917 carrying some 600,000 ounces of silver bullion.

Under the National Monuments (Amendment) Act 1987, at s 1(1) 'wreck' means a vessel, or part of a vessel, lying wrecked on, in or under the sea bed or on or in land covered by water, and any objects contained in or on the vessel and any objects that were formerly contained in or on a vessel and are lying on, in or under the sea bed or on or in land covered by water.

At s 3(1) of the 1987 Act:

> "Where the Commissioners are satisfied in respect of any place on, in or under the sea bed of the territorial waters of the State or on, in or under the sea bed to which section 2 (1) of the Continental Shelf Act, 1968, applies or on or in land covered by water that—
> (a) it is or may prove to be the site where a wreck or an archaeological object lies or formerly lay, and
> (b) on account of the historical, archaeological or artistic importance of the wreck or the object, the site ought to be protected,

---

[23] Lorna Siggins, 'Treasure hunters say Irish waters have valuable wrecks', *The Irish Times* <https://www.irishtimes.com/news/treasure-hunters-say-irish-waters-have-valuable-wrecks-1.610957> accessed: 21 August 2024.

they may by order (in this section referred to as "an underwater heritage order") designate an area of the sea bed, or land covered by water, around and including the site as a restricted area."

Where an underwater heritage order is in place the restricted area shall be specified in the order and shall be of such size as the commissioners think necessary for the protection of the site concerned, the order shall come into operation on the day specified in the order and with immediate effect a person may not tamper with, damage, remove, survey, attempt to detect, locate or dive on or salvage from any part of a wreck or any archaeological object in that restricted area.

Further, under the National Monuments (Amendment) Act 1994 s 7(1)(b) a member of the Garda Síochána may without warrant seize and detain any equipment being capable of surveying or detecting wrecks being used in contravention of s 3.

It is often cited that wrecks are not protected under National Monuments legislation if they are less than 100 years old. This interpretation seems to stem from s 3(4) of the 1987 Act which precludes tampering, diving, surveying, salvage operations and use of detection equipment at the site of a wreck 'being a wreck which is more than 100 years old'.

The interesting point is that under s 3(1), which describes underwater heritage orders, there is no age attached to the definition of wreck. Nor is there a 100-year interpretation in the definition of 'wreck' at s 1 (see above). The only requirement for designation of an area of seabed or land covered by water as a restricted area by an underwater heritage order is that there be a historical, archaeological or artistic importance to the wreck.

The National Monuments service has a freely available *Wreck Inventory of Ireland*[24] that contains details of some 18,000 known and potential wreck sites in Ireland. The *SS Mantola* is listed on the inventory as sitting 143 miles WSW of Fastnet. The source of the location is listed as "Hocking, 1969, 450."[25]

Given that the location of the wreck and its cargo was well known before

---

[24] National Monuments Service, 'Wreck Inventory of Ireland' <https://data.gov.ie/dataset/national-monuments-service-wreck-inventory-of-ireland> accessed 21 August 2024.
[25] Charles Hocking, 'Dictionary of Disasters at Sea During the Age of Steam: Including sailing ships and ships of war lost in action, 1824-1962', Lloyd's Register of Shipping, 1969.

Odyssey Marine began surveying for it in Ireland's exclusive economic zone, this begs the question why was there not an underwater heritage order in place? Indeed, why not place an underwater heritage order over the entire WW1 and WW2 wartime shipping lanes SW of Ireland which would preclude any surveying or salvage activity without a licence from the Irish government?

This issue was debated in the Dáil in 1999,[26] in relation to the discovery of the wreck of the *Carpathia*, most famous for coming to the rescue of the *Titanic*, which was torpedoed and sunk in 1918, 100 miles SW of Baltimore. The wreck of the *Lusitania*, some 11 miles off Kinsale and within the state's territorial waters had previously been designated under an underwater heritage order. In response to queries in the Dáil, the then Minister for Arts, Heritage, Gaeltacht and the Islands explained the difference between the *Lusitania* and *Carpathia* as being one of location. The *Lusitania*, lying within territorial waters, was straightforward to designate. The *Carpathia*, although lying within Ireland's exclusive economic zone, and therefore covered as part of the seabed to which section 2(1) of the Continental Shelf Act 1968 act refers, and therefore able to be designated, was not done so as the UNESCO Convention on the Protection of Underwater Heritage was at that time being negotiated.

As we have seen above Part 5 Chapter 2 of the Historic and Archaeological Heritage and Miscellaneous Provisions Act 2023 allows the state to ratify the 2001 convention. This may not solve the issue of wartime wrecks off the coast of Ireland though, as neither the UK nor the US have ratified the treaty and thus retain ownership rights over their respective wrecked shipping and its content and the treaty only places duties to notify and consult in relation to wrecks.

In an interesting twist, Odyssey Marine had started its salvage operation on the *Mantola* in 2015 (presumably to frustrate the 100-year limit) when its salvage contract with the UK Government (the owners of the ship) lapsed. In April of 2017, an "unspecified United Kingdom Entity"[27] retrieved the silver from the wreck and deposited it with the Receiver of Wreck in the UK. Odyssey Marine brought an action *in rem* against the *SS Mantola* in the US seeking disclosure of the entity that had salvaged the silver, presumably in anticipation of bringing proceedings against that entity, which was denied.

---

[26] 508 *Dáil Debates* Cols 1457-1459.
[27] *Odyssey Marine Expl Inc v Shipwrecked & Abandoned SS Mantola*, 333 F Supp 3d 292 (SDNY 2018).

Chapter 8

Tax

Tax on Cultural Objects

Tax is universally understood as one of the two inevitabilities, so there is no requirement to explain it in general conceptual terms here. There are however a number of tax issues that have specific application to the world of art and cultural heritage law that we shall investigate. By definition, many cultural objects, sites or properties that are in private hands are high value items, so much tax law is based around the minimisation of Capital Acquisitions Tax (CAT), currently set at 33% in Ireland, either at the point of inheritance, or part of estate planning to minimise taxes at the point of inheritance. Some tax law, as it relates to GLAM, is also designed to encourage the purchase and donation of cultural objects as a mechanism to ensure they remain in the state in cases where there are insufficient funds for the state to make a direct purchase. As we shall see in Chapter 9 there are some classes of object that require a licence to be exported, but at a maximum an embargo of one year from the date of the application for the licence can be imposed — after which the owners are free to export the object for sale or other purposes.

Tax and Inheritance

There is no CAT on money left to you by a spouse or civil partner on their decease.

There is also no requirement to pay tax on a gift or inheritance up to a certain limit depending on your relationship with the person leaving the inheritance or making the gift, known as the 'disponer.' The limits below are lifetime limits, so the threshold once passed is not reset by a new inheritance.

If you are the child of the disponer; the grandchild of the disponer if your parent has died and you are under 18, or; you are the foster child of the disponer then you pay CAT on any moneys over €335,000.[1] If you are a sibling of the disponer; a grandparent, grandchild or other relative

---

[1] To increase to €400,000 from 2025.

of direct descent of the disponer; a niece or nephew of the disponer or equivalent foster child relationships the CAT threshold is €32,500.[2] Any relationship not covered by the scenarios above has a limit of €16,250.[3] Prior to 2012, the maximum threshold was €542,544 and the CAT rate was 22%. The CAT thresholds outlined above will increase from January 2025 as announced in Budget 2025, after the government had previously indicated a willingness to address some of the "unfairness and anomalies in inheritance tax",[4] while opposition parties sought to increase it.

So, what mechanisms exist to reduce tax bills on inheritance for the owners (and in some cases creators) of cultural objects?

Gifts and Inheritances of Heritage Property

Sections 77 and 78 of the Capital Acquisitions Tax Act 2003 address the issue of exemptions to CAT for heritage property.[5] Under s 77, gifts and inheritances of pictures, prints, books, manuscripts, works of art, jewellery, scientific collections or "other things not held for the purposes of trading" are exempt from CAT where certain conditions are satisfied: the property is of national, scientific, historic or artistic interest; the property is kept permanently in the state; and, reasonable facilities for viewing are afforded to members of the public or to recognised bodies or to associations of persons.

The exemption also applies to houses and gardens in the state not held for the purposes of trading which are of national, scientific, historic or artistic interest; reasonable facilities for viewing were afforded to the public during the three-year period preceding the gift or inheritance; and, reasonable facilities for viewing continue to be afforded to the public after the inheritance.

Section 78 addresses instances where heritage property has been held in a family-controlled company. Where it would otherwise qualify for exemption on the basis above then a gift or inheritance of shares in that company will be exempt up to the value of the shares that relate to that heritage property.

---

[2] To increase to €40,000 from 2025.
[3] To increase to €20,000 from 2025.
[4] Cormac McQuinn, '"Unfairness" and "anomalies" in inheritance tax should be considered before budget, Taoiseach says' *The Irish Times* <https://www.irishtimes.com/politics/2024/07/16/unfairness-and-anomalies-in-inheritance-tax-should-be-considered-before-budget-taoiseach-says/> accessed 21 August 2024.
[5] Confusingly 'property' is used here in the same way as 'object' is in the Act of 1997, not in the way 'property' is used in the Historic and Archaeological Heritage and Miscellaneous Provisions Act 2023, to mean a monument or building.

Donation of Heritage Items

Section 1003 of the Taxes Consolidation Act 1997 provides relief to taxpayers who donate 'heritage items' to Irish national collections. Section 1003(2)(a) defines heritage items as "any kind of heritage item, including — any archaeological item, archive, book, estate record, manuscript and painting, and… any collection of cultural items and any collection of such items in their setting" that are determined by a selection committee consisting of an officer nominated by the minister,[6] the Chief Executive of the Heritage Council, the Director of the Arts Council, the Director of the National Archives, the Director of the National Gallery of Ireland, the Director of the National Museum of Ireland and the Director and Chief Executive of the Irish Museum of Modern Art and the Director of the Crawford Art Gallery Cork Ltd consider to be

> "an outstanding example of the type of item involved, pre-eminent in its class, whose export from the State would constitute a diminution of Ireland's accumulated cultural heritage or whose import into the State would constitute a significant enhancement of the accumulated cultural heritage of Ireland and must be suitable for acquisition by the Approved Bodies."[7]

The approved bodies are the National Archives, the National Gallery of Ireland, the National Museum of Ireland, the National Library of Ireland, the Irish Museum of Modern Art and the Crawford Art Gallery Cork Ltd, or, with the consent of the Minister for Finance, any other body wholly or partly funded by the State, public or local authority approved by the minister.

The open market value (OMV) of the item or collection of items must be €150,000 or more and in the case of a collection of items, one item must be worth at least €50,000. The exception to this requirement relates to collections of archives or manuscript materials that have been held together in a collection for at least 30 years, in which case there is no requirement for a single item to be worth €50,000 or more, but the baseline requirement for a valuation of €150,000 or more remains.

Next, a valuation is carried out by Revenue, who will usually engage a third-party expert to advise on the value of the heritage item or collection. The potential donee of the item or collection also places a value on the item or collection on the application form when applying for s 1003 relief. The OMV for the determination of tax credit is the lower of the two valuations.

---

[6] The Minister for Tourism, Culture, Arts, Gaeltacht, Sport and Media.
[7] Revenue, *Payment of Tax by Means of Donation of Heritage Items* (2023) p 3.

A tax credit of 80% of the market value of the item can then be set against taxpayers' liabilities for income tax, corporation tax, capital gains tax or gift and inheritance tax. Following Budget 2023, the maximum amount of tax credits available per year across all s 1003 donations is €8m. Any tax credit is first set against any arrears that may exist and then can be set against current or future liabilities. Tax relief may be assigned to family members and is in addition to the CAT thresholds ordinarily available on gifts/inheritances. In the event of the death of the donee, any tax credits remaining may be transferred to the donee's spouse.

A list of tax relief granted under s 1003 is available online,[8] with some notable entries including film maker Neil Jordan's archive at a valuation of €2.75m, WB Yeats' Nobel Prize Medal at a valuation of €1.5m and James Joyce's *Finnegan's Wake* manuscripts at a little under €1.2m.

An example of how a s 1003 donation worked in this way was the purchase of Old Masters from the Beit Collection at Russborough House by Denis O'Brien, John Gallagher and Lochlann Quinn. The three paintings were due to be sold by the Alfred Beit Foundation at auction, but were purchased by Quinn, Gallagher and O'Brien. O'Brien and Quinn donated their paintings to the National Gallery in return for tax breaks of a reported €2.8m and €1.6m respectively.

The painting purchased by Gallagher appears to be in Russborough House 'on loan from the Apollo Foundation.'[9] Gallagher is not listed as a trustee of the Apollo Foundation,[10] so the exact ownership of the painting is unclear. The governance documents available online state that the charity does not own and/or lease land or property,[11] so the painting may be on loan to the charity or held in trust by it, then loaned to Russborough House.

---

[8] The list of s 1003 reliefs granted so far is a direct download from <https://assets.gov.ie/283305/f5f00eb0-c315-4759-bba8-0cdd277b2f34.pdf> accessed 21 August 2024.

[9] Charity Commission for England and Wales, 'Register of Charities' <https://register-of-charities.charitycommission.gov.uk/charity-details/?regid=290351&subid=0> accessed 21 August 2024.

[10] Charity Commission for England and Wales, 'Register of Charities' <https://register-of-charities.charitycommission.gov.uk/charity-search/-/charity-details/290351/trustees> accessed 21 August 2024.

[11] Charity Commission for England and Wales, 'Register of Charities' <https://register-of-charities.charitycommission.gov.uk/charity-search/-/charity-details/290351/governance> accessed 21 August 2024.

Loan of Art Objects

Under s 236 of the Taxes Consolidation Act 1997, an art object meaning a picture, sculpture, print, book, manuscript, piece of jewellery, furniture or scientific collection which the Minister,[12] on application to them in that behalf by a person who owns or occupies a relevant building or a relevant garden, as the case may be, determines to be an object which is intrinsically of significant national, scientific, historical or aesthetic interest and is an object to which reasonable access is afforded and in which reasonable viewing facilities are made available to the public

> "provided for not less than 60 days (including not less than 40 days during the period commencing on the 1st day of May and ending on the 30th day of September) in any year and, on each such day, such access is afforded and such facilities for viewing are provided in a reasonable manner and at reasonable times for a period, or periods in the aggregate, of not less than 4 hours." (See section on 'approved buildings' below.)

Access must be available on the same days and the same times as access to the building or garden in which the object is kept. Any fees charged must be reasonable so as not to deter public access.

Once these conditions are satisfied and a body corporate incurs an expense solely in or solely in connection with, or is deemed to incur an expense solely in connection with the provision of a benefit or a facility in consisting of a loan of that art object to an individual then that benefit or facility is not taxable as a benefit in kind for the purposes of s 118 or a distribution for the purposes of s 436.

An authorised person may at any reasonable time enter a building or garden in which the art object is kept in order to inspect the art object.

Another benefit to loaning objects is contained under s 606 of the 1997 Act. This section applies to any object being any picture, print, book, manuscript, sculpture, piece of jewellery or work of art which is determined by Revenue to have an OMV of not less than €31,740 at the date when the object is loaned to a gallery or museum in the state and is the subject of or included in a display to which the public is afforded reasonable access in the gallery or museum to which it is loaned for a period of not less than ten years (or six years for loans prior to 2 February 2006[13]) from the date it is loaned.

---

[12] The Minister for Housing, Local Government and Heritage.
[13] Chartered Accountants Ireland, 'Revenue Note for Guidance: Disposals of work

Once these circumstances have been met at the end of the qualifying period if the object is disposed of by the person making the loan, then the disposal "shall be treated for the purposes of the Capital Gains Tax Acts as being made for such consideration as to secure that neither a gain nor a loss accrues on the disposal." The approved bodies, as we have seen above, include other bodies wholly or partly funded by the State, public or local authority approved by the minister.

Expenditure on Approved Buildings, Gardens and Objects

Section 482 of the Taxes Consolidation Act 1997 allows for tax relief for the owners of approved buildings including their surrounding gardens, approved gardens existing independently, approved buildings used in tourist accommodation subject to certain conditions and for approved objects in an approved building or garden.

An approved building is one in which determinations have been made by the minister[14] that it is a building which is of significant historical, architectural or aesthetic interest and has been determined by Revenue that reasonable access to the building is afforded to the public.

Similarly, an approved garden is one in which determinations have been made by the minister that it is a garden which is of significant horticultural, scientific, historical, architectural or aesthetic interest and has been determined by Revenue that reasonable access to the garden is afforded to the public. These determinations are made on the return of application forms, which are available online for Revenue and by writing to the Department for Housing, Local Government and Heritage.[15]

Reasonable public access comprises access to the whole or a substantial part of the building or garden being available at the same time; access available at reasonable times and in a reasonable manner subject to temporary closures for repair, maintenance and restoration works and access available for a minimum of 60 days per year, 40 of which must be in the period 1 May to 1 September inclusive. Further, access must be available for the whole of National Heritage Week (as far as it falls between 1 May and 1 September); daily viewing times must be for a period of at least four hours; admission

---

of art, etc, loaned for public display' <https://www.charteredaccountants.ie/taxsourcetotal/1997/en/act/pub/0039/nfg/sec0606-nfg.html> accessed 21 August 2024.

[14] The Minister for Housing, Local Government and Heritage.
[15] All details available in: Revenue, *Expenditure on Approved Buildings and Gardens* (2023).

prices where they are charged must be reasonable, so as not to dissuade visitors; opening times must be advertised in local and national newspapers and a sign must be erected outside the building or garden notifying visiting times. Claimants of tax relief under s 482 must also notify Fáilte Ireland in relation to access to the building or garden.

Revenue carries out annual checks of approved buildings and gardens to ensure that access requirements are met, and claimants must facilitate access by authorised officers of Revenue and the Department of Housing, Local Government and Heritage to examine any works in respect of which relief was claimed.

If the above requirements are met, then tax relief may be claimed on expenditure incurred on the repair, maintenance or restoration of an approved building, or the maintenance or restoration or any garden or grounds of an ornamental nature occupied or enjoyed within that building. This relief is only available where no other grants or reimbursements are recoverable from another source.

Additionally, relief up to €6,350 on aggregate is available for the installation, maintenance or replacement of a security alarm system in the approved house or garden, the provision of public liability insurance for the approved building or garden and the repair, maintenance or restoration of approved objects in an approved building or garden provided they have been on display for a period of at least two years from the year in which the expenditure was claimed.

In this instance, approved objects must meet the same criteria as for art objects (see above) but must be the property of the owner or occupier of the approved building or garden, rather than on loan to the owner or occupier.

All reliefs under s 482 are subject to High-Income Individuals Restriction, which determines the amount of relief available based on income and ring-fenced income. The calculations are outside the remit of this book, but Revenue have made a guide available online.[16]

---

[16] Revenue, 'High-Income Individuals' Restriction Tax Year 2010 onwards' <https://www.revenue.ie/en/tax-professionals/tdm/income-tax-capital-gains-tax-corporation-tax/part-15/15-02a-05.pdf> accessed 21 August 2024.

Imports, Exports and Tax

If moving cultural objects within the EU, they can be moved freely with no customs control. Objects travelling outside of the EU will need to be accompanied by sufficient customs documentation, for instance a pro-forma invoice, commercial invoice, single administrative document (SAD) or ATA Carnet.

A pro-forma invoice is a preliminary bill of sale sent to buyers when an order is placed and in advance of a shipment or delivery of goods. It will usually describe the purchased items, price, and other important information such as the shipping weight and transport charges. A commercial invoice is a request for payment for goods sold internationally and is the basis upon which taxes, tariffs, customs or duties are calculated.

In the EU, the SAD is a form used

> "for customs declarations in the EU, Switzerland, Norway, Iceland, Turkey, the Republic of North Macedonia and Serbia. It is composed of a set of eight copies each with a different function. Using one single document reduces the administrative burden and increases the standardisation and harmonisation of data collected on trade."[17]

It is used for trade with non-EU countries and for the movement of non-EU goods within the EU.

ATA Carnets are international customs and temporary import-export documents and are presented when entering a carnet country. At present the countries that are members of the ATA carnet chain or signatories to the Istanbul Convention are:

> "Albania, Algeria, Andorra, Australia, Austria, Bahrain, Belarus, Belgium, Bosnia & Herzegovina, Brazil, Bulgaria, Canada, Chile, China, Cote d'Ivoire, Croatia, Cyprus, Czech Republic, Denmark, Estonia, Finland, France, Germany, Gibraltar, Greece, Hong Kong, Hungary, Iceland, India, Indonesia, Iran, Ireland, Israel, Italy, Japan, Kazakhstan, Korea, Latvia, Lebanon, Lithuania, Luxembourg, Macao, Macedonia (Republic of), Madagascar, Malaysia, Malta, Mauritius, Mexico, Moldova, Mongolia, Montenegro, Morocco, Netherlands, New Zealand, Norway, Pakistan, Poland, Portugal, Romania, Russia, Senegal, Serbia, Singapore, Slovakia, Slovenia, South Africa, Spain, Sri Lanka (except for professional equipment), Sweden, Switzerland, Thailand, Tunisia, Turkey,

---

[17] European Commission, 'The single administrative document' <https://taxation-customs.ec.europa.eu/single-administrative-document-sad_en> accessed 21 August 2024.

Ukraine, United Kingdom, United States (except for international trade fairs and exhibitions), United Arab Emirates."[18]

There is no requirement for an ATA carnet for goods moving between any two EU countries on this list.

In Ireland, ATA carnets are guaranteed by Dublin Chamber of Commerce, to whom application must be made online.[19] Original paintings / works of art and antiques are two of the allowable categories of goods for an ATA carnet. There is no mention of heritage or cultural objects. Goods brought in under an ATA carnet are exempt from customs duties and VAT on condition that they are re-exported within 12 months.

VAT and Artists

Under s 195(12) of the Taxes Consolidation Act 1997, artists can apply for exemption from income tax on income earned from the sale of artistic works up to a limit of €50,000 per annum. Revenue can make determinations in relation to books or other forms of writing, plays, musical compositions, paintings or other pictures and sculptures. According to the "[g]uidelines drawn up under Section 195(12) of the Taxes Consolidation Act 1997 for the Artists Exemption Scheme by An Comhairle Ealaíon and the Minister for Arts, Heritage and the Gaeltacht,"[20] the work must be determined to be both original and creative and a work which is generally recognised as having either cultural or artistic merit.

This exemption does not apply to the application of VAT. Artists are required to register for VAT if they provide services worth more than €37,500 per annum or sell works in excess of €75,000 per annum. Services provided by artists, such as giving talks or facilitating workshops or classes are VAT exempt.

The sale of works is subject to VAT at the reduced rate of 13.5%.

---

[18] Dublin Chamber of Commerce, 'ATA Carnets' <https://www.dublinchamber.ie/Export-Services/ATA-Carnets> accessed: 21 August 2024.

[19] Dublin Chamber of Commerce, 'e-ATA Carnets' <http://www.e-ata.ie/> accessed 21 August 2024.

[20] An Comhairle Ealaíon and the Minister for Arts, Heritage and the Gaeltacht, 'Guidelines drawn up under Section 195 (12) of the Taxes Consolidation Act 1997 for the Artists Exemption Scheme' <https://www.revenue.ie/en/personal-tax-credits-reliefs-and-exemptions/documents/artist-exemption-guidelines.pdf> accessed 21 August 2024.

Basic Income for the Arts

In April 2022, a Basic Income for the Arts (BIA) scheme was launched which allocated funding of €25m to 2000 artists on a random selection basis. The definition of 'Arts' was extremely broad and included support workers – for instance hair designers, make-up artists circus artists and most oddly of all, architects. This is because the definition of arts from s 2(1) of the Arts Act 2003 was used.[21] There are 566 architects' practices listed on the RIAI website alone.[22] This contrasts with the artists' exemption scheme, which is allocated to those that produce 'works' that are original and creative and are generally recognised as having either cultural or artistic merit. To put it in context, 4426 works were determined by Revenue to have been created that met this requirement during the period 2017 to 2023.[23] While some artists have multiple entries — Turtle Bunbury for instance having 12 works during this period — each individual is limited to €50,000 per annum free of income tax.

The question in relation to BIA is why the criteria were different to those for a Revenue determination? Arguably the most logical way of determining who is an artist is by checking artists exemption records and assigning BIA to those individuals, but this is presumably problematic from a personal data perspective.

It was reported that for the initial BIA scheme over 9,000 applications were made and only 2,000 (chosen at random) were selected to receive the payment.[24] Of the 9,000 who applied 8,200 met the eligibility criteria. Calls were made to retain, extend and expand the existing scheme when it finished in 2025 and as part of Budget 2025 €35m was announced to fund the scheme beyond the end of the three-year pilot.[25]

---

[21] 'Arts' includes, in particular, visual arts, theatre, literature, music, dance, opera, film, circus and architecture.

[22] RIAI, 'Practice Directory' <https://www.riai.ie/work-with-an-architect/find-an-architect/practice-directory/eyJyZXN1bHRfcGFnZSI6Indvcmstd2l0aC1hbi1hcmNoaXRlY3RcL2ZpbmQtYW4tYXJjaGl0ZWN0XC9wcmFjdGljZS1kaXJlY3RvcnlcLyIsImxpbWl0IjoiMTAwIn0/P200> accessed 21 August 2024.

[23] Revenue, 'List of individuals who received a favourable determination under Section 195 Taxes Consolidation Act 1997 during the period 21 April 1998 to 31 December 2001, from 1 April 2002 to 30 December 2016, from 1 January 2017 to 31 December 2023 and from 1 January 2024 onwards' <https://www.revenue.ie/en/corporate/information-about-revenue/statistics/other-datasets/artist-exemption.aspx> accessed 21 August 2024.

[24] Irma McLoughlin, 'Why we should keep the Basic Income for the Arts' <https://www.rte.ie/culture/2024/0715/1459026-the-case-for-keeping-the-basic-income-for-the-arts/> accessed 21 August 2024.

[25] Performing Arts Forum, 'Retain, Extend and Expand Ireland's Basic Income for the Arts Pilot' https://performingartsforum.ie/ accessed 21 August 2024.

The Margin Scheme

Under s 2(1) of the EU VAT Directive

> "In respect of the supply of second-hand goods, works of art, collectors' items or antiques carried out by taxable dealers, Member States shall apply a special scheme for taxing the profit margin made by the taxable dealer, in accordance with the provisions of this Subsection."[26]

This scheme is known as the margin scheme and allows dealers to only pay VAT on the difference between the sale price and the purchase price of the goods.

Imports and Exports

Sales of goods to a business or VAT registered person in another EU country that has a valid VAT number are not liable for VAT. If the business to which the sale is being made does not have a valid VAT number, then VAT should be charged at the rate applicable in the country of the business or VAT registered person making the sale.

According to Revenue guidance "for VAT purposes, exports are goods directly dispatched to a destination outside the EU VAT area. The term EU VAT area means the EU, except for territories that are part of EU Member States. These territories are not regarded as being part of the EU for VAT purposes."[27] These exports are not liable for VAT.

If an item is transported for use in an exhibition, it is generally not liable for VAT and duties as long as it is returned within a set timeframe. In the EU this timeframe is two years, but varies from country to country outside the EU.

"Collector's pieces and works of art of an educational, scientific or cultural character" can be imported [into Ireland] free of VAT, but not from customs duty.[28] In order for this relief to be available they cannot

---

[26] Council Directive 2006/112/EC of 28 November 2006 on the common system of value added tax [2006] OJ L 347/1.

[27] Revenue, 'Goods and Services to and from abroad' <https://www.revenue.ie/en/vat/goods-and-services-to-and-from-abroad/vat-and-exports/index.aspx> accessed 21 August 2024.

[28] Revenue, 'Importation of collectors' pieces and works of art' <https://www.revenue.ie/en/customs/businesses/relief-duty-vat/collectors-art/index.aspx> accessed 21 August 2024.

be intended for sale, they must be imported by museums, galleries or other institutions approved by Revenue and they must be imported free of charge, or if imported for payment they cannot be supplied by a taxable person. Otherwise, the reduced VAT rate of 13.5% applies.

Free Ports

Free ports are designated areas that are subject to a broad array of special regulatory requirements, tax breaks and government support and are designed to specifically encourage businesses that import, process and then re-export goods. There is normally a physical boundary around the freeport that is staffed by customs officers who monitor all goods entering or leaving the freeport who must report and make written declarations to the customs officers in relation to the consignments they are carrying.

Within the EU, freeports are allowable under the Union Customs Code, which designates 'free zones' as:

> "enclosed areas within the customs territory of the Union where non-Union goods can be introduced free of import duty, other charges (i.e. taxes) and commercial policy measures. Such goods may, following the period in the free zones, be released for free circulation (subject to payment of import duty and other charges), or be placed under another special procedure (e.g. inward processing, temporary admission or end-use procedures – under the conditions laid down for these procedures) or re-exported. Union goods may also be entered into or stored, moved, used, processed or consumed in free zones. Such goods may afterwards be exported or brought into other parts of the customs territory of the Union."[29]

Free ports therefore act as storage places which offer a "temporary exemption of taxes for an unlimited quantity of time"[30] and are resultingly widely used within international art markets by collectors and dealers. A work can be purchased, stored in a freeport anonymously without paying any customs or duties and then re-exported to sell again without paying any customs or duties.[31] The London art dealer Inigo Philbrick, who was convicted of wire fraud in the US had been operating a scheme including

---

[29] European Commission, 'Free zones' <https://taxation-customs.ec.europa.eu/customs-4/free-zones_en> accessed 21 August 2024.
[30] 'Swiss Freeports Are Home for a Growing Treasury of Art', *The New York Times* <https://www.nytimes.com/2012/07/22/business/swiss-freeports-are-home-for-a-growing-treasury-of-art.html> accessed 21 August 2024.
[31] For more infomration see European Parliament, Directorate-General for Parliamentary Research Services, R Korver, *Money laundering and tax evasion risks in free ports* (European Parliament 2018).

selling shares in artworks comprising more than 100% of their value and selling artworks or using them as loan collateral without the knowledge of their owners. This was achieved, in part, by the fact that works were stored in freeports and never seen by their owners. On occasion, blank canvasses of the correct dimensions wrapped as valuable art pieces were moved into freeports used by their owners, thus allowing a single painting to simultaneously be in multiple collections, but as nobody unpacked the items the deception was not detected.[32]

NFTs

Since 2021, Non-Funigble Tokens, or NFTs, have introduced a new mechanism for trading digital or digitised artworks. 'Non-Fungible' means a unique item that is not interchangeable, such as an artwork, 'Token' refers to a line of code that represents a programmable digital unit of value that is recorded on a digital ledger. NFTs utilise Ethereum blockchain technology and specifically the ERC-721 Non-Fungible Token Standard. The code combines at its most basic level a token ID that is a unique identifier generated at the time of creation of the token and a blockchain address. These elements are unique, which makes the token saleable as a unique item. Most NFTs also include a link to the location of the actual digital asset.

What sorts of things can be sold as an NFT? Jack Dorsey, the former CEO of Twitter (as was) sold an NFT of his first tweet on the platform for $2.5m. The 'Nyan Cat' meme (a flying cat with a pop-tart body travelling through space leaving a rainbow in its wake) sold for 300 Ethereum, or $1,048,703 at the time of writing.

In Ireland, for the purposes of taxation, NFTs are treated by Revenue as 'crypto assets,' which are

> "any digital representation of value or a right that can be transferred or stored electronically using distributed ledger technology or similar technology — this generally includes cryptocurrencies, crypto-assets, virtual currencies and digital money, or any variation of these terms."[33]

Revenue's view of 'crypto assets' is that these do not differ from other assets in terms of how they are to be treated for tax.

---

[32] For more see Orlando Whitfield, *All That Glitters* (Profile Books 2024).
[33] Revenue, 'Taxation of Crypto-Asset Transactions' (June 2024), p 3.

"Where there is a tax event arising on any transaction involving the use of crypto-assets, a taxpayer is required to keep proper records2 [*sic*] of that transaction and the affect assets, similar to other transactions. Therefore, no special tax rules for crypto-asset transactions are required."[34]

We have already seen that ss 77 and 78 of the Capital Acquisitions Tax Act 2003 address the issue of exemptions to CAT for heritage property.[35] Under s 77 gifts and inheritances of pictures, prints, books, manuscripts, works of art, jewellery, scientific collections or "other things not held for the purposes of trading" are exempt from CAT where certain requirements are met.

As an NFT is not a picture or a work of art *per se*, but rather a token containing a link to the asset itself, it would appear that NFTs cannot be treated as exempt under ss 77 and 78. The fact that NFTs are specifically created and held for the purposes of trading would also appear to preclude them from this exemption. Similarly, an NFT cannot be displayed and is not an item *per se*, so relief under ss 236 and 1003 of the Taxes Consolidation Act 1997 would appear to be unavailable.

For VAT purposes, under article 135(1)(e) of the VAT Directive,[36] transactions involving currency, bank notes, and coins used as legal tender are exempt from VAT, including both regulated and centralised currencies guaranteed by a central bank and crypto-currencies.

In the EU case of *Skatteverket v David Hedqvist*, it was held that:

"Article 135(1)(e) of the VAT Directive also covers the supply of services such as those at issue in the main proceedings, which consist of the exchange of traditional currencies for units of the 'bitcoin' virtual currency and vice versa."[37]

Following a referral from Denmark, the European Commission VAT Committee produced a working paper on the issue of VAT on NFTs. The first question that was examined was whether NFTs were currencies and therefore exempt from VAT:

"An enquiry into the world of crypto art shows that works of crypto art are bought for many reasons ranging from spectating, collecting, supporting the

---

[34] ibid, p 4.
[35] Confusingly, 'property' is used here in the same way as 'object' is in the Act of 1997, not in the way 'property' is used in the Historic and Archaeological Heritage and Miscellaneous Provisions Act 2023, to mean a monument or building.
[36] Council Directive 2006/112/EC of 28 November 2006 on the common system of value added tax [2006] OJ L347/1.
[37] Case C-264/14 *Skatteverket v David Hedqvist*, (ECJ, 22 October 2015) at 53.

work of an artist to investing. Therefore, trade in which participants exchange goods or services for works of crypto art without using (crypto) currency consists in barter in which crypto art may be used as a means of payment but nonetheless does not qualify as a currency."[38]

The VAT Committee next examined the question of whether the margin scheme for art (see above) could apply to NFTs. The Committee found that:

> "A work of crypto art is in no case a tangible property and thus does not qualify as a good as provided for by the VAT Directive" and further that "there are therefore fundamental differences between the works of art featured in [Annex IX of the VAT Directive] and works of crypto art which indicates that they cannot be seen as comparable thereby fuelling the conclusion that the margin scheme for works of art cannot apply to crypto art."[39]

By the same logic, the Committee determined that crypto art cannot avail of reduced rates of VAT applied to other art (see above).

Lastly, the VAT Committee examined the exemption from VAT for supply of services by artists (see above) and found that:

> "The first thing to be noted is that crypto art did not exist back in 1978 or at the time of accession of most of the Member States joining later. It therefore appears that Member States could not continue to apply an exemption to something that did not exist, i.e. crypto art. Moreover Article 371 of the VAT Directive expressly excludes under point 2 (a) 'assignments of patents, trademarks and other similar rights.'"[40]

Case Study: The Rory Gallagher Stratocaster

According to Rory Gallagher's official site,[41] he bought his iconic Fender Stratocaster (strat) from Crowley's Music Store in Cork for £100 on credit in 1963. The guitar had previously been owned by Jim Conlon from the *Royal Showband* who had requested a candy apple red strat, but had received the sunburst model instead. Once the red strat eventually arrived from America (possibly allowing Jim to more closely resemble the iconic look of Hank Marvin from *The Shadows*), he resold the sunburst guitar to Crowley's, from where it was purchased by Gallagher.

---

[38] European Commission, *VAT Committee (Article 398 of Directive 2006/112/EC) Working Paper No 1080*, (March 2024) para 3.2.
[39] ibid, at 3.3.1.
[40] ibid, at 3.3.3.
[41] <https://www.rorygallagher.com/1961-stratocaster/> accessed 21 August 2024.

The guitar's famously battered looks came about from a combination of heavy usage and having been stolen after a gig in 1966 and subsequently retrieved from a garden on South Circular Road, Dublin, following a TV appeal on RTÉ's 'Garda Patrol.' For guitarists who want one that looks the same, Fender Custom Shop manufactured a Rory Gallagher custom strat which are now available second-hand for around €7,000.[42]

In July 2024, news emerged that Rory Gallagher's original strat was to be auctioned by Bonham's in London with an estimate of €800,000–€1.2m, the guitar currently belonging to Dónal Gallagher, his brother and former manager. Calls for the guitar to be kept in Ireland immediately started, with the Lord Mayor of Cork stating that the guitar is

> "… totemic, especially for Cork. Bought at Crowley's Music Store and memorably played many times in concerts at Cork City Hall, from where Rory went on culturally to take on the world. It would be and should be pride of place here… It's hoped that whoever gets to acquire it would make it available publicly in Cork."[43]

At the time of writing there were at least two GoFundMe campaigns trying to raise funds to purchase the guitar, one set up by Sheena Crowley of Crowley's Music in Cork and one by the Irish Rock'n'Roll Museum Experience. An Tánaiste Micheál Martin also expressed the desire for the guitar to be reunited with Cork and that he would speak to the Minister for Tourism, Culture, Arts, Gaeltacht, Sport and Media: "I would love if we could, obviously. I will talk to Catherine Martin and see what's possible, but it would be lovely if we could get that guitar back on Leeside."[44] The concept of the Irish state spending over €1m on a 1961 Stratocaster seems remote, especially when it balked at spending a smaller amount on a surrender letter of PH Pearse from 1916 (see Chapter 9).

The exact structure of the ownership of the guitar is unknown. Dónal Gallagher stated that

> "with the proceeds raised from this instrument sale we will continue to do

---

[42] <https://reverb.com/uk/p/fender-custom-shop-rory-gallagher-tribute-stratocaster> accessed 21 August 2024.
[43] Des O'Driscoll, 'Up for sale: Cork lord mayor calls for Rory Gallagher's guitar to stay in Ireland', *Irish Examiner* <https://www.irishexaminer.com/lifestyle/artsandculture/arid-41432932.html> accessed 21 August 2024.
[44] Elaine Whelan, 'Tánaiste "would love" Rory Gallagher's guitar back in Cork', *Echo Live* <https://www.echolive.ie/corknews/arid-41438422.html> accessed 21 August 2024.

further good for Rory's name and legacy, as well as assisting good causes, that my brother would have supported."[45]

Section 76(2) of the Capital Acquisitions Tax Act 2003 allows that:

"A gift or an inheritance which is taken for public or charitable purposes is exempt from tax and is not taken into account in computing tax, to the extent that the Commissioners are satisfied that it has been, or will be, applied to purposes which, in accordance with the law of the State, are public or charitable."

Availability of this relief would of course depend on whether the guitar has already been accounted for in probate or inheritance taxes have already been paid.

As we have seen above, under s 606 of the Taxes Consolidation Act 1997, an object, being a picture print, book, manuscript, sculpture, piece of jewellery or work of art, can be exempted from CGT at the point of sale if it has been on display for ten years (or six years for loans prior to 2 February 2006) in a display to which the public is afforded reasonable access in a gallery or museum approved by the Revenue commissioners.

Notably, the word 'continuous' is absent from s 606, though 'reasonable public access is defined at s 236 (see above) as

"provided for not less than 60 days (including not less than 40 days during the period commencing on the 1st day of May and ending on the 30th day of September) in any year and, on each such day, such access is afforded and such facilities for viewing are provided in a reasonable manner and at reasonable times for a period, or periods in the aggregate, of not less than 4 hours."

The guitar has certainly been on display along with Gallagher's other guitars in the Rory Gallagher Exhibition in Ballyshannon, but it's uncertain whether the above threshold has been reached and whether the owner of the guitar (Dónal Gallagher himself, or some form of trust or foundation) has applied for s 606 relief from CGT on the sale. This will, of course, not be at issue if s 76(2) (see above) is to be availed of.

A purchaser at an auction could theoretically take advantage of s 606 by displaying the guitar in an approved institution — for instance the Crawford Art Gallery Cork Ltd — for ten years and then reselling the guitar without attracting CGT on the increase in value that would presumably accrue during this time.

---

[45] Dónal Gallagher, 'Rory Gallagher Instrument Sale <https://www.rorygallagher.com/rory-gallagher-instrument-sale/> accessed 21 August 2024.

Availing of s 606 would of course depend on whether a guitar could be deemed a 'work of art.'

Alternately, the guitar could be purchased by an individual with tax liabilities in the state, then gifted back to the State under section 1003 of the Taxes Consolidation Act 1997, which would enable the donor to claim back 80% of its value in tax relief.

As we have seen above, s 1003 allows for the donation of "any kind of heritage item." We know that the guitar has an OMV of over €150,000 and is arguably an outstanding example of the type of item involved, pre-eminent in its class, whose export from the state would constitute a diminution of Ireland's accumulated cultural heritage or whose import into the State would constitute a significant enhancement of the accumulated cultural heritage of Ireland.

It must also be suitable for acquisition by one of the approved bodies. While Gallagher's connection with Cork would seem to make the Crawford Art Gallery Cork Ltd a suitable choice, it should be remembered that the National Museum hosted an exhibition celebrating 75 years of the electric guitar called RockChic in 2006/2007 that featured Rory Gallagher's guitars.

Chapter 9

Imports, Exports and Loans

There are a variety of import and export restrictions on the movement of cultural objects internationally, into the EU, out of the EU and within the EU.

International regulations include the 1970 UNESCO Convention, the UNESCO 1954 Convention (The Hague Convention) and the 1995 UNIDROIT Convention (see also Chapter 5 and Chapter 3).

Article 7(b)(i) of the 1970 UNESCO Convention states that Parties to the convention undertake to

> "*prohibit the import* of cultural property stolen from a museum or a religious or secular public monument or similar institution in another State Party to this Convention after the entry into force of this Convention for the States concerned, provided that such property is documented as appearing in the inventory of that institution" (emphasis added).

And at 7(b)(ii) that

> "at the request of the State Party of origin to take appropriate steps to recover and return any such cultural property imported after the entry into force of this Convention in both States concerned, provided, however, that the requesting State shall pay just compensation to an innocent purchaser or to a person who has valid title to that property. Requests for recovery and return shall be made through diplomatic offices. The requesting Party shall furnish, at its expense, the documentation and other evidence necessary to establish its claim for recovery and return."

Article 9 of the 1970 UNESCO Convention declares that:

> "Any State Party to this Convention whose cultural patrimony is in jeopardy from pillage of archaeological or ethnological materials may call upon other States Parties who are affected. The States Parties to this Convention undertake, in these circumstances. to participate in a concerted international effort to determine and to carry out the necessary concrete measures, *including the control of exports and imports* and international commerce in the specific materials concerned. Pending agreement each State concerned shall take provisional measures to the

extent feasible to prevent irremediable injury to the cultural heritage of the requesting State." (Emphasis added)

While the Hague Convention is the first treaty to provide for a system of protection of cultural property in the event of armed conflict, the First Protocol to the Hague Convention provides for a system of protection specifically adapted to situations in which the territory of one state is occupied by another state. The First Protocol of 1954 Hague Convention states at part I that:

> "Each High Contracting Party undertakes to prevent the exportation, from a territory occupied by it during an armed conflict, of cultural property... undertakes to take into its custody cultural property imported into its territory either directly or indirectly from any occupied territory. This shall either be effected automatically upon the importation of the property or, failing this, at the request of the authorities of that territory... undertakes to return, at the close of hostilities, to the competent authorities of the territory previously occupied, cultural property which is in its territory, if such property has been exported in contravention of the principle laid down in the first paragraph. Such property shall never be retained as war reparations."

Chapter III Article 5 of the 1995 UNIDROIT Convention sets out that:

> "[a] Contracting State may request the court or other competent authority of another Contracting State to order the return of a cultural object illegally exported from the territory of the requesting State." Article 10(2) sets out that "the provisions of Chapter III shall apply only in respect of a cultural object that is illegally exported after this Convention enters into force for the requesting State as well as the State where the request is brought."

Article 10(3) clarifies that

> "This Convention does not in any way legitimise any illegal transaction of whatever nature which has taken place before the entry into force of this Convention or which is excluded under paragraphs (1) or (2) of this article, nor limit any right of a State or other person to make a claim under remedies available outside the framework of this Convention for the restitution or return of a cultural object stolen or illegally exported before the entry into force of this Convention."

The Convention on International Trade in Endangered Species of Wild Fauna and Flora 1973 (CITES) is an international agreement that aims to ensure that international trade in specimens of wild animals and plants does not threaten the survival of the species. This trade is diverse, ranging from live animals, such as pets, and live ornamental plants to a vast array of wildlife products derived from them, including food products, exotic leather goods, wooden musical instruments, timber, tourist curios and medicines. Levels of exploitation of some animal and plant species are high, and the trade in them, together with other factors such as habitat loss, is capable of heavily depleting their populations and even bringing some species close to extinction. Specimens include live, dead, parts, derivatives and final products, as well as specimens produced through biotechnology.

For the purposes of the convention, the EU has the status of a member state and is a party to the convention, which thus includes Ireland under its requirements. CITES regulates international trade in specimens of listed species by enforcing controls as these items cross international borders. These specimens can range from whole animals or plants, whether alive or dead, to products containing parts or derivatives of the listed species, such as cosmetics or traditional medicines.

CITES recognises four types of trade: import, export, re-export (the export of specimens previously imported), and introduction from the sea (the transportation of marine specimens taken from areas beyond national jurisdiction into a state). The CITES definition of 'trade' does not necessitate a financial transaction. All trade involving CITES-listed species requires authorisation through a system of permits and certificates, which must be obtained before the trade occurs. These permits and certificates are issued by designated management authorities in each country, who administer the CITES system and are advised by scientific authorities on the impact of trade on the status of the species. These documents must be presented to border authorities to authorise the trade. The requirements for import certificates are set out at article 4, export and re-export permits at article 5, certificates issued by states not party to the Convention at article 10.

Article 10(6) sets out the exemption that the requirements for import, export or re-export licences

> "shall not apply to the non-commercial loan, donation or exchange between scientists or scientific institutions registered by a Management Authority of their State, of herbarium specimens, other preserved, dried or embedded museum specimens, and live plant material which carry a label issued or approved by a Management Authority."

Each CITES party must enact domestic legislation to implement the convention's provisions within their territories. Parties may also choose to enforce stricter measures than those required by CITES, such as requiring permits or certificates in additional circumstances or prohibiting trade in certain specimens altogether. In Ireland, legislative basis for CITES regulations is provided for by s 53A of the Wildlife Act 1976 (as amended), which gives effect to elements of the EU Wildlife Trade Regulation (Regulation 338/97).

Imports into the EU

Cultural objects imported into the EU are governed by EU Regulation 2019/880 which sets out to protect cultural heritage and prevent money laundering and financing of terrorism by regulating the import of cultural goods into one of the largest art markets in the world.

Article 3(1) of Regulation 2019/880 states that:

> "The introduction of cultural goods referred to in Part A of the Annex which were removed from the territory of the country where they were created or discovered in breach of the laws and regulations of that country shall be prohibited. The customs authorities and the competent authorities shall take any appropriate measure when there is an attempt to introduce cultural goods as referred to in the first subparagraph".

Part A of the Annex details the types of cultural objects covered by article 3(1) and includes detailed definitions of archaeological, archival, artistic, manuscripts, furniture, antiquities and instruments.

Article 3(2) addresses the requirement for import licences or importer statements for the import of cultural goods not removed from the territory of the country where they were created or discovered in breach of the laws and regulations of that country.

Article 8 sets out that

> "The storage and the exchange of information between the authorities of the Member States, in particular regarding import licences and importer statements, shall be carried out by means of a centralised electronic system."

The centralised electronic system that will deal with the exchange of information between Member States and the online licence applications is due to become operational by 28 June 2025.

Part B of the Annex details the minimum age and value of items in order for them to require such a licence, Part C of the Annex details the minimum age and value of items in order for them to require such a statement. Archaeological items and elements of dismembered monuments over 250 years old will require a licence whatever their value. Other types of cultural objects worth €18,000 or more per item and more than 200 years old will require an importer statement.

An import licence must be issued by the competent authorities of a member state — in Ireland the Department of Tourism, Culture, Arts, Gaeltacht, Sport and Media is the competent authority for the issue of a licence to export goods outside the EU,[1] so it is probable that the department will also be the competent authority to issue import licences under Regulation 2019/880. Article 4(1) states that:

> "The holder of the goods shall apply for an import licence to the competent authority of the Member State referred to in paragraph 1 of this Article via the electronic system referred to in Article 8. The application shall be accompanied by any supporting documents and information providing evidence that the cultural goods in question have been exported from the country where they were created or discovered in accordance with the laws and regulations of that country or providing evidence of the absence of such laws and regulations at the time they were taken out of its territory."

A derogation for material ordinarily requiring a licence is set out at article 4(4) which sets out that an

> "application may be accompanied instead by any supporting documents and information providing evidence that the cultural goods in question have been exported in accordance with the laws and regulations of the last country where they were located for a period of more than five years and for purposes other than temporary use, transit, re-export or transhipment, in the following cases:(a) the country where the cultural goods were created or discovered cannot be reliably determined; or (b) the cultural goods were taken out of the country where they were created or discovered before 24 April 1972."

Article 5 addresses the requirements for importer statements and states that:

> "The import of the cultural goods listed in Part C of the Annex shall require an importer statement which the holder of the goods shall submit via the electronic system referred to in Article 8... The importer statement shall consist of: (a) a declaration signed by the holder of the goods stating that the cultural goods have been exported from the country where they were created or discovered in accordance with the laws and regulations of that country at the time they were taken out of its territory; and (b) a standardised document describing the cultural

---

[1] Revenue, 'Exportation of Cultural Goods, Archaeological Objects, Documents and Pictures' <https://www.revenue.ie/en/tax-professionals/tdm/customs/prohibitions-restrictions/exportation-of-cultural-goods.pdf> accessed 21 August 2024.

goods in question in sufficient detail for them to be identified by the authorities and to perform risk analysis and targeted controls."

A similar derogation exists at article 5(2) whereby

"the declaration may instead state that the cultural goods in question have been exported in accordance with the laws and regulations of the last country where they were located for a period of more than five years and for purposes other than temporary use, transit, re-export or transhipment, in the following cases: (a) the country where the cultural goods were created or discovered cannot be reliably determined; or (b) the cultural goods were taken out of the country where they were created or discovered before 24 April 1972."

Items listed under parts B and C of the Annex are further derogated from the requirement for an import licence or importer statement under article 3(4)(c) in cases which involve

"the temporary admission of cultural goods... into the customs territory of the Union for the purpose of education, science, conservation, restoration, exhibition, digitisation, performing arts, research conducted by academic institutions or cooperation between museums or similar institutions."

Exports from the EU

Council Regulation (EC) No 116/2009 sets out at article 2(1) that:

"The export of cultural goods outside the customs territory of the Community shall be subject to the presentation of an export licence."

Article 2(2) explains:

"The export licence shall be issued at the request of the person concerned: (a) by a competent authority of the Member State in whose territory the cultural object in question was lawfully and definitively located on 1 January 1993; (b) or, thereafter, by a competent authority of the Member State in whose territory it is located following either lawful and definitive dispatch from another Member State, or importation from a third country, or re-importation from a third country after lawful dispatch from a Member State to that country."

The phrase "lawful and definitive despatch" was examined in the UK case of R *(Simonis) v Arts Council England*,[2] and it was held that this refers to the "law of the state of physical export or dispatch,"[3] in other words, the law of the country from which the cultural goods were despatched.

---

[2] R *(Simonis) v Arts Council England* [2018] EWHC 1822 (Admin).
[3] ibid, at 62-70.

A Member State is authorised not to require export licences for the cultural goods specified in the first and second indents of category A.1 of Annex I where they are of limited archaeological or scientific interest, and provided that they are not the direct product of excavations, finds or archaeological sites within a Member State, and that their presence on the market is lawful.

The export licence may be refused, for the purposes of the regulation, where the cultural goods in question are covered by legislation protecting national treasures of artistic, historical or archaeological value in the Member State concerned.

In Ireland, the Department of Tourism, Culture, Arts, Gaeltacht, Sport and Media is the competent authority for the issue of a licence to export goods outside the EU. It issues such licences directly after procuring appropriate professional/technical advice from the relevant National Cultural Institution (see below).

Annex 1(A) of Council Regulation (EC) No 116/2009 sets out the categories of cultural objects[4] to which the regulation applies, and the minimum ages that the objects must have attained before the regulation applies. For instance, printed books, singly or in collections, must be more than 100 years old before a licence is required. Archives and documents must be more than 50 years old. Printed maps must be more than 200 years old. Annex 1(B) details the minimum values different categories of cultural objects must hold before being required to apply for an export licence; for instance, there is no minimum value for archives, but mosaics or drawings must be worth at least €15,000.

Commission Implementing Regulation (EU) No 1081/2012 sets out the technicalities of how licences should be issued, their format, period of validity and the use of one off or open licences depending on the type of cultural good being exported and for what purposes.

Exports within the EU

Section 49(1) of the National Cultural Institutions Act 1997 sets out the cultural objects to which a requirement for an export licence applies:

> "(a) any document (other than a document wholly in print) which is not less

---

[4] The terms 'cultural objects' and 'cultural goods' are used interchangeably in the Regulation.

than 70 years old of a value exceeding such an amount (if any) as may be specified by order made by the Minister,
(b) any painting (other than a painting in the ownership of the person who painted it) not less than 25 years old of a value exceeding such amount (if any) as may be specified by order made by the Minister which is painted entirely by hand on any medium and in any material and which either—
  (i) originated in Ireland, or
  (ii) has been in the State for not less than 25 years,
(c) any document declared by an order made by the Minister under subsection (2) to be an article to which this Part applies,
(d) any cultural object entered in the register,
(e) any archaeological object,
(f) any object specified in the Third Schedule which is made in Ireland, is not less than 70 years old and the value of which is not less than £35,000,
(g) any cultural object falling within a class of cultural objects designated by order by the Minister."

The 'register' referred to at (d) above is described at s 48:

"Subject to the provisions of this section, the Minister shall, as soon as may be after the commencement of this Part, establish and maintain a register of cultural objects of a class or classes denoted in such manner (including by reference to monetary value) as may be determined by the Minister whose export from the State would constitute a serious loss to the heritage of Ireland (in this Act referred to as "the register")". This register comprises (at time of writing) 47 items, 46 of which are paintings in the National Gallery, and one of which is the "Surrender letter written by Padraig Pearse on 30th April 1916 in Arbour Hill Prison."[5] (See Case Study below)

Section 49(2) as referred to at (c) above sets out that:

"[t]he Minister may by order declare any document, which is in his or her opinion of national, historical, genealogical or literary interest, to be an article to which this Part applies."

Furthermore, at s 49(3):

"[t]he Minister may by order declare any object, which is in his or her opinion an archaeological object, to be an article to which this Part applies"

— in other words that requires an export licence.

Section 50 states that subject to the provisions of that section, the minister shall, on the application of a person in that behalf, grant to that person

---

[5] The register is available online at <https://www.gov.ie/pdf/?file=https://assets.gov.ie/96266/b0ff164e-53b7-4dea-a42b-472c5c7be08b.pdf> accessed 21 August 2024.

a licence authorising the person to export an article to which that part applies.

Section 50(2) lists a number of provisions that apply where an application is made to the minister for a licence in respect of an article referred to in s 49(1)(d): "any cultural object entered in the register."

> "(a) in the case of an article that for an uninterrupted period of 5 years before the commencement of this section was in the care of an institution specified in the Second Schedule or in any other institution owned or funded wholly or substantially by the State or by any public or local authority, the Minister may, at his or her discretion, grant or refuse to grant the licence and any such licence may be subject to such conditions and restrictions as the Minister determines and specifies in the licence,
> (b) in the case of a cultural object that comes into the care of an institution referred to in paragraph (a) after the commencement of this section and remains in such care for an uninterrupted period of 10 years, the Minister may, at his or her discretion, grant or refuse to grant the licence and any such licence may be subject to such conditions and restrictions as the Minister determines and specifies in the licence,
> (c) in any other case, the Minister shall grant the licence and any such licence may be subject to such conditions and restrictions as the Minister determines and specifies in the licence including the condition that the object shall not be exported before the expiration of one year from the date of the application for the licence."

Section 50(3) lists a number of provisions that apply where an application is made to the minister for a licence in respect of an article referred to in s 49(1)(e): 'any archaeological object':

> "Where an application is made to the Minister for a licence in respect of an article referred to in section 49(1)(e), the Minister may, at his or her discretion, grant or refuse to grant the licence and any such licence may be subject to such conditions and restrictions as the Minister determines and specifies in the licence."

A licence granted under s 50 shall remain in force for such period as may be specified therein, a person who holds a licence must comply with the conditions of the licence or be guilty of an offence and shall be liable on summary conviction to a fine not exceeding £1,500.

Sections 50(6) to (8) detail that, where an application is made to the minister for a licence to export an article, the minister may request the applicant to afford such facilities as they think necessary for the making within a reasonable time of copies of the article whether by photographic or other means, and in that case they shall not grant the licence unless the request has been complied with. The minister may then make copies of the article and use any copies in any manner which they think proper. Where copyright subsists in an article the making of copies pursuant to that subsection shall not constitute an infringement of that copyright.

Under s 51(1) of the National Cultural Institutions Act 1997, the minister may delegate one or more of their functions in relation to the granting of export licences as follows:

> "in relation to museum heritage objects, to the Board of the [National] Museum [of Ireland] or the Heritage Council, (ii) in relation to paintings, to the Governors and Guardians [of the National Gallery of Ireland], the Heritage Council or the Board of the Irish Museum of Modern Art Company, and (iii) in relation to documents, to the Board of the [National] Library [of Ireland], the Heritage Council or the Director of the National Archives."

According to the Department of Tourism, Culture, Arts, Gaeltacht, Media and Sport's, 'Export Licensing Guidelines" application for licences in relation to documents/manuscripts are issued directly by the Department in consultation with the National Library, applications for licences in relation to paintings/drawings are issued directly by the National Gallery and applications in relation to archaeological items are issued directly by the National Museum.[6]

Imports within the EU

The free movement of goods is a fundamental aspect of the European project. It has significantly contributed to the development of the internal market, benefiting European citizens and businesses alike, and remains central to EU policies. The current internal market facilitates the buying and selling of products across 27 Member States, encompassing a total population of over 490 million people.

The Treaty on the Functioning of the European Union (TFEU), which emerged from the Lisbon Treaty, evolved from the Treaty establishing the European Community (TEC or EC Treaty), originally instituted by the Treaty of Maastricht. The EC Treaty itself was founded on the Treaties of Rome, which established the European Economic Community (EEC) in 1957. The formation of the European Union through the Treaty of

---

[6] Department of Tourism, Culture, Arts, Gaeltacht, Media and Sport, 'Export Licensing Guidelines' <https://www.gov.ie/pdf/?file=https://assets.gov.ie/200031/b35e3951-b2cd-413d-b652-5473d2b840cb.pdf> accessed 21 August 2024.

Maastricht on 7 February 1992 marked a significant milestone toward the political unification of Europe.

The main Treaty provisions governing the free movement of goods are: Article 34 TFEU: This pertains to intra-EU imports and prohibits 'quantitative restrictions and all measures having equivalent effect' between Member States; Article 35 TFEU: This concerns exports from one Member State to another and similarly prohibits 'quantitative restrictions and all measures having equivalent effect'; and, Article 36 TFEU: This allows for derogations from the internal market freedoms outlined in Articles 34 and 35 TFEU, justified on specific grounds.

Articles 34 and 35 TFEU encompass all types of imports and exports of goods and products. The scope of goods covered is extensive, including any items with economic value: "goods, within the meaning of the ... Treaty, are products which can be valued in money and are capable of forming the subject of commercial transactions."[7]

The Court of Justice has clarified the classification of specific products in its rulings. For instance, works of art are considered goods.[8] Similarly, coins that are no longer in circulation as currency, as well as bank notes and bearer cheques, fall under the definition of goods.

A Member State's duty to protect its national treasures and heritage may justify measures that create obstacles to imports or exports. The definition of a 'national treasure' is subject to interpretation, but it is clear that such items must have genuine "artistic, historic, or archaeological value." within the meaning of article 36 TFEU. It is the responsibility of the Member States to determine which items qualify under this category. In Ireland, these are defined under s 49 of the National Cultural Institutions Act 1997 (see above).

Directive 2014/60/EU on the Return of Cultural Objects Unlawfully Removed from the Territory of a Member State is an update to Directive 93/7/EEC of 1993 that clarifies and extends existing rules on the return of all cultural objects considered by an EU country as national treasures which have been unlawfully removed from its territory after 1 January 1993. 2014/60/EU states at (9) that:

> "The scope of this Directive should be extended to any cultural object classified

---

[7] Case 7/68 *Commission v Italy* [1968] ECR 423.
[8] Case 7/78 *Thompson* [1978] ECR 2247.

or defined by a Member State under national legislation or administrative procedures as a national treasure possessing artistic, historic or archaeological value within the meaning of Article 36 TFEU. This Directive should thus cover objects of historical, paleontological, ethnographic, numismatic interest or scientific value, whether or not they form part of public or other collections or are single items, and whether they originate from regular or clandestine excavations, provided that they are classified or defined as national treasures. Furthermore, cultural objects classified or defined as national treasures should no longer have to belong to categories or comply with thresholds related to their age and/or financial value in order to qualify for return under this Directive."

Once alerted by another EU country of the discovery of an object, a country has six months to determine whether it is a national treasure.

The country from which the object was unlawfully removed has three years to initiate return proceedings from the moment it becomes aware of the object's location and the identity of its owner or holder.

Return proceedings cannot be initiated more than 30 years after the object's unlawful removal[9] from the requesting EU country. This time limit extends to 75 years for objects that are part of public collections or religious institutions in countries where they benefit from special protection rules.

The Historic and Archaeological Heritage and Miscellaneous Provisions Act 2023 addresses the issue of the export of Chapter 8 monuments (monuments to which general or special protection applies) at s 43 which states that a person shall not export, or direct or authorise the export of a Chapter 8 monument other than under and in accordance with a licence, unless the export is done under and in accordance with a licence which has been granted under section 50 of the National Cultural Institutions Act 1997 (see above), and the minister has approved the terms and conditions of such licence in so far as they relate to the export of the Chapter 8 monument the subject of the licence (at the time of writing this section has yet to be commenced).

International Loans

International loans involve a detailed and carefully managed process to ensure the safe transport, exhibition, and return of artworks between institutions across different countries. It is worth noting at this point

---

[9] 'Unlawfully removed' can also mean failure to return after temporary export / loan or breach of a relevant condition of an export or loan — see Article 2(2).

though, that most of what are referred to as loans within this context are in fact bailments (see Chapter 3).

International loans provide an important opportunity for cultural exchange as they facilitate the sharing of cultural heritage and artistic achievements between countries, enriching public knowledge and appreciation of different cultures. Loans also allow museums and galleries to offer diverse and comprehensive exhibitions that might not be possible without borrowed pieces supplementing their permanent collections, while allowing scholars and the public to study and engage with cultural objects that would otherwise be inaccessible.

Many institutions will have a loans policy that will detail the legislative basis under which they may make or receive loans, the process by which an application is made, the criteria under which a decision to lend may be judged — for instance, consideration of the

> "safety, security, physical condition and degree of rarity of the objects, the value of the loan to the recipient, the facilities required to service the loan, and the resources of either the borrower or [the recipient]"[10]

as well as

> "consideration of circumstances that would be damaging to the Museum's standing and reputation, or any exhibition which includes objects that are known to have been illegally or unethically acquired by the current holder."[11]

A code of practice outlining "General Principles on the Administration of Loans and Exchange of Works of Art Between Institutions"[12] were drawn up and accepted by the members of the international group of organisers of large-scale exhibitions which was founded by the Réunion des Musées Nationaux in 1992. Originally consisting of European institutions, the group was joined in 1993 by major museums in North America and elsewhere in the world. These guidelines were intended to inform, simplify and make more cost-effective the organisation and administration of major international exhibitions of works of art and were drawn up originally in

---

[10] National Museum of Ireland, 'Loans Policy' <https://www.museum.ie/en-IE/About/Corporate-Information/Policies-Guidelines/Loans-Policy> accessed 21 August 2024.
[11] ibid.
[12] International Group of Organisers of Large-Scale Exhibitions, 'General Principles on the Administration of Loans and Exchange of Works of Art Between Institutions' <https://www.readkong.com/page/general-principles-on-the-administration-of-loans-and-1475097> accessed 21 August 2024.

1995 and revised in 2002. The International Council of Museums (ICOM) drew up a set of guidelines for loans as a result of an ICOM working party set up to study this matter in 1971. The members of the working group met three times between 1972 and 1973 resulting in the 'ICOM Guidelines for Loan Agreements' in 1974.[13] The process of arranging international loans will usual usually follow some or all of the following steps:

Firstly the borrowing institution identifies the cultural objects it wishes to borrow and formally requests the loan from the lending institution. Both parties then negotiate and draft a loan agreement, detailing the terms and conditions, including loan duration, insurance, transport, display conditions, and responsibilities (see Chapter 6). Secondly, before shipping, a detailed condition report for each cultural object is created. This report documents the current state of the object with descriptions and photographs, serving as a reference to ensure the item is returned in the same condition. Thirdly, the borrowing institution typically arranges insurance, often 'nail-to-nail' coverage, which protects the artwork from the time it is removed from its original location until it is returned. Fourthly, the borrowing institution may also apply for legal immunity from seizure to protect the artwork from legal claims while in transit or on display (see below). Fifthly, packing and transportation will be undertaken by professional specialised art handlers and conservators who will pack the artworks using climate-controlled crates (provided by layers of insulation within the crate) and other protective measures to prevent damage during transport. The cultural objects are then transported by specialised shipping companies, often using climate-controlled vehicles to maintain optimal environmental conditions. Sixthly, necessary permits for the export and import of cultural property are obtained to comply with international and national regulations (see above). The shipment then goes through customs clearance in both the exporting and importing countries, facilitated by detailed documentation, carnets and permits. For more on taxes and customs (see Chapter 8).

Upon arrival, the borrowing institution's conservators and curators will unpack and install the cultural objects according to the agreed-upon display conditions, often under the supervision of a representative from the lending institution, the artworks are then exhibited for the agreed-upon period, with security and climate control measures in place to protect them during the display.

---

[13] International Council of Museums, 'ICOM Guidelines for Loan Agreements' <https://icom.museum/wp-content/uploads/2018/07/Loans1974eng.pdf> accessed 21 August 2024.

On completion of the exhibition period a condition check will be carried out and the cultural objects checked against the original condition report to ensure no damage has occurred, then packed and transported back to the lending institution, following the same procedures used during the initial shipment. Upon return, the lending institution conducts a final condition check to confirm the objects are in the same state as when they were loaned out.

Key considerations in international art loans include navigating legal and ethical concerns, including provenance research, to ensure the artwork is not subject to ownership disputes or cultural heritage laws; ensuring proper environmental conditions (temperature, humidity, lighting) during periods of transport and display; security measures during transport and exhibition to prevent theft or damage (for instance, recent high-profile cases of vandalism by 'Just Stop Oil' protestors); and respect for cultural heritage and sensitivity to the significance of objects to originating communities or original owners or creators of objects.

Immunity from Seizure

Anti-seizure legislation for cultural object loans refers to legal measures that protect artworks and cultural property on loan from one country to another from being seized by the borrowing country. These laws are crucial for facilitating international art loans, ensuring that museums and other cultural institutions can borrow and exhibit artworks without the fear of legal disputes leading to the seizure of the loaned items.

The United Nations Convention on Jurisdictional Immunities of States and Their Property began as an initiative to harmonise and clarify the laws regarding immunity. It adopts the restrictive doctrine of immunity, which differentiates between actions conducted in the exercise of sovereign power, or *acta de jure imperii* (which are immune), and actions of a commercial or private law nature, or *acta de jure gestionis* (which are not immune).

The Convention aligns with the 1972 European Convention on State Immunity, and the domestic laws of countries like the United States (Foreign Sovereign Immunities Act) and the United Kingdom (the State Immunity Act 1978 and the more recent Tribunals, Courts and Enforcement Act 2007). It establishes a general rule that states and their property are immune from the jurisdiction of foreign courts, but it also outlines exceptions to this rule, including waiver. Similar to these instruments, the Convention applies only to immunity from the civil jurisdiction (not criminal) of foreign courts.

The cornerstone of the Convention is found in article 5, which states: "[a] State benefits from immunity, both for itself and its property, from the jurisdiction of another State's courts, subject to the provisions of this Convention." The subsequent sections of the Convention serve to elucidate the scope and exceptions to this fundamental principle.

As of April 2019, the Convention had 22 of the 30 required parties for it to enter into force under article 30. Despite this, it has significantly influenced the development of state immunity law, with some of its provisions considered to codify customary international law.[14]

During the 45th session of the Committee of Legal Advisers on Public International Law (CAHDI), the delegation of the Czech Republic, supported by Austria and the Netherlands, proposed an initiative aimed to develop a declaration, endorsing the customary nature of relevant provisions within the United Nations Convention on Jurisdictional Immunities of States and Their Property. Its purpose was to ensure the immunity of cultural property belonging to states while on loan.

The declaration was formally introduced during the 46th CAHDI session, held in Strasbourg on 16-17 September 2013. It was emphasised that this declaration served as a non-binding legal document expressing a shared understanding on the principle of jurisdictional immunity, specifically for cultural property exhibited abroad. In Brussels on 18 November 2013, the declaration was signed jointly by the Minister of Foreign Affairs of the Czech Republic and the Federal Minister for European and International Affairs of Austria. It was subsequently made available for signing by other states. Currently, the declaration has been signed by a total of 18 states, including Ireland, alongside Austria and the Czech Republic.

The key provisions of the declaration state that:

> "property of a State forming part of its cultural heritage or its archives or forming part of an exhibition of objects of scientific, cultural or historical interest, and not placed or intended to be placed on sale cannot be subject to any measure of constraint, such as attachment, arrest or execution, in another State; and therefore, such measures of constraint can only be taken if immunity

---

[14] Philippa Webb, 'United Nations Convention on Jurisdictional Immunities of States and Their Property' <https://legal.un.org/avl/ha/cjistp/cjistp.html> accessed 21 August 2024

is expressly waived for a clearly specified property by the competent national authorities of the State owning the property or if the property has been allocated or earmarked by that State for the satisfaction of the claim which is the object of the proceeding concerned."

The Draft Convention on Immunity from Suit and Seizure for Cultural Objects Temporarily Abroad for Cultural, Educational or Scientific Purposes by the International Law Association, as approved by the ILA in April 2014, provides for immunity from suit and seizure of all cultural objects which are temporarily present in a receiving state for cultural, educational or scientific purposes, unless the cultural object is placed or intended to be placed on sale.

There is one key exception to the above, namely that the rule does not extend to those cultural objects which have been the subject of a serious breach of an obligation arising under general international law, or which are already subject to return obligations under international or European law.

International Examples

Anti-seizure laws typically grant immunity from seizure to artworks that are temporarily imported for public exhibition. This immunity protects against claims such as ownership disputes, debt recovery, or other legal actions. Borrowing institutions usually need to apply for immunity status before the artworks enter the borrowing country. This process often involves providing detailed information about the artworks, the terms of the loan, and the exhibition.

These laws can vary significantly in their scope. Some protect only artworks loaned by foreign governments or public institutions, while others extend protection to loans from private collections.

Conditions under which immunity is granted can include: assurance that the artworks will be returned to the lender after the exhibition; confirmation that the artworks are not subject to legal claims or disputes at the time of the loan; and documentation proving the provenance of the artworks.

United States

The Immunity from Judicial Seizure Statute 1965 states at title 22 that:

"Whenever any work of art or other object of cultural significance is imported into the United States from any foreign country, pursuant to an agreement entered into between the foreign owner or custodian thereof and the United States or one or more cultural, educational, or religious institutions with the capacity to appropriately curate such object within the United States providing for temporary storage, conservation, scientific research, exhibition, or display within the United States at any cultural exhibition, assembly, activity, or festival administered, operated, or sponsored, without profit, by any such cultural, educational, or religious institution with the capacity to appropriately curate such object, no court of the United States... may issue or enforce any judicial process, or enter any judgment, decree, or order, for the purpose or having the effect of depriving such institution, or any carrier engaged in transporting such work or object within the United States, of custody or control of such object if before the importation of such object the President or his designee has determined that such object is of cultural significance and that temporary storage, conservation, scientific research, exhibition, or display within the United States is in the national interest, and a notice to that effect has been published in the Federal Register."

United Kingdom

Under Part 6 of the Tribunals, Courts and Enforcement Act 2007 (the '2007 Act'), cultural objects from outside the UK on loan to approved museums and galleries are protected from court-ordered seizure for a period of up to 12 months from the date the objects enter the UK, providing that the borrowing museum or gallery complies with the conditions of the 2007 Act.

Objects on loan from abroad in temporary exhibitions in UK museums are protected from seizure by the UK courts when they are on display in a museum or gallery which has been approved by the Culture Secretary and where the museum or gallery has published information about the objects on loan.

An object is only protected if it is: usually kept outside the UK; not owned by a person resident in the UK; not in contravention of a prohibition or restriction on import; brought into the UK for temporary public display by an approved museum or gallery; and publicised for exhibit in line with the regulations.[15]

European Union

EU Directive 2014/60/EU (see above) sets out a framework for the return

---

[15] UK Government Department of Culture, Media and Sport, 'Guidance: Protecting cultural objects on loan' <https://www.gov.uk/guidance/protecting-cultural-objects-on-loan> accessed 21 August 2024.

of cultural objects unlawfully removed from the territory of a member state. Article 2(2)(b) states that

> "'unlawfully removed from the territory of a Member State' means... not returned at the end of a period of lawful temporary removal or any breach of another condition governing such temporary removal."

Australia

The Protection of Cultural Objects on Loan Act 2013 encourages international loans for temporary public exhibition in Australia by limiting the circumstances in which lenders, exhibiting institutions, exhibition facilitators and people working for them can lose ownership, physical possession, custody or control of objects while they are in Australia. Under the Act, most types of legal action including seizure and suit and the enforcement of judgments and orders are prevented. Museums and galleries must provide detailed information about the loan and confirm that the objects are not subject to ownership disputes.[16]

In summary, anti-seizure legislation is a crucial tool to facilitate international art loans, offering legal protection that enables the sharing and exhibition of cultural treasures worldwide while balancing the need to address legal and ethical considerations.

Case Study: The Padraig Pearse Surrender Letter

In 1916, Padraig Pearse wrote a letter from Arbour Hill prison stating

> "In order to prevent further slaughter of the civil population and in the hope of saving the lives of our followers, the members of the Provisional Government present at headquarters have decided on an unconditional surrender, and commandants or officers commanding districts will order their commands to lay down arms. P.H. Pearse, Dublin 30 April 1916."

In 2017 the letter left Ireland for good.

The ownership of the letter had been the subject of some controversy. It was initially believed to have been part of the Irish Capuchin Provincial Archives which contain the records of the Order of Friars Minor Capuchin

---

[16] Australian Government Department of Communications and the Arts, 'Protection of cultural objects on loan scheme guidelines' <https://www.arts.gov.au/sites/default/files/documents/protection-of-cultural-objects-on-loan-scheme-guidelines_aug_17_0.pdf> accessed 21 August 2024.

in Ireland from 1615 to circa 1980. According to the order, Capuchin priest Fr Columbus Murphy received the letter from Pearse just three days before his execution, with instructions to deliver it to the rebels' commander stationed at the Four Courts[17] but the order was unable to prove title and prevent the auction.

After a publicity garnering stint on display at the 'GPO: Witness History' exhibition in Dublin's General Post Office, the headquarters of the 1916 Easter Rising, between September and November 2016, the letter was put up for auction by Adam's auctioneers with an asking price of €1 to €1.5 million, but it found no buyers from either the state or private sector; the state having previously ignored overtures from the seller to purchase the object, on the basis of its high valuation and the fact that similar material was already held by the National Museum of Ireland. Bidding stopped at €770,000, the owner having originally paid €800,000 at auction in 2005, presumably in confidence of a smart uptick in value on the occasion of the centenary of the Easter Rising.

Suggestions that the owner might avail of a section 1003 tax break (see Chapter 8)[18] were not practicable as the seller had no business interests in the state and therefore paid no taxes here against which they might avail of a potential relief of €1.2m.

Subsequently, the owner, who resided abroad, sought an export licence. However, Heather Humphreys, then the Minister for Arts, Heritage and the Gaeltacht included the Pearse letter in the Register of Cultural Objects described at s 48 of the National Cultural Institutions Act 1997. No other privately owned object has ever been placed on the register and, to date, the only other objects on the register are paintings belonging to the National Gallery of Ireland (see above).

As we have seen s 50(2) of National Cultural Institutions Act 1997 lists a number of provisions that apply where an application is made to the minister for a licence in respect of an article referred to in s 49(1)(d): any cultural object entered in the register, specifically in the case of items in private ownership that

---

[17] For more information on the Fr Columbus Murphy papers see list of documents at this website <https://catholicarchives.ie/index.php/the-papers-of-fr-columbus-murphy-ofm-cap> accessed 21 August 2024.
[18] Revenue, 'Payment of tax by means of donation of heritage items' <https://www.revenue.ie/en/tax-professionals/tdm/income-tax-capital-gains-tax-corporation-tax/part-42/42-05-01.pdf> accessed 21 August 2024.

> "in any other case, the Minister shall grant the licence and any such licence may be subject to such conditions and restrictions as the Minister determines and specifies in the licence including the condition that the object shall not be exported before the expiration of one year from the date of the application for the licence."

Heather Humphries granted the export licence with a one-year restriction, presumably in the hope that an Irish buyer might come forward and the item might remain in the state.

The end result of this process was that, after the one-year period had elapsed, the minister had to allow export, as the statute is worded in the imperative — "The Minister shall grant the license…"

The Pearse surrender letter ended up being exported from Ireland and it is unclear where it is now — though the owner at one point suggested he would keep it in his collection and bequeath it to his children. What is clear is that the only item on the s 48 register in private hands (and that is not a painting) "whose export from the State would constitute a serious loss to the heritage of Ireland" is now gone, with nothing but the entry on the register remaining.

Appendix

SI No 252 of 2024 the Historic and Archaeological Heritage and Miscellaneous Provisions Act 2023 (Commencement) Order 2024

In one of the most significant changes to the law as it applies to archaeology and monuments, under SI No 252 of 2024, the Historic and Archaeological Heritage and Miscellaneous Provisions Act 2023 (Commencement) Order 2024, the Minister for Housing, Local Government and Heritage ordered that, on 31 May 2024, the following provisions of the Historic and Archaeological Heritage and Miscellaneous Provisions Act 2023 came into operation (references to sections below refer to sections of the act). Any sections of the Historic and Archaeological Heritage and Miscellaneous Provisions Act 2023 that are not mentioned below have not been commenced and therefore have not come into force.

The following is a list of commenced provisions in the order in which they appear on SI No 252. Items in bold are the sections that have been commenced and an explanation of the impact of the commencement of each is included below each commenced section.

Sections 1 to 6

These sections comprise the short title and commencement, interpretation, performance of functions, the area of territorial application of the act, regulations and payment of expenses.

Section 7 insofar as relates to the Architectural Heritage (National Inventory) and Historic Monuments (Miscellaneous Provisions) Act 1999 (other than section 5);

Section 7 addresses repeals, in the case of this commencement the Architectural Heritage (National Inventory) and Historic Monuments (Miscellaneous Provisions) Act 1999 apart from s 5.

Section 5(2) of the Architectural Heritage (National Inventory) and Historic Monuments (Miscellaneous Provisions) Act 1999 details the requirement for a sanitary authority "as soon as practicable after serving or proposing to serve a notice under section 3(1) of the Act of 1964 in respect of a monument" to "inform the Minister of the particulars of the notice." A monument has the meaning ascribed to it by the National Monuments (Amendment) Act 1987, which defines a historic monument as

> "a prehistoric monument and any monument associated with the commercial, cultural, economic, industrial, military, religious or social history of the place where it is situated or of the country and also includes all monuments in existence before 1700 A.D. or such later date as the Minister may appoint by regulations."

Section 5(3) states that a sanitary authority which carries out works on a monument shall, as far as possible, preserve the monument in as much as its preservation is not likely to cause a danger to any person or property and s 5(4) details the requirement for a sanitary authority to inform the minister of the works which have been carried out.

Under the terms of section 3(1) of the Local Government (Sanitary Services) Act 1964,

> "a sanitary authority may, if they so think fit, give a notice to the owner who occupies or is entitled to occupy a dangerous structure situate in their functional area or from whom it is held by a person who is not the owner and, if he can be ascertained by reasonable inquiry, to the occupier of the structure, requiring such owner, within such period specified in the notice as the authority may consider appropriate to (a) to carry out such works (including the demolition of the structure or any part of it and the clearing and levelling of the site thereof) specified in the notice as will ,in the opinion of the authority, prevent the structure from being a dangerous structure, to remove any debris and to erect a wall or barrier between any open area created by the works and any road, street or public place, and (b) to terminate or modify any use of the structure or any part thereof."

Section 3(2) allows for the entry onto lands by the agents of the sanitary authority to prevent a structure being dangerous to carry out works up to and including demolition or levelling that may be required to make the structure safe.

Part 3

Part 3 addresses measures to assist in implementing the 1972 Convention Concerning the Protection of the World Cultural and Natural Heritage. Part 3 states that a property included in the World Heritage List under article 11 of the Convention, and which is situated in the state, shall be known as 'World Heritage Property,' that the Minister for Housing, Local Government and Heritage is the competent authority for submitting to the World Heritage Committee, on behalf of the state, the inventory referred to in article 11 of the convention, and arranging, on behalf of the state and in co-operation with such other ministers of the government as may be appropriate, participation in the work of the World Heritage Committee. Provision is also made for the minister to carry out such consultation with such persons, or the public, as appears appropriate to him or her and may specify procedures for the carrying out of such consultation before preparing an article 11 list.

Article 11 of the 1972 Convention states that every state party to the Convention shall, in so far as possible, submit to the World Heritage Committee an inventory of property forming part of the cultural and natural heritage, situated in its territory and suitable for inclusion in the 'World Heritage List.' This list includes: monuments; architectural works; works of monumental sculpture and painting; elements or structures of an archaeological nature; inscriptions; cave dwellings and combinations of features, which are of outstanding universal value from the point of view of history, art or science; groups of buildings: groups of separate or connected buildings which, because of their architecture, their homogeneity or their place in the landscape, are of outstanding universal value from the point of view of history, art or science; and sites, works of man or the combined works of nature and man, and areas including archaeological sites which are of outstanding universal value from the historical, aesthetic, ethnological or anthropological point of view.

At the time of writing there were three entries on the World Heritage List for Ireland — Brú na Bóinne, the Giants Causeway and Causeway Coast and Sceilg Mhichíl.

The inclusion of a property in the World Heritage List requires the consent of the state concerned. The inclusion of a property situated in a territory, sovereignty or jurisdiction over which is claimed by more than one state shall in no way prejudice the rights of the parties to the dispute.

Article 11 goes on to state that:

> "The Committee shall establish, keep up to date and publish, whenever circumstances shall so require, under the title of 'List of World Heritage in Danger,' a list of the property appearing in the World Heritage List for the conservation of which major operations are necessary and for which assistance has been requested under this Convention. This list shall contain an estimate of the cost of such operations. The list may include only such property forming part of the cultural and natural heritage as is threatened by serious and specific dangers, such as the threat of disappearance caused by accelerated deterioration, large-scale public or private projects or rapid urban or tourist development projects; destruction caused by changes in the use or ownership of the land; major alterations due to unknown causes; abandonment for any reason whatsoever."

At the time of writing there were no entries on the list of World Heritage in Danger for Ireland.

Part 8

Part 8 relates to Inventories, Records and Research, Publication and Promotion of Public Knowledge and Awareness.

Part 8 chapter 1 sets out that the minister may carry out or caused to be carried out inventories of or in relation to historic heritage, World Heritage Property or property which is situated in the state that the minister is satisfied may have the potential to become World Heritage Property as he or she considers appropriate. In addition, the minister shall establish and maintain, or cause to be established and maintained, inventories in respect of each of the following: (a) relevant things of archaeological interest; (b) architectural heritage; (c) wrecks of archaeological or historic interest.

The inventories may include searching for previously unidentified "relevant things of a relevant interest,"[1] the minister may determine the form, content and title or description of any such inventory; designate classes of the archaeological or architectural heritage or historic objects to be included in any particular inventory; and amend, add to or delete from any such inventory. The minister may make information from inventories

---

[1] Historic and Archaeological Heritage and Miscellaneous Provisions Act 2023, s 158 (3).

available to public or local authorities or disseminate such information at their discretion, with a prohibition on the disclosure of personal data.

Part 8 Chapter 2 sets out provisions to secure the records of companies engaged in archaeological works that hold records relating to archaeological objects, or results or findings of any work or activity related to archaeological excavations or to the recording of such results or findings or the preparation of a report on them. There is a requirement to notify the relevant authority if a company is wound up or an individual dies and they hold such records no later than 21 days after the order or resolution of winding up or the death of the individual, unless an administrator is appointed to that individual's estate in which case notice shall be given not later than 7 days after that appointment. Relevant records in the possession of the company or individual shall not be damaged, destroyed, sold, transferred or disposed of without the consent of the minister. The same provision applies to archaeological objects as to records. Crucially this provision is retrospective, so applies even when a death or winding up occurred before the commencement of this section on 31 May 2024.

Part 8 Chapter 3 sets out provisions for the promotion of knowledge, interest and awareness of historic heritage, stating that a relevant authority may commission, compile, publish and distribute materials in any format relating to that authority's functions under the Act. A relevant authority may furthermore provide advice, technical, financial or other assistance to any person in the protection of any element of historic heritage. Lastly, a relevant authority may acquire and make use of copyright, patents, licences, privileges and concessions as may be appropriate to any matter connected with the authority's functions under the act.

Part 9

Part 9 details the issuing of guidelines and matters relating to historic heritage. The minister is empowered to issue guidelines relating to dealing with historic heritage in the course of the preparation or carrying out of an Environmental Impact Assessment (EIA) under the EIA Directive. Under the EU's EIA Directive 2011/92/EU as amended by 2014/52/EU, major building projects, such as long-distance railways, motorways, express roads or waste disposal locations for hazardous waste, must first be assessed for their impact on the environment. One of the environmental factors to be considered for impact is "cultural heritage." The project developer must provide the relevant authority with a report detailing a description of the project, potential significant effects, reasonable alternatives and "features of the project and/or measures to avoid, prevent, reduce or offset likely significant impacts on the environment."

Under Part 9, the minister may also issue guidelines to local authorities relating to their dealings with historic heritage. These guidelines may, without prejudice to ss 28 and 52 of the Planning and Development Act 2000 relate to objectives which fall within s 10(2)(c) of the 2000 Act in so far as such objectives relate to the conservation and protection of historic heritage, World Heritage Property, or property which is situated in the state that the minister is satisfied may have the potential to become World Heritage Property.

Section 28 of the Planning and Development Act 2000 enables the minister to issue guidelines to planning authorities regarding any of their functions under that Act; s 52 states *inter alia* that the Minister for Arts, Heritage, Gaeltacht and the Islands shall

> "issue guidelines to planning authorities concerning development objectives —
> (a) for protecting structures, or parts of structures, which are of special architectural, historical, archaeological, artistic, cultural, scientific, social or technical interest, and
> (b) for preserving the character of architectural conservation areas, and any such guidelines shall include the criteria to be applied when selecting proposed protected structures for inclusion in the record of protected structures."

Section 10(2)(c) of the Planning and Development Act 2000 sets out that a development plan shall include "the conservation and protection of the environment including, in particular, the archaeological and natural heritage and the conservation and protection of European sites and any other sites which may be prescribed for the purposes of this paragraph."

Further provisions of Part 9 include defining as general functions of the minister in conjunction with the Heritage Council in so far as the council's functions relate to historic heritage (as distinct from their environmental remit) to co-ordinate and promote the development of public policy on historic heritage. Promotion of best practice in relevant disciplines and professions which may include the Minister or the Board of the National Museum co-operating with or assisting any body that has been established for the purpose of regulating any discipline or profession relating to the protection of historic heritage shall also be a function of the minister. In consultation with the Board of the National Museum, it shall also be a function of the minister to promote the protection of historic heritage by public authorities in the course of the performance of their functions under any enactment other than this act and the minister may enter into an agreement with a public authority on foot of that function. It shall also be a general function of a public authority or local authority to have regard to historic heritage in the performance of their respective functions under any enactment.

Section 172

Section 172 states that

> "A person shall not knowingly or recklessly make a statement (whether orally or in writing), when providing information to another person pursuant to a provision of this Act, that is false or misleading in any material respect."

Section 174

Section 174 sets out that a person shall not interfere with or obstruct, including withholding information or knowingly or recklessly providing false or misleading information, the Minister, the Commissioners of Public Works, the Board of the National Museum, a local authority, the Revenue Commissioners, their officers, servants or agents, a member of An Garda Síochána or a member of the naval service in the performance of their functions under the Act.

Subsections (3) and (4) of section 175 insofar as they apply to sections 159 (4), 172 and 174

Section 175 (3) states that

> "A person who contravenes any provision of this Act to which this subsection applies by virtue of subsection (4) shall be guilty of an offence and shall be liable—
>
> (a) on summary conviction, to a class A fine or imprisonment for a term not exceeding 6 months or both, or
>
> (b) on conviction on indictment, to a fine not exceeding €10,000 or imprisonment for a term not exceeding 3 years or both."

Subsection (4) sets out the sections of the Act that this offence relates to. The only sections commenced are sections 159(4), 172 and 174. Section 159(4) states that

> "Relevant records in the possession of the company or individual shall not be

damaged, destroyed, sold, transferred or disposed of without the consent of the Minister. The same provision applies to archaeological objects as to records".

Sections 172 and 174 are addressed above.

Subsections (7) and (8) of section 175 insofar as they apply to section 159 (2)

Section 175(7) sets out that

> "A person who, without reasonable excuse, contravenes any provision of this Act to which this subsection applies by virtue of subsection (8) shall be guilty of an offence and shall be liable on summary conviction to a class A fine."

A class A fine is a fine not exceeding €5,000.

Section 159(2) sets out the requirement that

> "where a company is ordered to be wound up or a resolution is passed for the voluntary winding up of a company or an individual dies and such company or individual, as the case may be, has or had, at the time of such order, resolution or death, as the case may be, relevant records or relevant archaeological objects in his or her possession, then the company (or, as appropriate, the liquidator or receiver thereof) or the personal representative of such individual, as the case may be, shall notify the relevant authority."

Sections 178(2) and 179

Section 178(2) sets out that a party who is convicted of an offence under s 159(2) who continues to contravene that section shall be guilty of a further offence on each day that they continue to contravene that section and be liable on summary conviction to a class E fine for each day of continued contravention. A class E fine is a fine not exceeding €500.

Section 179(1) states that

> "Where an offence under this Act is committed by a body corporate and it is proved that the offence was committed with the consent or connivance, or was attributable to any wilful neglect, of a person who was a director, manager, secretary or other officer of the body corporate, or a person purporting to act in that capacity, that person, as well as the body corporate, shall be guilty of an offence and may be proceeded against and punished as if he or she were guilty of the first-mentioned offence."

Section 179(2) states that "where the affairs of a body corporate are managed by its members" the same provisions apply to those members as to directors, managers secretaries or other officers of a body corporate.

Section 182

Under s 182 if a person is charged with an offence under this Act and the alleged offence occurred at sea or on water it shall be a defence for the person to show that the act was urgently required to protect human life, protect persons from serious injury or prevent serious damage to the environment.

Sections 188 to 190

Section 188 sets out the right of relevant authorities, their officer, servants or agents, exercising powers under the Act to "enter on, in, over or go across freely any land (including dwellings) and carry out works there or carry out all forms of survey, recording or investigation (including archaeological excavation)," to bring machinery, equipment or materials, to secure any site for further investigation (including archaeological excavation), to be accompanied by any persons it is reasonable to require. They can also require any person encountered to give assistance or provide information about archaeological, architectural or other historic heritage as may reasonably be sought. Entry into a private dwelling under this section requires the consent of the occupier or a District Court warrant.

Under section 189, the Minister may inspect or cause to be inspected sites or "a relevant thing of a relevant interest or a relevant thing that the Minister reasonably believes may be of such interest," including archaeological investigation or the examination of any archaeological or historic object which was found or identified in that site.

Section 190 assigns powers to the Board of the National Museum to inspect or cause to be inspected any site where an archaeological or historic object has been found or the Board reasonably believes such an object may have been found, or where such an object is situated, or the board reasonably believes is situated. For the purposes of s 190, 'inspect' incudes archaeological excavation, any other form of investigation or recording that may be appropriate or the examination of any archaeological object or historic object in the site inspected or that was found or identified in that site.

Chapters 7 and 8 of Part 10

Chapter 7 of Part 10 relates to enforcement notices. After a section on interpretation s 194 sets out the High Court's jurisdiction in relation to enforcement notices issued in respect of s 175(4) — that records are not to be damaged, destroyed, sold, transferred or disposed of without the consent of the Minister. Any other proceedings in relation to an enforcement notice are within the jurisdiction of the Circuit Court. The Circuit in question shall be "the circuit in which the monument, archaeological object, historic object, wreck, licensable activity or other thing to which the enforcement notice concerned relates is situated at the time the application concerned is made," or in the case of the whereabouts of the person or the thing to which the enforcement notice relates being unknown at the time the application concerned is made, the Dublin Circuit Court.

Section 195 sets out that where a relevant authority is of the opinion that a person has contravened, is contravening or is continuing to contravene a relevant provision then without prejudice to s 154 (which has not yet been commenced) or the other provisions of Part 10, then that authority may issue that person with a notice in writing stating their name and address, the relevant opinion, the relevant provision and the reasons why they are of the opinion that the person is in contravention, directing the person to take such steps as are specified in the notice to remedy the contravention and specifying a period ending not earlier than 30 days after being given the notice within which the person may make an application under s 196(1) and being a reasonable period under the circumstances. Under s 195(6) where a person fails to take the steps set out in an enforcement notice issued to them the relevant authority may (on notice to the person) apply in a summary manner to the court of relevant jurisdiction for an order compelling that person to take those steps or varied steps as specified in the order.

Section 196 allows a 30-day period under which a person to whom an enforcement notice has been delivered may make application to the court of relevant jurisdiction for the cancellation of any direction specified in the notice. The decision of the court shall be final, unless by leave on a point of law to appeal to the High Court for matters before the Circuit Court, or the Court of Appeal for matters before the High Court.

Under s 197 where an enforcement notice has been issued the relevant authority may make application for an interim or interlocutory order directing the relevant person to do or cease doing the relevant act due to the nature or gravity of the possible contravention referred to in the enforcement notice. An interim or interlocutory order may also be made by the court under s 195(6) or s 196 proceedings.

The burden of proof in relation to all matters arising under the hearing of proceedings under Chapter 7 shall be on the balance of probabilities. Rules of court may make provision for the expedition of the hearing of proceedings under this Chapter.

Chapter 8 of Part 10 sets out arrest, search and seizure powers which are in addition to the powers arising under the Criminal Law Act 1997. Under Chapter 8, a member of An Garda Síochána or the Naval Services of the Defence Forces may arrest without warrant any person committing, or whom the member believes to be committing an offence under the Act. Similar arrest powers extend to suspicion of committing or having been involved in committing if the member of An Garda Síochána or the Naval Services has reasonable grounds to believe that search a person may abscond.

Powers of search and seizure without warrant extend to land, premises, vehicles, vessels and aircraft (other than a private dwelling, which still requires a warrant from the District Court).

Section 204 sets out that a member of An Garda Síochána or the Naval Services may accompany or assist any officer, agent or servant of the Minister, the Commissioners of Public Works, the Board of the National Museum or a local authority in performing any of their functions under the Act. Any person encountered in the course of a search under this Chapter may be requested to render assistance or to give their name and address, with which request they must comply. Similarly, where a member of An Garda Síochána or the Naval Services suspects that a person has committed an offence under the Act and so alleges to the person, that person must give their name and address. Where a member of An Garda Síochána or the Naval Services has reasonable grounds for believing an offence under the Act has been committed and finds any person in possession of an archaeological object, historic object, monument or wreck and that thing relates to the suspected offence they may request an explanation as to how that person came into possession of the thing. The person in question must comply with this request, provided they have had the consequences of a refusal to comply explained to them in ordinary language. Any information thus given shall not be admissible in evidence in any civil or criminal proceedings, other than proceedings for refusal to provide such information.

Sections 207, 209 and 210

Section 207 sets out that anything done by a person in the course of his employment, or as an agent of another person shall be treated as also done by that employer or person (vicarious liability). It shall be a defence for an employer to demonstrate that the employer took such steps as were practicable to prevent the employee from doing that act or from doing in the course of their employment acts of that description, however this defence is not available to proceedings seeking an interim or interlocutory order under s 197.

Under s 209 an offence under the Act may be prosecuted summarily by the Minister, the Board of the National Museum if the offence relates to an archaeological or historic object, or the local authority concerned in the case of an offence relating to a national monument.

Section 210 sets out that summary proceedings may be brought within 12 months after the date on which the offence was committed or within 6 months after the date on which evidence sufficient in the opinion of the person instituting the proceedings to justify proceedings comes to that person's knowledge, whichever is the later. A cutoff period of 2 years after the date on the offence concerned was committed, notwithstanding s 10(4) of the Petty Sessions (Ireland) Act 1851 which sets out a 6-month maximum timeframe for a complaint to be made in summary proceedings. Section 210(3) states that the no provisions of s 210 shall be construed to prejudice the generality of s 7 of the Criminal Justice Act 1951, which states that the time limits for the making of complaints of summary jurisdiction s 10(4) of the Petty Sessions (Ireland) Act 1851 shall not apply to a complaint in respect of an indictable offence.

Chapters 10 and 11 of Part 10

Chapter 10 sets out that where a court convicts a person of an offence under the Act, or the person is the subject of a s 197 order it shall, unless satisfied there are special and substantial reasons not to do so, order the person to pay the Minister, the Commissioners of Public Works, the Board of the National Museum, the local authority or other person as appropriate the costs and expenses of the action as measured by the court. These costs shall include any costs or expenses reasonably incurred by any persons in relation to the investigation, detection and prosecution of the offence or seeking of the order, including costs of employees, consultants and advisers.

Appendix

Chapter 11 states that the minister may prepare and publish a code of practice for the purposes of setting out the manner in which the minister proposes to perform any function conferred upon them by the Act and to assist persons or classes of persons in complying with a provision of the Act that applies to that person or class of persons. Where the minister wishes to prepare and publish such a code they shall before publication make available a draft to such persons that the Minster considers appropriate having regard to the matters to which the code relates and invite those persons to make representations in writing on it.

Any document bearing the seal of the Minister and purporting to be a code of practice that code shall be admissible in evidence in any proceedings before a court or tribunal or in any proceedings concerning the provisions of the Act to which the code relates.

Sections 217 and 218

Section 217 states that the minister for any purposes under the Act may require, by notice in writing, any occupier or person receiving rent from any land to inform the minister of particulars of the estate, right or interest by virtue of which they occupy such land or receive such rent, within a specified period not less than 14 days.

Under s 218, a relevant body may for the purposes of protection and management of historic heritage to the extent necessary and proportionate to those purposes share information, notably including personal data with another relevant body in accordance with law. The minister may prescribe 'relevant bodies' but these include *ab initio* Departments of State, local authorities, the Heritage Council, An Garda Síochána, the Office of Public Works, the National Museum of Ireland, Tailte Éireann, the Revenue Commissioners, the Coroner Service, the Defence Forces, any authority in another state that has responsibilities as regards historic heritage in that state.

Sections 220 and 221

The Board of the National Museum may derogate any or all of the Board's functions under the Act to the Director of the National Museum in writing under s 220, other than the requirement under s 3(2) to cooperate with the Minister, the Commissioners of Public Works, the Heritage Council and each local authority in the implementation of the Act. A function of the Board of the National Museum so delegated shall continue to be vested in the Board but concurrently with the Director, so that they may act jointly or severally. Where such a delegation is made the Director may, if expressly permitted in the delegation, appoint a person by notice in writing to perform a function so delegated.

Section 221 details the methods of serving a notice, including delivery in person, by leaving at an address at which the person resides, by registered post or by email where the recipient has given permission to have notice served on them by that means.

Schedule 3

Schedule 3 is the full text of the 1972 Convention Concerning the Protection of the World Cultural and Natural Heritage see Part 3 above.

Index

Abbey Theatre, 42–43
Access to information. *See* **Freedom of information**
Acquisition of title, 45–46
Acta de jure gestionis, 173
Acta de jure imperii, 173
Actus reus, 71
Advanced Research Projects Agency Network (ARPANET), 24
Adverse possession, 106, 107
African art and artefacts, 93, 94, 100
'After', 117
AI generated artwork, 10
An Taisce, 132–133
Annexation to realty, 131
Apollo Foundation, 144
Appellate jurisdiction, 70–71
Appropriation without consent, 73–74
Archaeological heritage
   Grenada Convention, 129
   national inventory, 123–124, 130
   national monuments. *See* National monuments
   protected structures. *See* Protected structures
Archaeological objects
   disposal powers, 89–90
   duty to report finds, 128n
   illicit traffic. *See* Illicit traffic in archaeological/cultural objects
   State ownership. *See* State ownership of archaeological/cultural objects
Archives
   copyright exemptions, 11–12
   data protection issues. *See* Data protection

Archives—*contd.*
   freedom of information issues. *See* Freedom of information
   re-use of public sector information, 40–41
   s 1003 donation, tax relief, 143–144
   use of out-of-commerce works, 12–14
Armed conflict. *See* **War**
Art crime
   criminal and civil law distinguished, 69
   elements of crime, 71–73
   fraud, 74
   handling stolen property, 46–47, 74
   jurisdiction, 69–71
   money laundering, 75–76, 118
   possession of stolen property, 47–48, 75
   proceeds of crime, 76–77
   proof, 69
   theft, 73–74
Artist's resale right, 18–19
Artistic work
   advertising for sale, 10
   AI generated, 10
   copying, in another work, 11
   copyright. *See* copyright
   resale right, 18–19
Artists Exemption Scheme, 149, 150
Arts Council, 42–43
Ashurbanipal library, 6
ATA carnet, 148–149
Attornment, 49
'Attributed to', 117
Attribution right, 17
Auctions, 117–118
Audio books, 15–17

Australia
    Protection of Cultural Objects on
        Loan Act 2013, 177
Author
    definition, 5
    copyright. *See* Copyright
    moral rights, 17–18

Bailment, 48–50
Barakat Galleries case, 57–58
Basic Income for the Arts, 150
Battle of Cúl Dreimhne, 1
Battle of the Book, 1
Battle of the Booksellers, 2
Battlefield sites, 133–134
Beit Collection, 144
Benin Bronzes, 94
Berne Convention, 3, 4, 10, 17
Bewley's Café, 132
Blockchain technology, 153
Boğazköy Sphinx, 99
Brexit, 113
British Library, cyber-attack, 25
British Museum
    disposal of objects vested in
        trustees, 89
    Elgin Marbles, 88, 89
    translation, moral rights case, 18
Broadcast, copyright, 4, 7
Bruce, Thomas, 88
Buildings at Risk Register, 133
Bunbury, Turtle, 150
Burden of proof, 69
Byrne, Charles, 91

Capital acquisitions tax (CAT)
    case study: Rory Gallagher
        Stratocaster, 155–158
    current rate, 141
    exemptions for heritage property,
        142
    NFTs, 154
    s 1003 relief for donation of
        heritage item, 143–144
    thresholds for gifts/inheritances,
        141–142
Capuchin archives, 177–178
Caricatures, 10
Carney, Mark, 121
Cartoons, 18
Case stated, 70

Casement, Roger, 93
Cassirer family, restitution claim,
    106–108
Catalogue raisonné, 118
Cataloguing contract, 115
Central Criminal Court, 70
Chattels and fixtures, 55, 62, 131–132
Chinese antiquities, 99
Circuit Court jurisdiction, 70
Civil recovery of object
    accrual of cause of action, 61
    circumstances requiring, 53
    civil and criminal law distinguished,
        69
    claim in conversion, 54–55, 61–62
    detinue claim, 54, 61, 65–66
    further conversion or detinue, 61–62
    law of location applicable, 55–56
    limitation periods, 60–62
    proof, 69
Clarke, Harry, 132
Codes of ethics, 81–83
Cold War, 24
Commercial invoice, 148
Commercially sensitive information,
    37
Committee of Legal Advisers on
    Public International Law
    (CAHDI) declaration, 174–175
Compulsory acquisition, 58–60
Confidential information
    confidentiality clause, 112
    freedom of information exemption,
        37, 42–43
Confiscation of proceeds of crime,
    76–77
Consent, element of theft, 73–74
Consideration, 109
Constantinople, sack of, 87
Continental shelf, 135
Contract
    assignment or subcontracting, 113
    auctions, 117–118
    common forms, 110
    confidentiality clause, 112
    consideration, 109
    copyright issues, 111–112
    digitisation and cataloguing
        contracts, 115
    dispute resolution, 113
    entire agreement clause, 113

Index

Contract—*contd.*
  essential terms, 110–111
  extension clause, 112
  force majeure clause, 113
  framework agreements, 116
  governing law, 113
  incapacity to enter, 109–110
  international obligations, 112
  key personnel clause, 112
  loan agreements. *See* Loans
  offer and acceptance, 109
  overview, 109
  privity, 109
  public procurement contracts, 116
  sale of goods, 110
  termination clause, 112
  terms and conditions, 111
  warranties and indemnities, 111
  written contracts, 110
Convention on International Trade in Endangered Species (CITES) 1973, 80–81, 160–162
Conversion, 54–55, 61–62
Copyright
  definition, 4
  archivists' exemptions, 11–12
  artist's resale right, 18–19
  artistic works, 4, 10–11
  assignment or licence, 111–112
  audio books, and PLR, 15–17
  'author' defined, 5
  Berne Convention, 3, 4, 10, 17
  broadcasts, 4, 7
  caricature, parody and pastiche, 10
  catalogues and inventories, 115
  'copying' defined, 6
  Copyright and Related Rights Act 2000, 3, 4–6
  Copyright Term Directive, 7
  databases, 4
  Digital Single Market, 12–14
  digitised images, 19–20, 115
  duration, 7–8, 21–22
  e-books, and PLR, 15–17
  early legislation, 2–3
  exhaustion, 6
  fair dealing exception, 9–11
  films, 4, 7
  history, 1–3
  InfoSoc Directive, 3
  infringement, acts constituting, 6

Copyright—*contd.*
  Irish Copyright Licensing Agency licences, 10
  James Joyce, 7
  librarians' exemptions, 11–12
  lists or tables, 5
  literary works, 4
  'making available' defined, 6
  Mickey Mouse, 8
  moral rights, 17–18
  musical works, 4, 7
  originality, 4–5, 19
  orphan works, 8–9
  out-of-commerce works, use by cultural heritage institutions, 12–14
  performers' rights, 7
  PLR, 14–15
  preservation of works, 11
  proof, 5–6
  public domain, 7
  quotations, 10
  rental and lending rights, 14
  rights protected, 6
  scope of works etc protected, 4
  sound recordings, 4, 7
  Spain, 7
  State records, 5
  typographical arrangement of published edition, 4
  underlying ideas and principles, 4
  United States, 7, 21–22
  Winnie-the-Pooh, 21–22
Costume display, 114
Court of Appeal, 70
COVID-19 pandemic, 10, 113, 132
Creative commons licences, 20
Creep holes, 133–134
Crime. *See* **Art crime**
Criminal Assets Bureau, 77
Crypto assets, 153–155
Cultural heritage institution
  definition, 12
  use of out-of-commerce works, 12–14
  work permanently in collection, 45–46
Cultural objects
  definition, 88
  deaccession. *See* Deaccession

Cultural objects—*contd.*
  illicit traffic. *See* Illicit traffic in archaeological/cultural objects
  import-export controls. *See* Import-export of cultural objects
  international protection laws, 56–58
  power to dispose of, transfer or exchange, 90
  repatriation. *See* Repatriation of cultural objects
  restitution. *See* Restitution of cultural objects
  State ownership. *See* State ownership of archaeological/cultural objects
Cyber-attack, 25

Data protection
  'appropriate authority' defined, 30
  civil servants as data controllers, 30–31
  culture of monetised fear, 28
  cyber-attacks and ransom, 25
  data controllers, 26, 30–32
  data processors, 26
  data protection officers, 32–34
  data subject access requests, 27–28
  data subjects' rights, 27
  deceased person's data, 28–29
  EU Charter, 26
  GDPR, 26–29
  historical archives, 28
  history of data sharing, 23–25
  impact assessment, 31–32
  Individual Health Identifiers, 28–29
  information to be kept, 31
  'new technology' defined, 32
  'personal data' defined, 26
  private institutions as data controllers, 31
  'processing' defined, 27
  processing for archiving purposes in the public interest etc, 29–30
  processing for crime prevention, detection etc, 30
  processing purposes and restrictions, 29–30
  pseudonymisation, 30
  records less than 100 years old, 29–30

Database
  copyright, 4
  data protection. *see* Data protection
Dating of artworks, 119–121
David Bowie Is **exhibition**, 114
Deaccessioning
  ethical and legal considerations, 88–90
  ICOM guidelines, 89, 90–91
  NMI policy, 90
Dealers' code of ethics, 82–83
Death
  deathbed gift or gift in contemplation, 52
  inheritance tax. *See* Capital acquisitions tax
Defence Data Network (DDN), 24
Delivery, 51
Derrynaflan hoard, 50, 54, 64–68
Detinue, 54, 61, 65–66
Digitisation
  contract for digitisation work, 115
  copying, as, 6
  copyright over digitised materials, 19–20, 115
  e-books, and PLR, 15–17
  Getty Museum images, 20
  NFTs, 120–121, 153–155
  orphan works, 9
  preservation or archival purposes, 11–12
Dishonesty, 73, 84–85
District Court jurisdiction, 69–70
Donatio mortis causa, 52
Donative intent, 51
Dorsey, Jack, 153
'Draped Seated Woman', 61–62
Dust and pollutants, 114

E-books, 15–17
Easter Rising 1916, 133–134, 177–179
Egyptian antiquities
  law protecting, 56
  repatriation of mummified remains, 94
  sale of *Sekhemka* sculpture, 89
  smuggling into the US, 56–57
Elgin Marbles, 88, 89
Emms, Norman, 118
Endangered species, 80–81, 160–162
Entire agreement clause, 113

Index

Eskenazi, John, 83–86
Ethereum, 153
Ethics of acquisition
   codes of ethics, 81–83
   international conventions, 77–81
Ethnological items, 91–94
European Union (EU)
   Copyright Term Directive, 7
   EU VAT area, 151
   fraud affecting financial interests, 69
   free ports, 152–153
   GDPR, 26–29
   import-export controls. *See* Import-export of cultural objects
   InfoSoc Directive, 3
   Maastricht Treaty, 168–169
   money laundering, 75, 118
   movement of cultural objects within, 148
   Open Data Directive, 40–41
   public procurement, 116
   TFEU, 168–170
   VAT margin scheme, 151
European Union Intellectual Property Office (EUIPO), 13
Exhaustion of copyright, 6
Export controls. *See* **Import-export of cultural objects**
Extension clause, 112

Fair dealing, 9–11
Film, copyright, 4, 7
Finnegan's Wake, 144
Fixtures and chattels, 55, 62, 131–132
'Follower of', 117
Force majeure, 113
Forgeries, 83–86
Formaldehyde-vitrine works, 119–121
Framework agreements, 116
Fraud
   affecting financial interests of the EU, 69
   art crime, 74
   Qatar Investment v Eskenazi case, 83–86
Free ports, 152–153
Freedom of information
   amendment of personal information, 35
   appeals, 39–40
   case study, 42–43

Freedom of information—*contd.*
   certificate exempting records from disclosure, 38
   commercially sensitive information, 37
   confidential information, 37, 42–43
   Council of Europe recommendation, 35
   deceased person's information, 37–38
   disclosure of personal information, 37–38
   Freedom of Information Act 1997, 35
   Freedom of Information Act 2014, 35
   internal review of decision, 39
   legal right of access, 35
   Open Data Directive, 40–41
   origins and development, 34–35
   overview, 34
   prescribed classes of exempt records, 38
   publication scheme, 36, 38–39
   reasons for decision, 35
   'record' defined, 35–36
   refusal of access request, 36–38
   re-use of public sector information, 40–41
   UN resolution, 34
   US FOIA, 34–35
   1998 cut-off date, 35

Gairsoppa, 136–139
Gallagher, John, 144
Gallagher, Rory, 155–158
Galleries
   copyright issues. *See* Copyright
   data protection issues. *See* Data protection
   freedom of information issues. *See* Freedom of information
   non-application of Open Data Directive, 40
General Data Protection Regulation (GDPR), 26–29
Geneva Convention 1864, 63
Getty Museum images, 20
Gifts
   deathbed, or in contemplation of death, 52

Gifts—*contd.*
  delivery, 51
  loans distinguished, 51–52
  power to accept, 50
  real or movable property, 50
  tax issues. *See* Tax
  trust conferring, 50–51
'Goods' defined, 169
Greek antiquities, 88, 89
Grenada Convention, 129
Guban Saor, 64
Gutenberg, Johannes, 1

Hague Conference on Laws and Customs of War 1899, 63, 87
Hague Convention for the Protection of Cultural Property 1954, 63–64, 78, 160
Handling stolen property, 46–47, 74
Hari Hara statue, 85
Harvesting of user data, 25
Hawaiian human remains and sacred objects, 94
Head of Krodha, 84
Heritage Council loan documentation, 52, 115
High Court jurisdiction, 70
High-Income Individuals Restriction, 147
High-value datasets, 41
Hirst, Damien, 46, 117, 119–121
'His Circle', 117
'His Studio', 117
Historic and Archaeological Heritage Act 2023
  accession to UNIDROIT Convention 1995, 98–100
  acquisition of archaeological objects for the State, 60
  battlefields, 133
  commencement, 98, 123, 124, 134
  export of Ch 8 monuments, 170
  inventories, power to carry out, 123–124
  limitation periods, 62
  monuments, power to prescribe, 124
  objects, 123
  ownership of archaeological objects for theft and fraud purposes, 74

Historic and Archaeological Heritage Act 2023—*contd.*
  ratification of illicit trafficking convention (1970), 98–99
  ratification of underwater heritage convention (2001), 134, 139
  sale of archaeological objects without authorisation, 48
  State ownership of archaeological objects, 45, 58, 128
  wrecks and underwater sites, 134
Historic Monuments Council, 125
Hollerith Machine, 23, 24
Holocaust expropriated art. *See* Nazi-era spoliation
Horses of Saint Mark, 87–88
Horses of the Hippodrome of Constantinople, 87–88
House or garden of significant historical interest etc
  CAT exemption, 142
  reasonable public access, 146–147
  tax relief for expenditure on maintenance etc, 146–147
Human remains, 91–94
Humidity control, 114
Humphreys, Heather, 178–179
Hunt Museum, 94
Hunterian Museum, 91
Hypertext Markup Language (HTML), 25
Hypertext Transfer Protocol (HTTP), 25

IBM, 23–24
Illicit traffic in archaeological/cultural objects
  codes of ethics, 81–83
  international conventions. *See* International conventions protecting cultural property
Immunity from seizure
  Australian law, 177
  CAHDI declaration, 174–175
  EU Directive, 176–177
  International Law Association draft convention, 175
  UK law, 176
  UN Convention on jurisdictional immunities, 173–174
  US Immunity from Judicial Seizure Statute 1965, 175–176

Index

Import-export of cultural objects
    ATA carnet, 148–149
    case study: Padraig Pearse Surrender Letter, 177–179
    commercial invoice, 148
    customs documentation, 148–149
    exports from EU, 164–165
    exports within EU, 165–168
    imports into EU, 162–164
    imports within EU, 168–170
    national treasures, 165, 169–170
    pro-forma invoice, 148
    SAD, 148
    VAT, 151–152
    2023 Act, 170
Income tax
    Artists Exemption Scheme, 149
    Basic Income for the Arts Scheme, 150
    s 1003 relief for donations of heritage items, 143–144
Indemnities, 111
Indigenous peoples' rights, 81, 91, 92
Individual Health Identifiers, 28–29
InfoSoc Directive, 3
Inheritance tax. *See* **Capital acquisitions tax**
Inishbofin remains, 91–92
Installation conditions, 114
Insurance, 114, 172
Intangible cultural heritage
    international convention, 79–80
    national inventory, 80
Integrity right, 17
Interest in property, 45
Intermediary's money laundering obligations, 118
International Association of Dealers in Ancient Art (IADAA) code of ethics, 83
International conventions protecting cultural property
    armed conflict/occupation, 63–64, 78, 160
    endangered species, 80–81, 160–162
    illicit trafficking of cultural property, 78, 83–84, 94–95, 159–160
    intangible cultural heritage, 79–80
    overview, 77–78
    return of stolen or illegally exported cultural objects, 78, 88, 95–100, 160

International conventions protecting cultural property—*contd.*
    underwater heritage, 78–79, 134, 139
International Council of Museums (ICOM)
    code of ethics, 81–82
    deaccessioning guidelines, 89, 90–81
    loan guidelines, 115, 172–173
International cultural object protection laws
    Egypt, 56
    Iran, 57–58
    Turkey, 57
    UNIDROIT Model Provisions, 58
    US, 56–57
    2023 Act, 58
International Group of Organisers' loan principles, 171–172
International loans
    condition report, 172
    ICOM guidelines, 172–173
    immunity from seizure. *See* Immunity from seizure
    import-export permits. *See* Import-export of cultural objects
    importance, 171
    insurance, 172
    International Group of Organisers' general principles, 171–172
    loan agreements. *See* Loans
    National Museum loan policy, 171
    overview, 170–171
    packing and transportation, 172
International Meteorological Organisation, 23
International Register of Cultural Property under Special Protection, 64
Internet
    data protection. *See* Data protection
    origins and development, 24–25
Inventories
    intellectual property rights, 115
    national inventories. *See* National inventories
    terms of contract, 115
    Wreck Inventory of Ireland, 138
Iranian antiquities
    Barakat Galleries case, 57–58
    unauthorised excavations and digging, 57

Irish Giant, 91
Istanbul Convention, 148–149

Jackson, Andrew, 87
Jewish property. *See* Nazi-era spoliation
Jordan, Neil, 144
Joyce, James, **7**, 144
Jurisdiction, 69–71
Jury trials, 70
'Just Stop Oil', 173

Key personnel clause, 112
King Diarmaid, 1

Laches or delay, 103–104
Law of the Sea, 135, 137
'Lawful and definitive despatch', 164
Lending of works
  definition, 14
  author's rights, 14
  e-books and audio books, 15–17
  PLR, 14–15
Lex situs, 55
Libraries
  copyright exemptions, 11–12
  data protection issues. *See* Data protection
  freedom of information issues. *See* Freedom of information
  public libraries. *See* Public libraries
  re-use of public sector information, 40–41
  use of out-of-commerce works, 12–14
Licensing of the Press Act 1662, 1
Limitation periods
  detinue and conversion claims, 60–62
  HEAR Act, 104–105
  Proceeds of Crime (Amendment) Act 1995, 77
  restitution claim under UNIDROIT Convention 1995, 96–98
  return of cultural object to EU member state, 170
  Statute of Limitation 1957, 60–61
  2023 Act, 62
Literary work
  definition, 4
  copyright. *See* Copyright

Loans
  bailment, 49
  borrower's undertakings, 114
  condition check, 114
  creation, 52
  gifts distinguished, 51–52
  Heritage Council documentation, 52, 115
  ICOM guidelines, 115, 172–173
  installation conditions, 114
  insurance, 114, 172
  international loans. *See* International loans
  National Museum loan policy, 53, 171
  power to make or receive, 53
  State indemnity, 53
  tax relief, 145–146
  terms and conditions, 113–115
  UK Museums Association guide, 115
Looted art and artefacts
  context, 87–88
  deaccession. *See* Deaccession
  Nazi era. *See* Nazi-era spoliation
  repatriation. *See* Repatriation of cultural objects
  restitution. *See* Restitution of cultural objects
Lusitania, 139
Lux of light exposure, 114

Maastricht Treaty, 168–169
Mantola, 136–139
Maori artefacts, 56
Marcy, William L, 87
Margin scheme, 151
Mens rea, 71–73
Metal detectors, 127
Meteorological data, 23
Mickey Mouse, 8
Milne, AA, 21–22
Minister responsible, 60n
Misappropriation of public funds, 69
Money laundering, 75–76, 118
Monuments. *See* National monuments
Moore, Henry, 61–62
Moore Street, Dublin, 133–134
Moral rights, 17–18
Movable property, 51

Index

Museums
    copyright issues. *See* Copyright
    data protection issues. *See* Data protection
    deaccessioning guidelines, 89, 90–91
    freedom of information issues. *See* Freedom of information
    human remains and ethnological items, 91–94
    ICOM code of ethics, 81–82
    Nazi-looted art. *See* Nazi-era spoliation
    re-use of public sector information, 40–41
    use of out-of-commerce works, 12–14
Musical work, copyright, 4, 7

Napoleon, 88
National Archives
    certificate exempting departmental records from disclosure, 38
    'departmental records' defined, 36
National Heritage Week, 146
National inventories
    architectural heritage, 123–124, 130
    intangible cultural heritage, 80
National Library
    James Joyce copyright case, 7
    sale, exchange or gift of library material, 90
National monuments
    definition, 124–125
    acquisition powers, for access purposes, 126
    battlefields, 133
    byelaws, power to make, 127
    decision-maker unclear, 125
    entry and inspection powers, 127
    Historic Monuments Council, 125
    legislative framework, 124
    notice of proposed works, 126
    possession, purchase or sale, non-reporting or failure to hand over, 128
    prohibited works, 126
    register of historic monuments, 125–126
    removal to museum, 127
    State ownership, 68, 127
    2023 Act, 124

National Museum of Ireland (NMI)
    collections disposal policy, 90
    Derrynaflan Hoard, 50, 54, 64–68
    ethnographic objects, 92–94
    loans policy, 53, 171
    power to dispose of archaeological objects, 90
National treasures, 165, 169–170
National Trust for Ireland, 132–133
Natural History Museum, 18
Nazi data collection, 23–24
Nazi-era spoliation
    case study: Rue Saint-Honoré in the Afternoon, 106–108
    context, 100
    Foreign Sovereignties Immunities Act (US), 105–106
    Holocaust Expropriated Art Recovery (HEAR) Act 2016 (US), 103–105
    Holocaust (Return of Cultural Objects) Act 2009 (UK), 89, 101
    replevin, 100–101
    Terezin Declaration, 101–102
    Washington Principles, 101–103
Negligence, 72
Nemo dat quod non habet, 48, 56, 95
Non-fungible tokens (NFTs), 120–121, 153–155
Northampton Borough Council, 89
'Nyan Cat' meme, 153

O'Brien, Denis, 144
Odyssey Marine, 136–139
Omissions, 71
Open Data Directive, 40–41
Open market value of heritage item, 143–144
Originality, for copyright purposes, 4–5, 19
Orphan work
    copyright exemption, 8–9
    Qatar Investment v Eskenazi case, 83–84
Ottoman Sultan Murad II, 87
Ottoman Sultan Selim III, 88
Out-of-commerce work
    definition
    use by cultural heritage institution, 12–14

Parody, 10
Parthenon marbles, 88, 89
Pastiche, 10
Paternity right, 17
Pearse, Padraig, 177–179
Performers' rights, 7
Philbrick, Inigo, 152–153
Photographs
   copyright, 3
   paintings or antiques, 20
   silkscreens based on, 111
Pissarro, Camille, 106–108
Pomes Penyeach, 7
Possession of stolen property, 47–48, 75
Possessory title, 45
Prince, 111
Printing press, 1
Privity of contract, 109
Pro-forma invoice, 148
Proceeds of crime, 76–77
Promissory estoppel, 109
Property Services Regulatory Authority, 117
Proprietary rights, 73
Proprietary title, 45
Protected structures
   definition, 129–130
   battlefields, 133–134
   declaration as to works materially affecting character, 131
   designation of part, 130
   effects of registration, 130
   fixtures and chattels, 131–132
   Grenada Convention, 129
   Moore Street, Dublin, 133–134
   planning permission for normally exempted development, 130
   record of protected structures, 129, 130
   'structure' defined, 129
Provenance
   concept, 46
   Qatar Investment v Eskenazi case, 83–86
Public domain, 7
Public Lending Remuneration (PLR)
   definition, 14
   e-books and audio books, 15–17
   statutory scheme, 14–15
Public libraries
   definition, 15
   copyright exhaustion, 6
   e-books and audio books, 15–17
   PLR, 14–15
Public procurement, 116

Quinn, Lochlann, 144

Real property, 50
Recklessness, 46, 72, 76
Register of Cultural Objects, 166, 178–179
Relevant things of archaeological interest
   inventory, 123
   'relevant things' defined, 123–124
Repatriation of cultural objects
   advisory committee, 99
   Chinese antiquities, 99
   Elgin Marbles, 88
   ethical and legal considerations, 88–90
   EU Directive, 169–170, 176–177
   human remains and ethnological items, 91–94
   national treasures, 169–170
   request for, 88
   restitution distinguished, 88
   sack of Constantinople, 87–88
   Turkish antiquities, 99
Replevin, 100–101
Replicas, 117
Resale right, 18–19
Restitution of cultural objects
   advisory committee, 99
   ethical and legal considerations, 88–90
   Nazi-looted art. *See* Nazi-era spoliation
   repatriation distinguished, 88
   request for, 88
   UNESCO Convention 1970, 94–95, 159–160
   UNIDROIT Convention 1995, 95–100, 160
Re-use of public sector information, 40–41
Rhysida, 25
Royal College of Surgeons, 91

Index

Rue Saint-Honoré in the Afternoon—Effect of Rain, 106–108
Russborough House, 144

Saatchi, Charles, 119
Sack of Constantinople, 87–88
Sale
  archaeological/cultural objects, ethical considerations, 88–90
  stolen goods, 48
  written contract, 110
Scans of documents and paintings, 20
Schiele, Egon, 103
Science Ltd, 120–121
Sculptures, whether chattels or fixtures, 62, 131–132
Seizure, immunity from. *See* Immunity from seizure
Sekhemka sculpture, 89
Silver bullion, 137
Silver ingots, 136
Single administrative document (SAD), 148
Sound recording, copyright, 4, 7
Sovereign immunity, 105–106, 173–175
Spain
  Cassirer family, restitution claim, 106–108
  copyright duration, 7
Special Criminal Court, 70
Spoils of war, 87
St Columba, 1
St Finian, 1
St Mark's Basilica, 87–88
Stained glass windows, 132
Standard of proof, 69
State ownership of archaeological/cultural objects
  constitutional provisions, 67
  Derrynaflan hoard, 64–68
  legislative framework, 90
  National Monuments (Amendment) Act 1994, 68, 127
  UNIDROIT Model Law, 58, 91
  wrecks and underwater sites, 134
  2023 Act, 45, 58, 128
State records, 5
Stationers' Company, 1

Statute of Anne, 1–2
Statute of Frauds, 51, 110
Steamboat Willie, 8
Stolen property
  cultural objects. *See* Cultural objects
  handling, 46–47, 74
  possession, 47–48, 75
  recklessness as to whether stolen, 46
  restoration to person entitled, 47–48
  sale/transfer of title, 48
Storage agreement, 49
Stratocaster, 155–158
Strict liability, 73
Summary trial, 70
Supreme Court, 70–71
Surrender letter of Padraig Pearse, 166, 177–179

Tax on cultural objects
  case study: Rory Gallagher Stratocaster, 155–158
  CAT. *See* Capital acquisitions tax
  NFTs, 154
  overview, 141
  relief. *See* Tax relief
Tax relief
  expenditure on approved buildings, gardens and objects, 146–147
  loans of art objects, 145–146
  s 1003 donations of heritage items, 143–144
Tendering process, 116
Terezin Declaration, 101–102
Termination of contract, 112
Terms and conditions of contract, 111
Territorial waters, 135
Testamentary gift, 52
Testamentary trust, 51
The Three Graces, 131
Theft
  elements of offence, 73–74
  found archaeological object, 74
  handling etc stolen property. *See* Stolen property
  penalty, 74
Three certainties, 50–51
Thyssen-Bornemisza Foundation, 106–108
Title, 45–46
Title deeds, 45

Transfer Control Protocol/ Internetwork Protocol (TCP/IP), 24
Translations, 18
Treasure trove, 64–68
Treaty on the Functioning of the EU (TFEU), 168–170
Trial on indictment, 70
Trinity College Dublin (TCD), 91–92
Triumphal Quadriga, 87–88
Trusts, 50–51
Turkish antiquities
  law protecting, 56
  repatriation, 99
  sack of Constantinople, 87–88

Ulster Museum, 94
Ulysses, 7
Underwater heritage
  definition, 78
  case study: *SS Gairsoppa* and *SS Mantola*, 136–139
  duty to report finds, 136
  international convention, 78–79, 134, 139
  legislative framework, 134–135
  prohibited diving, salvage or survey operations, 135–136
  underwater heritage order, 135, 137–139
  2023 Act, 134
UNESCO Conventions
  illicit trafficking of cultural property, 78, 83–84, 94–95, 159–160
  intangible cultural heritage, 79–80
  underwater heritage, 78–79, 134
UNIDROIT Convention on Stolen or Illegally Exported Cultural Objects 1995
  Circuit Court jurisdiction, 99
  'cultural objects' defined, 88
  Irish accession, 98–100
  limitation periods, 96–98
  not retroactive, 95–96
  overview, 78
  right of return under, 95, 99–100, 160
UNIDROIT Model Provisions on State Ownership of Undiscovered Cultural Objects, 58, 91

Uniform Resource Locators (URLs), 24
United Nations Convention on Jurisdictional Immunities of States and Their Property, 173–175
United States (US)
  copyright duration, 7, 21–22
  Foreign Sovereign Immunities Act (FSIA), 105–106
  Freedom of Information Act (FOIA), 34–35
  Immunity from Judicial Seizure Statute 1965, 175–176
  National Stolen Property Act, 56–57
  Nazi-looted art. *See* Nazi-era spoliation
  termination rights for authors, 21–22
Usucapion, 107

Valuation of heritage items, 143–144
VAT
  art services, 149
  EU VAT area, 151
  imports and exports, 151–152
  margin scheme, 151
  NFTs, 154–155
  sale of works, 149
Vienna International Meteorological Congress, 23

War
  laws and customs, 63, 87
  protection of cultural property 1954, 63–64, 78, 160
Warhol, Andy, 111
Warranties, 111
Washington Principles, 101–103
Watergate, 34–35
Weather information, 23
Webb, Michael, 64–68
Welfenschatz, 105
Wildlife trade, 80–81, 160–162
Windows, whether chattels or fixtures, 132
Winnie-the-Pooh, 21–22
Wire fraud, 152–153
World Heritage Property inventory, 123
World Wide Web, 24–25

Index

Wreck
definition, 137
Carpathia, 139
case study: *SS Gairsoppa* and *SS Mantola*, 136–139
duty to report finds, 136
legislative framework, 134–135
Lusitania, 139
prohibited diving, salvage or survey operations, 135–136
relevant wrecks, 134
State ownership, 134
unclaimed, notice to Director of National Museum, 136

Wreck—*contd.*
underwater heritage order, 135, 137–139
Wreck Inventory of Ireland, 138
2023 Act, 134
Written memorandum of contract, 110
Wrongful detention of goods. *See* **Civil recovery of object**

Yeats, WB, 144
Young British Artists, 119
Yusuf, Abdulqawi Ahmed, 93, 99–100